Group
Leadership Skills

4th Edition

 **Carolyn Chambers Clark, EdD, ARNP, FAAN,** holds a doctorate from Teachers College, Columbia University. Dr. Clark has conducted research on group processes, simulation gaming and wellness self-care. Since 1966, she has conducted a private practice in group therapy and provided consultation on group work topics. She is a prolific contributor to the literature of group process, simulation gaming, teaching-learning, assertiveness, empowerment, health promotion, wellness and complementary health.

Dr. Clark is editor-in-chief of *The Encyclopedia of Complementary Health Practice* (Springer, 1999), editor of *Health Promotion in Communities: Holistic and Wellness Approaches* (Springer, 2002), and author of *Wellness Practitioner* (Springer, 1996) and *Integrating Complementary Procedures into Practice* (Springer, 2000).

Group
Leadership Skills

4th Edition

Carolyn Chambers Clark, EdD, RN, ARNP, FAAN

 **Springer Publishing Company**

Title of earlier editions: *The Nurse as Group Leader*
First edition published, 1978
Second edition published, 1987
Third edition published, 1994

Springer Publishing Company, Inc.
536 Broadway
New York, NY 10012-3955

Acquisitions Editor: Ruth Chasek
Production Editor: Pamela Lankas
Cover design by Joanne Honigman

03 04 05 06 07 / 5 4 3 2

Library of Congress Cataloging-in-Publication-Data

Clark, Carolyn Chambers.
  Group leadership skills / Carolyn Chambers Clark.—4th ed.
    p. cm.
  Rev. ed. of: The nurse as group leader / Carolyn Clark Chambers. 3rd ed. 1994.
  Includes bibliographical references and index.
  ISBN 0-8261-2334-1
    1. Nursing services—Administration. 2. Leadership. 3. Small groups. I. Clark, Carolyn Chambers. Nurse as group leader. II. Title.

RT89 .C56 2003
362.1'73'068—dc21

                                  2002036571

Printed in the United States of America by Maple-Vail Book Manufacturing Group.

Contents

Preface to the Fourth Edition

This book contains information that will help you be an effective group leader whether you work in task, support, psychotherapy or educational groups, with groups of students or clients, in organizations or even communities. Despite the kind of group, and whether you are the designated or informal leader, the only way to learn group skills is to practice. That is why I have included many simulated situations. Please practice using them to try out your group skills prior to undertaking leadership of a real-life group. The simulated situations will give you the feel for real-life groups, but without the risk. They will allow you to try out different approaches and study your reactions and group members' responses. Consider them laboratory experiments that allow you plenty of freedom to play various roles.

I have added a great deal of new information to this edition, including:

- New information on self-help support groups and computer-mediated groups.
- Research evidence supporting the use of role playing and simulations as powerful tools for learning group skills.
- More methods and forms for studying group behavior.
- More focus group information and related research results.
- More information on the history, theory, and research related to group process.
- More information on group conflict, group problem solving, group decision making, types of leadership, and team building.
- A checklist for beginning a group.
- Methods for warming up groups and working with large groups.
- Tips on how to tune into group process and use it to move the group forward.

- Additional information on groups for older adults.
- The chapter entitled "When the Organization is the Group" has been almost entirely rewritten to include parliamentary procedure, successful delegation, how to conduct interactions and "Doings" (rather than "meetings"), how to lead from within, and how to heal the betrayal of trust.
- The chapter entitled "When the Community is the Group" now contains a wellness view of community and updated examples of community organization efforts and research.

I believe these changes and other reader-friendly approaches make this book a most useful manual that will help make you an effective group leader, if you take part in the suggested simulations and apply the theory and comments provided.

Best wishes in all your group work,

Carolyn Chambers Clark

Carolyn Chambers Clark, ARNP, EdD

Acknowledgments

I wish to thank the many students who have helped me learn about groups, and who shared in the development of the course, Group Dynamics and Leadership, on which this book is based.

I also wish to thank my peer support group, Susan DiFabio, RN, MS, and Judith Ackerhalt, RN, EdD, who helped me develop my own peer group skills.

C.C.C.

1
Introduction to Group Work

GROUPS ARE IMPORTANT

Groups are important to people from the moment they are born until their lives end. Socialization first takes place in the group called the family. Later, peer groups, social groups, religious groups, work groups, and political groups become important vehicles for learning and obtaining satisfaction.

The quality of peoples' lives often depends on their ability to perform effectively in the groups to which they belong. You, as a social being, also belong to many groups. Your effectiveness in these groups depends on your ability to assess and intervene in the ebb and flow of processes that affect the internal workings of each group.

Group skills are important for at least two reasons. First, many tasks, such as planning, cannot be accomplished without the cooperation and collaboration of group members. You must learn to work effectively with your colleagues and with other personnel. Group skills in this kind of cooperation and collaboration are especially important now if you are striving to be recognized as a peer by others. Effective group skills can assist you to be clear and assertive when working with various groups of personnel without resorting to aggressive or helpless behavior, withdrawal, or apathy.

Second, work functions include teaching and supportive assistance to supervisees and clients—two functions that can often best be provided within a group format. Such a format affords a number of experiences that the one-to-one relationship cannot provide. Group experiences can also supply a more intense and different type of support; assistance in observing a wide range of responses; positive and negative feedback in a supportive way; pooling of resources and solutions to problems; knowledge that others share the same difficulty, fear, or anxiety; validation of one's own perceptions; and more efficient use of time.

Group skills, then, are important not only when you form and lead groups that include clients or families but also when you are a member of a planning or task group. In the latter case, you may or may not be the designated leader; if you are not, you can learn to provide *informal leadership* and thus help the group to function more effectively; in these cases, you become an emergent or situational leader.

THE GROUP AND SYSTEMS THEORY

The Group as a System

Systems theory provides an overriding theoretical framework for understanding and intervening in groups. A *theoretical framework* helps organize group information into an understandable whole. It provides categories to assist group leaders to organize their thoughts and observations. A framework is like a clothesline upon which group leaders can hang their observations in an organized manner. It provides a perspective or specific way of looking at what is happening in a group.

A group is a *system* because it has identifiable parts (members) yet is a whole entity (a group) with each part influencing each other part (if one member is angry, other group members will react to the anger). Systems also have *subsystems*. In groups, these are subgroups or pairs of individuals who cluster together around shared interests. The group is a whole and different from the sum of its parts; even if one group member remains silent throughout a group session, the group as a whole can achieve a goal; even if a group is composed of mature individuals, the group as a whole must struggle to be a mature group and develop ways to work together. Systems also have the property of openness and closedness; human systems are believed to be open systems, exchanging energy, matter, and information with their environment. Groups can be influenced by their environment too: For example, if the room is too warm, energy levels of group members may be low; if group leaders bring in handouts for the group there can be an exchange of information with the environment; and if group leaders serve refreshments from the cafeteria, matter from the environment (food) can be exchanged for energy. Systems have inputs (people, energy, information), throughputs (what goes on in the group), and outputs (products, such as decisions that are carried out between group meetings, influence on interactions outside of the group). A system has interactive parts: the leader influences the group members and vice versa. Leaders and group members are continually influencing each other, even when there is silence in the group.

From a systems point of view, growth occurs in a unidirectional fashion; a group does not reverse itself or regress; some behaviors or sessions may seem nonconstructive, but eventually, the group will move forward if the leader exerts helpful leadership behaviors.

Open systems show a regularity and predictability. If you're observant you will begin to notice behavior patterns in specific groups. In one group, every time one of the group members speaks, a silence may follow, or laughter or encouragement.

Living systems have these common elements, but they also have their unique patterns; no two groups are the same; there are processes that occur, but each group may display them in unique ways.

Using systems theory can enable you to view group problems as systems issues, not as personal attacks or attitude problems, but as patterns that have been developed and are maintained by the system. In other words, many of the system problems discussed in Chapter 3 are best viewed as patterns that serve a purpose for the group. This does not mean that a pattern cannot be disrupted; suggested interventions for system pattern change are found in Chapters 3 and 4.

TYPES OF GROUPS

There are three types of groups: task groups, teaching groups, and supportive or therapeutic groups. Table 1–1 lists the types of groups, their primary purposes, effective group size, and examples of groups belonging to each type.

Task Groups

The primary purpose of *task groups* is to accomplish a given task; they place high priority on decision making and problem solving. Planning committees, service committees, teams, conference groups, staff meetings, community organizational meet-

TABLE 1–1 Types of Groups

Group Type	Primary Purpose	Examples
Task	Accomplishing the task	Curriculum committee meeting Service planning committee Team meeting Conference Staff meeting Community organizational meeting political action meeting
Teaching	Imparting information	Group continuing education Nutrition group for clients Sex education group for adolescents Sensory-motor group for preschoolers Reality orientation group for nursing home residents
Supportive/ Therapeutic	Dealing with emotional stress	Group for infertile spouses Group for expectant spouses Group for middle-aged people in midcareer crisis Group for people with chronic illness processes Group for rape victims

ings, and political action meetings are all examples of task groups. (see Table 1–1).

Task groups are often formed to solve a given problem; for example, how can the consumer have input into health care planning? Consider breaking task or teaching groups over 12 members into subgroups for maximum interaction and learning. Groups of six or fewer are more productive (Imel, 1997). What is the most effective way for the team to function? How can personnel best provide services for a group of 25 clients? How can the staff deal more constructively with Mr. A's behavior? How can members of this community be assisted to improve their level of wellness? How can professionals take political action?

Task groups are usually under pressure to complete the task within an allotted time period. There is also a tendency to ignore, deny, or try to smooth over any existing conflict.

Teaching Groups

The primary purpose of *teaching groups* is to impart information to the participants. Although the tendency to separate the learner from the teacher always exists in these groups, research has shown that students learn as much—or more—when teaching their peers as their peers do.

You may participate in a number of teaching/learning groups. Hospitals, institutions, and agencies often present continuing education courses to teach new skills or to enhance previously learned basic skills. You may utilize the group format in a program designed to teach others.

When you lead a group in which the primary purpose is to teach or to learn, the following questions need to be considered: Which material is best suited to group or individual learning? Are the students ready to learn? What do they already know? Do the members of the group have similar levels of knowledge? How much repetition of material is needed to enhance learning? How can students be helped to plan and evaluate their own learning experiences? Is the pace of instruction too fast or too slow? How can the teacher provide the students with adequate feedback about how well they are learning the material? How can effective learning behaviors be increased?

Innumerable subjects are suitable for handling via the group-teaching format: labor and childbirth techniques, birth control methods, nutrition, the management of diabetes, the management of colostomies or ileostomies, effective parenting, orientation to nursing home living, appropriate exercises for nursing home residents, sensorimotor skills for preschoolers, preparation of families to enable them to care for discharged family members, and more.

Supportive or Therapeutic Groups

The primary purpose of *supportive or therapeutic groups* is to assist members in dealing with emotional stresses due to hospitalization, illness processes, growth and development crises, situational crises, or socially maladaptive behavior. Supportive or therapeutic groups focus on the examination of members' thoughts, feelings, and subsequent behavior. Clients often benefit from ventilating their feelings, from seeing that others share and accept these feelings, and from learning healthy and constructive ways of coping with them. Supportive or therapeutic groups should not be thought of as a form of group psychotherapy or of psychoanalysis; rather, their concern is to prevent possible future upsets by educating participants in effective ways of dealing with emotional stress arising from situational or developmental crises.

Supportive or therapeutic groups are usually under less pressure than teaching and task groups to complete the task during one or two meetings. Another difference is that conflict among the group members may be pursued and explored because it is often related to the ways members deal with emotional stress. The leader may even choose to maintain anxiety and conflict at fairly high levels if this serves to assist the group to continue focusing on their feelings, rather than to cover over or withdraw from the discomfort. New tasks, such as how to deal with the entrance of a tardy or new group member, may be generated spontaneously and dealt with by the group.

In convening a supportive or therapeutic group, you frequently gather together people who are undergoing similar emotional stresses. Such groups may, for example, consist of families of the dying; individuals with a chronic illness and/or their families; individuals who have recently lost a body part through surgery or accident; the severely burned; individuals awaiting diagnosis, admission, surgery or hospital discharge; involuntary nursing home residents; rape victims; parents of infants with birth defects; clients with a drug or alcohol problem; prison inmates; those with suicidal or homicidal tendencies; middleaged men or women facing a career or midcareer crisis; anxious preschoolers who fear going to school; child-abusing parents; adolescents with inadequate knowledge of their current physiological changes and the ramifications; and identified or potential juvenile delinquents.

Leaderless or Self-Help Support Groups

Support groups can be leader-led or leaderless. Self-help groups or SHGs (Jacobs & Goodman, 2002):

- are leaderless groups that have a common problem
- meet for the purpose of exchanging psychological support
- charge minimal or no fees,
- are member-governed, although they may use professional consultation.

SHGs are growing in numbers and members. Somewhere between 7 and 15 million people belong to such groups. Groups such as Weight Watchers or groups run by hospital staff are not really SHGs because they are not member-governed. A study by Ouimette and colleagues (2001) found evidence that participants with substance abuse and posttraumatic stress disorder benefited from participation in a 12–step self-help group.

SHGs may have arisen due to the erosion of the family, the increasing number of people still living with significant disease, eroding confidence in care providers, lack of mental health services, increased faith in the value of social support as a buffer against stress, and the increased media attention provided by TV docudramas (Jacobs & Goodman, 2002).

SHGs can often work as well as leader-led groups. Three facts can explain their likely success:

1. Members are highly motivated to change. They join the groups because they want relief.
2. The unique focus of each SHG creates a reciprocal exchange, a balance of give and take and risk and reward.
3. Because of the focus and balanced exchanged, higher levels of self-disclosure are triggered; this leads to empathy, cohesion, and feelings of success (Jacobs & Goodman, 2002).

As long as SHGs stick to support and empathy, they can be useful. SHGs that turn to the popular media for self-help materials can have a detrimental effect. Zimmerman, Haddock, and McGeorge (2001) analyzed and critiqued the best-selling self-help book, *Men are from Mars, Women are from Venus.* Their analysis revealed that the author's materials are inconsistent with family therapy research findings and encourage unequal power differentials between women and men.

Computer-Mediated Support Groups

The computer can also serve as a support group. Robertshaw (2000) discussed the use of support groups in distance education. Social support groups can address teaching and learning needs and social needs in the distance education system where time, distance and/or opportunity isolate learners from their teacher and fellow students. Hettinger (1995) presented evidence from a survey of 17 adults enrolled in a course at Pennsylvania State University. Eighty-four percent of the students believed that computer-mediated communication interaction caused them to move in a positive direction in both the personal and cognitive areas of learning. The researcher found that after class, e-mail was insufficient for increasing critical thinking skills and affecting the group dynamic.

Dangers of incorporating groups into a support system include students developing dependency on the group, succumbing to peer pressure, and crossing the line between collaboration and plagiarism.

The Internet has even bred a form of addiction called Internet addictive disorder or pathological Internet use. Several forms of Internet addiction appear to exist, categorized according to the type of misuse they are subjected to: cybersex, chat rooms, net gaming, with the pathological search for information or video games being the most frequent. Bipolar disorders are the most common psychiatric condition linked with Internet addictive disorder (Dejoie, 2001).

CONCERNS OF ALL GROUP LEADERS

Although at first glance it would seem that each group would demand different group skills, actually, to be effective, *all three types of groups require that a balance be maintained between adhering to the task and meeting the interpersonal needs of group members.* For example, if task group leaders are so concerned about following the agenda that they fail to note how upset the curriculum committee is about a proposed cut in faculty salaries, the group will not function effectively. Likewise, if leaders in teaching groups are so concerned about giving information that they forget to find out whether all members understand the information, or if they support dependency on the leader by always giving the correct answer themselves, group functioning will not be as effective as it should be. Even in supportive or therapeutic groups, leaders have to maintain a balance between giving support and working toward a task; since the task may be to understand one's thoughts and feelings and to learn effective ways of dealing with them, leaders cannot be too supportive as this may prevent group members from learning new ways of coping with their thoughts and feelings. Thus, in all three types of groups, leaders are concerned with achieving a balance between interpersonal and task functions, and with system difficulties. Some questions to ask in this regard are:

- What patterns of behavior are developing in the group?
- Which patterns promote positive growth and which seem to promote negative growth?
- What can be done to promote primarily positive growth?
- How can subsystems be influenced to have congruent interests with the larger group system?
- What can be done to enhance openness in the group system?
- What is contributing to closedness in the group?
- What common group patterns and what unique group characteristics does this group have?

QUALITIES OF AN EFFECTIVE GROUP LEADER

Group leaders must have a high tolerance for anxiety, frustration, and disorganization. They must be capable of accepting group confrontation, hostility, and conflict without directly or indirectly punishing group members or ignoring the fact that such processes are occurring. (Cook, 1997).

A group leader needs to be able to accept and organize a great deal of information and be capable of observing both verbal and nonverbal messages and making sense out of both. Group interactions can be intense and quick-moving, and the amount of input can overwhelm the novice group leader. With practice and supervision by a skilled group leader, you can learn how to organize extensive amounts of information and when and how to intervene in group interaction. At times, you must be able to stop listening to what is being said in the group and instead "tune in" on the nonverbal communication that is being conveyed.

You have to engage in a certain amount of preparation for each session. This includes becoming informed about the task at hand and thinking of ways of structuring the meeting to delegate some responsibility to group members and to enlist their aid before and between meetings. Effective teaching requires that the teacher digest the information about the topic to be taught and plan how to present it to the learners "in their language" and on cue. Further, effective teachers are able to establish a give-and-take rapport with learners and to provide feedback and support in order to help group members feel comfortable when talking, practicing, or demonstrating in the group. A supportive or therapeutic group leader has to reread logs or recordings of past sessions, look for evidence of nonparticipation by members who may need attention or for strong feelings or opinions that need exploration in future sessions, and be alert for patterns of interaction that seem to be developing. Supportive or therapeutic group leaders are quite likely not to have an agenda or teaching plan in mind, but are aware of potential problem areas and move to intervene when appropriate. They must be willing and able to seek out assistance in understanding group processes; knowing when supervision from a more experienced group leader is needed is a very important quality to have.

A sense of humor is also a great asset to a group leader. Despite adequate preparation for group sessions, unforeseen circumstances can disrupt the best-laid plans. Being able to detect the humor in unexpected situations allows the group leader to ride with the ebb and flow of group processes without becoming irritated, angry, punitive, or withdrawn. Such a leader can often use humor as a way of decreasing group tension levels.

In theory, you may promote independent action in clients but, in practice, you may "do for" group members and are comfortable in the role of authority or expert. In a group setting, if you can promote independence and more effective behavior and encourage group members to be more responsible for what takes place in the group you will be the more effective group leader. In the beginning, limits need to be set on who will be part of the group, where the group will meet, and what topics will be discussed. You will also need to decide how group members will be prepared to enter the group. These somewhat competing goals of fostering independence yet structuring the group require a blend of skill that can be acquired through practice in group leadership and through the study of group processes.

Another asset of effective group leaders is the ability to blend their own style of relating to constructive communication techniques. Some leaders may believe that asking, "What's with

Betty and Tom?" seems too informal, even rude. Others may think that saying, "It seems the group has some feeling about what John said," sounds stilted or too formal. Develop your own choice of words and your own ways of conveying the same idea. Learning to apply communication principles in a clear, direct manner takes quite a bit of practice.

Your willingness to examine your own expectations for the group and to deal with them realistically is an important aspect of group leadership. You may deny wanting the group to progress in a certain way, yet feel quite frustrated when it does not proceed as expected. For example, the leader of a health discussion group may have in mind that 10 preplanned health topics will be covered in 10 weeks. If the group members have many questions, cannot absorb the information, or are concerned about other issues, the group will probably not proceed as the leader expected, who is then likely to react with anxiety, frustration, anger, and resentment. Effective group leadership requires that you examine your own expectations and acquire the ability to correct or change them if they turn out to be unrealistic. This may evoke further anxiety in you, but it is a necessary side effect of learning. Decisions about how or when to intervene with a group are based on group needs and system patterns, not your need for security, self-esteem, or support.

Being appointed a group leader does not mean that the respect and influence of the title necessarily follow. Acquiring a leadership title brings with it unexpected disappointments and uninvited problems. You must be prepared to encounter suspicion, distrust, hostility, subservience, passive resistance, insecurity, jealousy, and resentment.

Employees who went to lunch with you may now avoid, exclude, act defensively, become more guarded in their conversations, make more critical comments, or "apple Polish." Stubborn resistance and negativism to new plans or helpful suggestions may emerge.

Becoming a group leader invariably brings about significant changes in relationships with group members. Negative reactions to those in power and authority are part of everyone's behavior—even the group leader's. Children develop ways of coping with authority figures, including crying, getting sick, becoming compliant, withdrawing, buttering up, forming alliances, lying, hiding feelings, bullying or dominating, striking back, ridiculing, resisting, defying, showing aggression, perfectionism, blaming others, tattling, and cheating.

Identifying your own and group members' reactions to authority figures is the first step in becoming an effective group leader. Using the unique dynamic interplay between leader and group members without taking member reactions personally will assist you to help the group move forward effectively.

EFFECTIVE AND INEFFECTIVE GROUPS

Effective groups are capable of changing goals and matching individual needs to group goals. The leader is aware of how effective groups work and strives to promote behaviors that lead to effective functioning. In order to accomplish their task, all group members must be aware of exactly what this task is.

In ineffective groups the goals are unclear, the group remains uninvolved or uninterested, and the given tasks often seem to promote competition rather than cooperation and collaboration.

In effective groups, communication between the leader and the group members and among the group members themselves is open, direct, and clear. Accurate expression of thoughts and feelings is encouraged. Individuality is supported, while activities that foster a closer working relationship and enhance the "common good" are encouraged. In such groups a high level of trust, support, safety, creativity, and constructive controversy is evident.

In ineffective groups, communication is usually a one-way affair, from the leader to the group. Ideas are expressed, while feelings are denied or ignored. No attempt is made to involve group members in group functions. The emphasis is on conformity, and the leader seems most interested in the control of the group, in making sure that there is order and stability, and in maintaining the status quo.

Power and leadership are shared by all members in effective groups. The leader teaches the group members how to be effective, and members participate in decisions according to their ability. Controversy and conflict are assessed as possible clues to involvement and interest in the task. Members learn how to recognize problems and how to solve them with a minimum of energy and a maximum of satisfaction; they also learn how to evaluate the effectiveness of their solutions and, finally, the effectiveness of their group.

Leadership in ineffective groups is often based on seniority or authority. Participation of members is unequal; authoritarian members dominate the group and make decisions. Controversy and conflict are ignored, avoided, or squelched. Group members do not learn how to solve problems or how to evaluate their effectiveness as group members or as a group. The status quo is maintained.

In summary, the group leader promotes effective functioning by:

- Clarifying the group task
- Changing the group task to match individual and group goals (when necessary)
- Promoting collaboration and cooperation
- Promoting security, trust, support, and creativity
- Encouraging constructive controversy
- Teaching group members to share leadership and responsibility in the group
- Teaching group members to problem solve and to evaluate group functioning and resultant outcomes

WAYS OF LEARNING ABOUT GROUP FUNCTION

Learning to be an effective group leader cannot be accomplished merely by reading about group concepts and processes. An effective group leader has to have not only the theoretical knowledge about how groups work, but also the ability to assess group concepts and processes and to intervene in real-life groups. Assessing and intervening in group processes requires practice supervised by an experienced leader.

Obtain Experience

The best way to learn about group functioning is to join a task, teaching, supportive, or therapeutic group. As a participant, you can observe and study group concepts and processes in action. You also study group processes more effectively by becoming an observer/reporter for the group. In this role you can focus your energies on listening and recording and not participating verbally in the group interaction.

Prior to intervening in real-life group situations, you can practice interacting in simulated situations; these have many learning advantages that real-life situations do not have. First, simulations contain less risk than real-life situations; learners know they are only "pretending." Less risk in simulations can often lead to less anxiety about an unknown situation, and to more potential for learning. Second, simulations allow learners to receive feedback for group behavior and skills; they can observe the consequences of their behavior without being so concerned about disclosing their feelings, receiving disapproval from authority figures, or psychologically "damaging" clients. Third, since group simulations are structured to contain elements of possible real-life group situations, experience in simulation is likely to increase your ability to handle real situations more easily. Fourth, simulations are a "fun" way to learn, and motivation is usually high. By practicing some or all of the group simulations found at the ends of the first seven chapters of this book, you can achieve all four of these benefits.

Role playing and simulations are important and powerful tools for learning group skills. Knowles and colleagues (2001) demonstrated that students who role played upcoming interactions with clients and received feedback on their performance improved their communications skills and applied knowledge more effectively than a control group.

Rubino and Freshman (2001) also found that simulated exercise inspired dialogue and program improvement. A simulation exercise that was found especially helpful to group leaders was to role play a therapy session during which the people playing the clients speak a language that is not understood by the therapist-in-training. This exercise assists students to become more cognizant of the need to be cautious and curious in the cocreation of meaning in therapy. In addition, the exercise builds confidence and clinical skills, such as learning about nonverbal communication while observing group process (Helmeke & Prouty, 2001).

These research findings provide evidence that simulated learning can be highly beneficial to students learning group skills. Seven chapters in this book provide simulated practice. Be sure to participate fully and learn as much as you can in the protected and powerful learning environment of the simulations presented. Using experienced undergraduate students as peer learning assistants can also improve group performance and satisfaction with the learning process (Grocia & Miller, 1996).

The next step in learning to be an effective group leader is actual practice in assessing and intervening in group process. This can occur through taking the role of designated group leader either in a new group or in an already established group of clients, families, or health personnel. Being designated leader requires the output of more energy and the assumption of more responsibility, at least initially, than does assuming a group member role, a recorder role, or an observer role. Ultimately, the designated leader in an effective group shares responsibility and teaches group members how to assume responsibility for group decisions. You can also practice being a group leader by taking the informal leader role in a group; once you are aware of how and when to intervene, you can assume formal leadership functions in a group.

Studying Ongoing Group Behavior

The *sociogram* was one of the early methods of systematically studying groups. This form of relationship charting shows the differential relationships that exist between members (Stock & Thelen, 1958). Liking, prestige, and influence (among other relationships) can be charted using a sociogram. As leader, you ask for members' reactions to other members, and then chart them on a chalkboard or large sheets of paper. For example, at a specific point in group functioning, you might ask, "Whose ideas do you feel most sympathetic to so far during this meeting (session)? Please take a slip of paper and write down the name of the person you feel most sympathetic to." Collect the slips of paper and read the names; for example, Carol named Ezra as the person she felt most sympathetic to and Charles named Susan, and so on. Chart the relationships on the board or sheet of paper. When the charting is complete, ask the group to discuss the implications and interview members about why they named the people they did.

The persons most named often take on spokesperson, bridge or informal group leadership. There are risks. Members who are not named may feel unworthy or unacceptable. To avoid negative feelings, use cooperative planning; avoid hurrying or pushing decisions. Your job is to support the group to clarify and make plans about which everyone feels good.

You can use sociograms throughout the life of the group to show developmental changes in a graphic way. Avoid asking, "Who is the most likable?" or "Who is the best leader?" questions. Focus on group-relevant behaviors, not personality factors. Items such as "Person who thinks most like I do," and "Person who I think clarifies others' idea most frequently" are

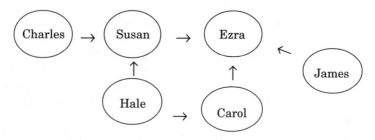

FIGURE 1-1 Sociogram.

useful. You can use these two items at the same time and then compare the results to show the group that different group members have different kinds of skills that help the group move along.

To study communication blocks in a group, use an item such as "Person who I think understands me least well." Once results are in, ask individuals who don't understand each other well to sit in pairs and discuss and clarify factors leading to misunderstanding. Ask each pair to report back to the group once reasons for communication difficulty have been identified. Figure 1-1 provides an example of a sociogram.

SIMULATED EXERCISES

Each of the three simulated exercises that follow includes an experiential and a discussion component. When using Exercises 2 and 3, large groups should be divided into subgroups of not more than 15 members. Following the simulation, the entire group reconvenes for the discussion.

Ample space should be provided for subgroups to spread out, and chairs should be movable. When subgroups are too close there is a tendency to listen to others' discussions.

EXERCISE 1 Perceived Problems of Being in a Group

Objectives
1. To provide practice as leader, recorder, and listener in groups.
2. To compare and contrast the listening and telling skills of various participants.
3. To examine common concerns regarding being in group situations.

Procedure
1. The group or the instructor appoints a timekeeper.
2. The group or the instructor appoints a leader who directs the exercise.
3. The leader says, "Arrange yourselves into subgroups of three. One will be the recorder who writes down what is said, one will be the listener, and one will be the speaker who tells what problems one faces in group situations." (Variation: have the speaker tell what problems are anticipated as group leader.)
4. When the small subgroups are arranged, the leader asks the timekeeper to call time when 15 minutes are up. The leader gives the signal to begin.
5. When the timekeeper calls time, the groups scramble, so that each person plays a different role for the next 15 minutes.
6. When the timekeeper calls time, the entire group convenes for a group discussion.
7. The group may appoint a leader to focus the discussion.
8. The leader asks the timekeeper to remind the group when only 10 minutes remain for discussion. Generally, 25 to 50 minutes is an adequate length of time to cover the issues, but the amount of time required will increase with an increase in the size of the group.
9. The following issues can be used as topics for discussion:
   a. What did the recorders in each group observe?
   b. What helpful or not helpful attitudes did the speakers in each group perceive in their listeners, i.e., nonverbal clues of attention, support, boredom, etc.?
   c. What did the listeners observe about the speakers?
   d. How does a listener encourage a speaker to speak?
   e. What skills are required by a recorder as compared to a speaker or listener?
   f. Did the recorder interfere with speaking and/or listening; if so, in what way?
   g. What concerns were expressed about being in (or leading) a group? (These may be written on a chalkboard or shown in overhead projection transparencies and used for reference purposes.)
   h. How could each concern be handled in the most effective way? (Refer to Chapters 1–3 and 5 for specific interventions.)
   i. How can what was learned in this exercise be applied in actual group situations?

EXERCISE 2 Introductions

This exercise is designed to give the nurse leader practical experience in giving, hearing, and analyzing group introductions without the risks that would be involved in actual patient or staff group situations.

Objectives
1. To practice introducing self to others.
2. To observe how others present themselves to the group.
3. To observe group processes characteristic of the orientation phase of groups.

Procedure
1. The group or instructor appoints a timekeeper. The timekeeper makes sure that each person's introduction does not exceed 3 minutes. Whenever a group member takes more than 3 minutes, the timekeeper turns to the next member and says, "Next, please."
2. The group or the instructor appoints a leader for each group.
3. The group leader appoints a recorder from among her group members. The recorder is asked to jot down observations regarding how people introduce themselves, how group members react toward being asked to introduce themselves, and the level of and changes in group cohesiveness.
4. The group leader asks the group members, "Will each of you introduce yourself to the group, say what you do, who you are as a person, and why you are participating in this exercise? Who will start?"
5. When all group members, including the leader, have introduced themselves, the entire group convenes.
6. A discussion leader volunteers or is appointed by the group. This leader asks the recorder to assist by helping the group to present their observations concerning the following issues:
   a. Did people tend to use socially acceptable, rational introductions? If so, is this characteristic of the orientation phase of a group? If not, what explanations does the group have for the presence or lack of more openness?
   b. Do nurses seem more likely to stereotype themselves than others might? Why?
   c. Why do people seem hesitant and cautious about expressing themselves in the group? If some people gave too much personal information, what might be an explanation for that type of behavior?
   d. Did group members really seem to get acquainted during the introductions? Why, or why not?
   e. What information seems most helpful for the leader to give during her introduction?
   f. What information seems most helpful for group members to give other group members during introductions?
   g. How can what was learned in this exercise be applied to actual group situations?

Variation: Two leaders can work together to lead the discussion. In this case, the following discussion question can be added:
   h. What advantages and disadvantages were there to coleadership? (Refer to Chapter 6.)

EXERCISE 3 Paraphrasing

This exercise provides practice in listening to and restating what others say. Many times the receiver of a message makes judgments about what the other has said and responds to these judgments rather than to the other's message. Because effective leadership requires expert listening and restating skills, this exercise can be redone whenever the group leader begins to notice a tendency toward interpreting group members' messages without sufficient basis for the interpretation.

Procedure

1. The group or the instructor appoints a timekeeper, who is to make sure that time limits set for each step are kept; the timekeeper also is to remind the group at appropriate intervals how much time remains.

2. The group decides on time limits for each step.

3. The group or the instructor appoints a leader for each group.

4. Each member is asked to talk about the best thing that happened this week. One member starts by telling the person to the right in the group the best thing that happened. The second person paraphrases what the first person has said, using different words to describe what happened without adding new information. The exercise continues in this manner, with one person recounting the best thing that happened, and the next person paraphrasing, followed by another person telling about a best experience and another person paraphrasing that experience until everyone has either told or paraphrased. (Variation: Use a highly controversial topic.)

15–30 minutes
5. The leader then asks group members to reverse roles and have the person who told of the experience become the paraphraser.

15–30 minutes
6. The entire group discusses the following points:
   a. What is difficult about paraphrasing another person's statements?
   b. Who in the group found it easier to tell a story than to paraphrase a story? Who found the reverse to be true? What ideas does the group have about why this might occur?
   c. What do the "speakers" have to tell the "paraphrasers" that may help them be more effective reflectors of what was said?
   d. What was learned from this exercise that can be applied in real-life group situations?
   e. (Optional) What effect did the controversial subject have on the ability to paraphrase?

REFERENCES

Cook, S. T., & Matheson, H. (1997). Teaching group dynamics: A critical evaluation of an experiential programme. *Nurse Education Today, 17*(1), 31–38.

Dejoie, J. F. (2001). Internet addiction: A different kind of addiction? *Revue Medicale de Liege, 56*(7), 523–530.

Groccia J. E., & Miller, J. E. (1996). Collegiality in the classroom: The use of peer learning assistants in cooperative learning in introductory biology. *Innovative Higher Education, 21*(2), 87–100.

Helmeke, K. B., & Prouty, A. M. (2001). Do we really understand? An experiential exercise for training family therapists. *Journal of Marital and Family Therapy, 27*(4), 535–544.

Hettinger, G. (1995). Raising the level of the debate: The effects of computer mediated communication on group dynamics and critical thinking. *Proceedings of the 1995 Annual National Convention of the Association for Educational Communications and Technology (AECT),* Anaheim, CA.

Imel, S. (1997). Adult learning in groups. Practice application brief. East Lansing, MI: National Center for Research on Teacher Learning. ERIC (Document Reproduction Service No: ED404569).

Jacobs, M. K., & Goodman, D. (1989). Psychology and self-help groups: Predictions on partnership. *American Psychologist, 44,* 536–545.

Knowles, C., Kinchington, F., Erwin, J., & Peters, B. (2001). A randomized controlled trial of the effectiveness of combining video role play with traditional methods of delivering undergraduate medical education. *Sexually Transmitted Infections, 77*(5), 376–380.

Ouimette, P., Humphreys, K., Moos, R. H., Finney, J. W., Cronkite, R., & Federman, B. (2001). Self-help group participation among substance use disorder patients with posttraumatic stress disorder. *Journal of Substance Abuse Treatment, 20*(1), 25–32.

Robertshaw, M. (2000). Support groups in distance education. Knowledge series. For full 2 of 2 learning about groups. [Available]: http://www.col.Knowledge/KSsupportgroups.pdf.

Rubino L., & Freshman, B. (2001). An experiential learning simulation exercise for health care management students. *Journal of Health Administration and Education, 19*(2), 155–172.

Stock D., & Thelen, H. A. (1958). *Emotional dynamics and group culture.* Washington, DC. National Training Laboratories.

Zimmerman, T. S., Haddock, S. A., & McGeorge, C. R. (2001). Mars and Venus: Unequal planets. *Journal of Marital and Family Therapy, 27*(1),55–68.

2

Basic Group Concepts and Process

GROUP PROCESS THEORIES AND RESEARCH

Although groups have been studied for centuries, it was not until 1890 that James put forward the theory of social identity. In 1897, Durkeim published his classic work *Suicide,* showing that an individual's action can be explained by social forces. The first laboratory experiment took place a few years later.

Group Processes

In the 1920s, the famous studies at the Hawthorne plant showed the "Hawthorne effect" or how group processes dramatically influence production when one group is given special attention from researchers. By 1936, Sherif had demonstrated that a purely social phenomenon, a social norm, could be created in the laboratory. In 1937, Lewin, Lippitt and White studied group members' reactions to autocratic leaders (task-oriented people who decide what needs to be done and then work hard to convince others to reach the same decision), democratic leaders (who look to the group for direction, promote cohesive group functioning, and train others to assume leadership), or laissez-faire leaders (who provide information and materials, but do not give direction, exert control, or evaluate results).

By the 1940's researchers and theorists began to understand group process in terms of fluidity and/or order, and many of the crucial developments in the field occurred from the late 1940s to the early 1960s (Whitaker, 2001). In 1946, Bales started work on his Interpersonal Process Analysis, a way to observe and categorize actions of small problem-solving groups. He eventually developed 12 mutually exclusive categories: shows solidarity, shows tension release, agrees, gives suggestions, gives opinion, gives orientation, asks for orientation, asks for opinion, asks for suggestion, disagrees, shows tension, and shows antagonism (Strodtbeck & Hare, 1954).

The next year, Lewin (1947) published a paper describing the group in terms of a "driving" and a "restraining" force. The driving forces pushed in one direction while the restraining forces exerted a counterpressure. A change in a driving or restraining force, according to Lewin, resulted in a change in the total system. This model portrayed the equilibrium in a group as a passive end product of two counterforces.

Bion (1952) published a paper on the successive cycles of group interaction: dependency, pairing, or flight-fight. While Bales' system was developed from observing task groups, Bion used psychotherapy groups. According to Bion, when the group was functioning in one of the three cultures, the other two remained in a latent state. The rational, organized state Bion called the "work group." He hypothesized that one of the "cultures" could exist simultaneously with the "work group."

Bales (1953) also developed a theory of group equilibrium. He theorized that group movement occurred as a result of a disturbance and a subsequent reestablishment of equilibrium when the group resolved a task. The cycle that arose between one disturbance (introduction of a task) and another was composed of activities that Bales termed orientation, evaluation, and control—-three types of action by group members directed toward resolution of the task.

By 1956, Ezriel theorized that the shift or movement in groups occurred due to emotional, nonrational events. Ezriel hypothesized that three kinds of "object relations" existed in a psychotherapy group. The group members idealized the therapist ("required relationship") in order to avoid attacking the therapist ("avoided relationship") for fear of harming the therapist or the therapist harming them ("the calamity").

In 1964, Whitaker and Lieberman developed an equilibrium model to account for the manner in which the psychotherapy group moved toward and away from preoccupation with a theme and shifted from one theme to another. The group situation was conceptualized in terms of opposing forces called "a disturbing motive," "a reactive motive," and "the group solution." The latter force was believed to represent the group's efforts to cope with the forces in conflict. They called this conflict situation "group focal conflict." By 2001, Whitaker had expanded her theory of focal conflict to include Lewin's concepts of life space, frontier and preoccupying concern, and Fritz Redl's cueing and altercasting concepts (to help understand how individuals occupy particular positions in groups).

Lamoureux and Debbane (1997) described the use of group-as-whole theory in groups. The phenomena developing in the group are related to the prevailing levels of therapeutic regression occurring. They suggest that the most regressive phenomena tend to be experienced as group-wide, with individual members assuming the position of part objects. Lesser degrees of regression center on the experience of whole-object relations. They show how anxiety relates to regression, the creation of objects and symbolization in group meetings. Rosen, Stukenberg, and Sacks (2001) also discussed the group-as-whole-object relations model of group psychotherapy and offer clinical examples of how to apply these principles in short-term inpatient settings in groups with open membership.

Aviram and Rosenfeld (2002) applied social identity theory in group therapy for adults with mild mental retardation. Social identity theory holds that social group membership (collective identity) impacts self-esteem and that individuals try to maintain self-esteem by thinking positively about social groups. They concluded that being in a group that supports positively viewing other group members can lead to positive self-esteem.

Developmental Phases of Groups

Several theorists concerned with long-term order of group interaction have identified developmental phases in psychotherapy groups. Bach (1954) identified seven developmental phases from an initial testing phase to a relatively stable work phase: (1) Initial Situation Testing, (2) Leader Dependence, (3) Familial Regression, (4) Associative Copeering, (5) Fantasy and Play, (6) In-Group Consciousness, and (7) The Work Group. Bach cautioned that during any given two-minute period when observing a therapy group meeting, a team of astute observers could find a simultaneous overlap of phases.

Martin and Hill (1957) identified six developmental phases in group interaction: (1) individual shared behavior in the imposed structure; (2) reactivation of fixated interpersonal stereotypes; (3) exploration of interpersonal potential within the group; (4) an awareness of interrelationships, subgroupings, and power structures; (5) responsiveness to group dynamics and group process problems; and (6) the group as an integrative-creative social instrument. In contrast to Bach, Martin and Hill hypothesized a more orderly progression from phase one through phase seven.

Geller (1962) focused on the development of a group from its beginning to the working relationship. His stages took from six to thirty sessions to occur. They included (1) uncertainty, marked by diffuse anxiety and avoidance of involvement with others; (2) overaggression; (3) regression; and (4) adaptation.

Each of these systems of thought has its limitations. Phases of group movement are not clear cut. The group moves in a fluid process so that behavior listed as characteristic of one phase may also appear in another phase. This means any statement about when a phase occurs must be qualified. Bach's developmental phase system comes closest to allowing for these transitions. Yet, his system prohibits knowing what phase to expect next and is not strictly predictive. Martin and Hill, and Geller have developed more predictive theories, yet their systems of classification do not allow for transitions.

Seating Arrangement

Steinzor (1950) focused on seating arrangement and its correlation with verbal behavior rather than on the content of the members' communication. He compared two different discussion groups for ten sessions. He hypothesized that people sitting in a position that allowed them to observe more of each other's behavior would follow one another in verbal behavior more often than people whose view of each other was limited. This hypothesis, though supported, does not deal with the multiplicity of other variables operating in the group situation (content verbalized, nonverbal behavior, or shared behavior), and consequently is limited in value as a group research method.

Group Size

Hare, Borgotta, and Bales (1955) studied group size and its effect on participation of group members. Four groups of each size, two through seven, were observed for four sessions each. Each group was presented with a problem to solve (task groups). The researchers found that relative talking time per member decreased as the group size increased and that more pressure was applied to each member to maintain relationships with each other member as group size increased.

Geller (1951) found that size of group may also have some influence on the establishment of relationships among group members in supportive or psychotherapeutic groups, too. For example, in a group containing fewer than six or seven members, participants tend to relate to the leader one by one rather than to other members. In larger groups (size eight to fifteen), more interacting occurs among group members, a more continuous process is identifiable, and more relationships among members are maintained as group size increases to an end point of fifteen.

Hare (1952) also studied the relationship between group size and interaction among task groups (Boy Scouts). He found that groups of twelve members tended to split into factions, but groups of five members tended toward consensus.

Sequence of Speaking

Haley (1964) studied the small group called the family. He used the sequence of speaking in single family group sessions to compare forty "disturbed" families with forty "normal" families. He theorized that the "normal" families would not have to resort to "pathological ententes" where two members shut out the other from speaking. He also hypothesized that "normal" families would speak in sequences approaching randomness, but "disturbed" families would speak in more fixed sequences, deviating widely from randomness. Sequence of speaking is an objective measure that requires minimal inference and it can be related to psychiatric theory. Ruesch (1957) described patterns of communication in terms of their flexibility. The more fixed patterns of communication are, and the more vested the interests, the more difficult they are to alter.

Fixed patterns of interaction are learned in the family, but are practiced in other small groups. After the initial testing phase in therapy groups, group members also develop rules for interacting (Whitaker, 2001). Chambers (1966) used sequence of speaking to compare hospitalized (psychotic diagnoses) and nonhospitalized (neurotic diagnoses) therapy groups, using a session halfway between six and thirty in the working phase, when patterns of interaction had already formed. Chambers found fixed patterns of interaction in both types of group, tending to negate theories that state there is a sharp differentiation between neurotic and psychotic interaction, and to support the theory that mental health and illness are on a continuum rather than being distinct categories.

GROUP CONTENT AND PROCESS

Content, or *group content*, is a term used to describe topics discussed in a group session. Content may be straightforward and explicit, or it may convey a symbolic meaning. Both explicit and symbolic meanings are assessed when one group member comments, "Boy, is it hot in here!" at a time when other group members are arguing with one another. Overtly, the room may be warm temperature-wise; symbolically, the group member may be commenting on the "hot" issue being discussed. With practice, you can tune in to both straightforward and symbolic meanings being expressed in the group.

In groups there is constant movement toward and away from the goal as group members seek to reduce the tension that arises when people attempt to have their individual needs met, yet engage in group tasks or interactions. This movement is referred to as *group process*. Group process refers to the way group members interact with one another: interruptions, silences, judgments, glares, scapegoating, and more are all group processes. Because so much activity occurs in some groups, the inexperienced leader often has difficulty identifying group process. In the group process approach you assume that the group is not only an aggregate of individuals, but a dynamic, ever-changing ebb and flow of energy. When tension levels are too high or too low, group process is impeded. For each group you must be able to identify what group processes are occurring, what will impede and what will assist group process, when to intervene in the process, and when to remain silent.

The following excerpt from an adolescent health discussion group points up the leader's lack of awareness of group process and shows how he impedes effective group movement:

> LEADER: "You guys shouldn't drink, you know."
> TONY: "What do you know about it?"
> LEADER: "Drinking is bad for your health."
> TONY: "That's what everyone says."
> LEADER: "So why not listen?"

TONY (burps loudly):   "Pass the beer, please."

SAM: "Enough talk for today."

LEADER: "O.K., since you don't want to talk, we'll end for today."

Here, the leader seems to be at war with the group and tries to use logic to convince the members that drinking is unhealthy. Had the leader realized that the members of this group would be likely to resist logical arguments (which they would probably have heard before from authority figures), he might have taken a different tack, such as asking them what drinking did for them, what they knew about the physiological effects of alcohol, or even whether they thought that he would tell them what everyone else had told them. In this way, the leader might have decreased group resistance to his statements and possibly begun to convince the group that he was interested in listening to them and understanding their perceptions. By taking such a role, he would not only potentially reduce group tension, but also serve as a role model for effective group interaction. The leader also assumes the group does not want to talk, when only one member indicated there had been enough talk (Sam). Querying the other group members would have been a useful intervention. Also, the leader makes a unilateral decision to end the group. It would have been helpful to either (a) stick to the limits of time the group had agreed on, or (b) get a group consensus on whether or not to end.

As you continue to observe group process over time, you will find it useful to ask a few questions:

- What seems to lead to increased tension levels?
- What indicates conflict?
- When does the group seem to be apathetic?
- How are decisions arrived at?
- What types of leadership occur?
- What rules for behavior are in operation?
- What factors lead to effective movement toward and away from group goals?
- What signs of aggression and assertiveness are evident?
- What phase of group process does the group seem to be in?
- What themes recur?

Process comments focus on the here and now of what is happening. Some general process comments are: "I wonder what is really going on in the group now." "Why are we doing this?" and "I believe we are getting bogged down by feelings right now." More specific process comments depend on what is occurring, but some possibilities are: "Were you all aware that only two people voiced their opinions, yet we made a decision?" "Did you know that Jim and Betty have formed their own discussion group?" and "I think we're really all very confused and angry by what just happened; let's discuss it."

This chapter describes key group concepts and the dynamics of group process.

TENSION AND ANXIETY IN THE GROUP

At times, all group members, including the leader, show signs of tension or anxiety. Mild and even moderate anxiety can be useful in promoting group movement. When the tension level becomes too high, the leader takes steps to lower it, after noting which indicants, of anxiety increase and which decrease, and at what points during the session this happens.

Anxiety is an unexplained feeling of discomfort that one experiences when expectations are not met. New group members may experience anxiety when they expect the group experience to be of one sort, and it turns out to be something else. Group members can also experience anxiety when asked questions about any topic on which they lack information or feel unsure of themselves. For example, a group member who is obese may experience anxiety when diet is discussed, and a group leader who does not have correct information on a certain drug may feel anxious when asked to discuss that drug. Anxiety is a common reaction in unfamiliar or new situations; the first meeting of a group may result in such feelings both in group members and the leader. Some people are quite sensitive to disapproval and may feel anxious when the leader or other group members indicate disapproval of their words or actions. Any situation that interferes with basic needs can create anxiety. Not being respected or recognized can lead to feelings of anxiety; leaders who are challenged by group members or group members who are called by inappropriate or incorrect names may experience anxiety.

Anxiety can occur whenever human needs are threatened. *Maslow's hierarchy of needs* provides a framework for assessing group members' anxiety. The lowest level of human needs is physiological in nature. A group member who complains of being tired or hungry is exhibiting Level 1 human needs. When group members are afraid of censure or feel insecure in their jobs or statements, Level 2 human needs for safety are threatened. When group members are talking and joking with one another, they may be attempting to meet their need for acceptance (Level 3). Group members who seek approval of their work or press to get the group moving to accomplish the work may be working on Level 4 needs for esteem. Group members who evolve creative solutions to problems may be working toward Level 5 needs for self-development and self-actualization (Maslow, 1987).

Many groups and organizations do not provide sufficient opportunities for their members to satisfy Level 4 and 5 needs. When leaders exercise arbitrary power, group members may be unable to move past Level 2 because their needs for security and safety are constantly being threatened. Group members who are not provided with sufficient opportunity to meet higher level needs will seek opportunities off the job. This may explain work situations in which workers slack off and use only enough energy to keep their jobs and receive their pay.

Signs of anxiety include restlessness, lack of eye contact, body tenseness, stiff or repetitive gestures, rapid shallow breathing, perspiration, rapid or unclear speech, changing the topic of conversation, silence, distorting or overreacting to others' comments, griping, daydreaming, or being forgetful.

You can follow several procedures to reduce anxiety in new group members. First, spending time with the members prior to the first group session will help them feel more comfortable, because they will then know at least one person who will be in the group. Also, you can share with group members the reasons they are leading the group and what their feelings are at that moment. Admission of your own feelings of tension or anxiety about starting a new group will often help the members to feel more comfortable in sharing their own thoughts and feelings. You can anticipate that in an unknown situation group members will be curious about the role they will play. Inviting comments from the group about what they expect of the leader and stating specifically the functions the leader plans to perform can decrease tension.

Warming-up exercises may be quite helpful in decreasing anxiety in a new group (Hunter, 1996). One exercise consists of having members write down and/or verbally explain the reason they are there and what they hope to get from the group experience. Or, to get the group started, the members can be asked to draw pictures of themselves and then pair off to talk about their drawings and possibly to express their fears about being in the group. Films and other audiovisual materials can be used to stimulate discussion. The innovative leader can devise many such warming-up exercises.

When group members are unable to talk about their discomfort, yet you sense that tension is high, one of the following comments can be made: "It seems we're all a little tense," or "I guess we're all a little nervous since we don't know each other yet," or "I sense this subject worries you," or "This is hard to learn, but it will be worth the effort."

You can prepare yourself and group members for meeting anxiety-provoking situations as they arise. One way to do this is to think through, or even write down, a summary of what you expected to happen in the coming session. This technique will help identify hidden fears, and once this is accomplished further self-questioning can include such queries as: "So what if that does happen?" "What could I do to handle that if it did occur?"

Role playing can also be used to decrease anxiety. Suppose a group member becomes anxious when asking for a raise, when setting a limit on a child's behavior, or when asking for a favor. Two group members, or the leader and one group member, can preplay the problematic situation; then the two role players can exchange roles to find out how it feels to "be in the other's shoes." Group members can serve as coaches to the role players and give feedback after the role play about how the situation could best have been handled.

Progressive relaxation can be used to reduce group anxiety at the beginning, middle, or end of a group session or meeting. Group members can be asked to close their eyes, get comfortable in their chairs, and concentrate on the leader's voice. The following words can then be said in a slow, monotone voice:

Each time you exhale, let your breathing move lower in your body, moving effortlessly toward your abdominal area. (Pause.) Focus your attention on your feet now; let your feet sink into the floor, becoming more relaxed and comfortable. (Pause.) Let that feeling of relaxation and comfort move up your feet into your lower legs. (Pause.) Continue to let your breathing move effortlessly toward your abdominal area, so that each time you exhale, your breathing becomes easier and more relaxed. (Pause.) Continue to let that feeling of relaxation and comfort move up your legs. You might want to picture the relaxation moving up your body as a color or symbol; use whatever is right for you. (Pause.) Let the feeling of relaxation and comfort move up your legs and into your buttocks; let your buttocks and groin relax and sink into the chair. (Pause.) Let your lower back and spine sink comfortably into your chair; let all the muscles in your back relax and get longer and wider. (Pause.) Let anything you're carrying on your shoulders roll down your shoulders, down your arms, and out your fingertips. (Pause.) Let your neck relax and float between your shoulders and head. (Pause.) Let that feeling of comfort and relaxation move up your scalp and hair, over the top of your head, and down your forehead; let your eyebrows relax. Let your eyelashes and eyes relax and the space behind them and the space behind that. Release all unwanted thoughts from your mind, getting more relaxed and more comfortable. Let your cheeks relax. (Pause.) Let your nose relax. (Pause.) Let your mouth relax, unlock your jaw and let it relax. (Pause.) Let your teeth and tongue relax. (Pause.) Scan your body and find any areas that need more relaxation; send some peaceful relaxation there. (Pause.) When you're ready, slowly open your eyes, keeping the sense of relaxation and comfort with you.

Imagery can also be used to assist group members to relax. Ask the members to close their eyes and take a trip to a relaxing, comforting place. It can be a place they have been before or someplace they have never been. Encourage the group to smell the smells associated with the peaceful and relaxing place; hear the sounds associated with the peaceful and relaxing place; taste the tastes and experience the sensations associated with the peaceful and relaxing place. Be silent for 2 to 3 minutes as the group totally immerses itself in the peaceful and relaxing place. After several minutes, ask the participants to come back through time and space to the group, keeping the relaxation and comfort with them. Remind group members that they can become more relaxed and comfortable at any time by closing their eyes and returning briefly to their peaceful and relaxing place.

In addition to anxiety in the early stages of a group, there may be upsetting situations that occur. At these times, group leaders can use either of the relaxation exercises described above to assist group members to relax and to communicate better with others in a calm and thoughtful manner.

These relaxation exercises can also be used to decrease anxiety about upcoming situations. The first step is consciously to contract and then relax the various body muscles. This allows learners to get the feel of tension and relaxation. Next, they imagine a pleasant scene. When they are completely relaxed, the anxiety-provoking situation is called to their attention, and, as soon as they feel their bodies becoming tense, they are asked to focus again on relaxing their muscles and imagining the pleasant scene. With practice, learners will be able to go through an entire tension-provoking scene mentally without experiencing overwhelming anxiety. Once they have mastered relaxation in role-playing situations, they can practice the exercise in actual anxiety-provoking experiences.

You can reduce group members' anxiety by assisting them to meet low-level human needs and by allowing them to share in creative problem solving.

Finally, humor can be used to dissipate tension. However, it should be used cautiously so that group members are not made to feel degraded, and it should never be used to avoid confronting important issues.

GROUP CONFLICT

Conflict caused by opposing forces within the group can occur in an individual member, or it can be shared by subgroups or by the entire group. Once group members have settled in and become acquainted with one another, conflict often begins to develop. It may be disguised and covered up at first, but it may soon burgeon into hostility or even out-and-out warfare. Group members may not voice their concerns, but they are probably worried about learning what they want to learn and getting their needs met. They may try to prove themselves or hassle the group leader about the agenda. As group leader, it is important that you note and express differences among group members in their motivation, knowledge of group processes, willingness to experiment, and rate of learning. It is also important to realize that resolution of group conflict cannot be rushed.

Group members may resist with long intellectual discussions, statements that whatever you say doesn't apply to them, withdrawal into silence, or superior assertions that they already know whatever you've said. Subgroupings may next appear with one or more group members vying for control of the group as conflict and resistance deepen. Although the goings on may appear chaotic, factional conflict is a good sign. The group is progressing, building working agreements and organizing itself. Through it all, you must trust the developmental group process and try to help participants work out the limits of what can be decided. Rational discussions of authority and group process can only prolong group conflict (Coleman, 2000).

Group conflict can be very useful. Without it, points of view are probably being masked and good solutions probably cannot be made. Help the group learn the difference between disagreement, which is to be encouraged because it enriches productivity and problem solving, and conflict (Nasmith, 1995).

The more inhibited group members are in expressing their feelings, the more frustration they will experience due to suppressed conflict. This builds tension, and conflict can provide an outlet for hostility. A group must find ways to vent hostility to reach and maintain cohesiveness. Social conflict need not be threatening to a group as long as the leader stays calm.

Conflict also increases the interdependence of group members. Groups will often permit and even encourage deviant behavior because it strengthens group norms and standards. A member who deviates from the norm also gives the group a focus—that group member—doing something about the deviation.

Feelings associated with conflict include helplessness, anger, and rejection. Wise leaders obtain experience in conflict simulations and role playing so they understand conflict more clearly and have experienced the feelings that go with it (Gross & Guerrero, 2000). This practice and the actual group sessions provide the best learning situation when they take place out of the usual stream of work. When the sessions are psychologically safe and "not for keeps," participants can feel free to admit inadequacy, to explore and to try out ways of handling conflict they may never dare to try in real-life situations.

Managing conflict doesn't mean a group necessarily resolves the conflict or even controls it. Conflict management means the group develops a consistent action when conflict occurs. The conflict may occur again, but often in a different form.

Perhaps the first step in conflict management is to acknowledge there is a conflict. By acting as if it is not occurring, the group's forward movement will be stymied. Next, a series of questions can be asked by the group leader to facilitate group resolution of conflict, including:

- What did you think of what happened when I tried to smooth over the conflict?
- How did you feel when I gave my own opinions?

- Is the group getting anywhere in resolving this conflict?
- The group went off on a tangent at one point. Was that due to something I did?
- What incidents in this session bothered you the most?
- Did you notice we've divided into two factions?
- How do you think we should handle group conflict?
- Do you get worried when group conflict appears?
- What would help you to notice the buildup before group conflict appears?
- How can we recognize the difference between healthy conflict and antagonism?
- Can you say what you've learned about how to handle group conflict?

Tape Recording Group Conflict

In the heat of an interchange, it is difficult to understand and choose healthier ways of reacting. When learning about group conflict and how to handle it as a leader or group member, it is useful to tape record segments of the group that display conflict and replay them later for discussion and analysis. Try not to make an issue of taping; just present it in a matter-of-fact way as a good method to learn about group process. Discussing tapes is time-consuming, so allow time for it.

Once tapes have been made of sessions or portions of sessions, you can play back a segment and the group can use checklists or process recording devices to analyze what occurred. You can also provide role-playing situations that demonstrate conflict and assign roles or have group members draw role descriptions out of a hat and then role play the situations you introduce. This kind of learning can even occur in large groups by dividing participants into smaller subgroups for the role playing and discussion segments and bringing the whole group back together to discuss what has been learned and what is left to be discovered in future sessions (Campbell, 1999).

Skill practice in conflict resolution (as well as for any other group process) includes the following elements (Miles, 1959):

1. isolate the behavior and define the desired reaction
2. try out the behavior
3. obtain feedback from the group on how the new behavior worked

4. note discrepancies from the desired reaction and use it as a basis for further practice

Here are some possible situations that could be role played to understand group conflict:

- The group has been offered no choice in a decision and progress is slow because members ridicule, criticize, and in general resist instituting the procedure.
- The group is working at cross purposes: one faction wants to solve one problem, while another faction has its own agenda.
- A clique that controls all activities has taken over the group and the other members are dissatisfied, ignored, and feel left out.
- The group leader sets up two factions, for example, "salary enhancement" vs. "professional integrity" and assigns half the group to each faction to play out which is more important. In this case, the leader can advise one faction on how to reduce conflict, thus demonstrating the importance of a liaison person who has membership in both factions (Miles, 1959).

Individuals can experience conflict within themselves when they wish to be singled out for special treatment by the leader yet at the same time fear the leader's disapproval; this conflict can be resolved when individuals conform to the behavior of the other group members. Another solution to bids for special attention by one group member is for the group to take over and interfere with the attention-getting behavior.

Sources of conflict in the group as a whole include being given an impossible task, having conflicting loyalties within and. outside the group, jockeying for power or status, dislike of one another, and involvement in the task assigned. Whether the group leader should intervene in a group conflict depends on whether group process seems to be impeded or assisted by it. Intervention may be necessary when some group members attack others' ideas before they are completely expressed, take sides and refuse to compromise, attack one another's personal attributes or behavior, insist that the group does not have the knowledge or experience to resolve its difficulties, or accuse one another of not understanding. Whenever any of these symptoms of conflict occur, you can intervene by stating the group goal more clearly, defining smaller steps that can be taken to assure obtaining the goal, suggesting that more time be allowed to achieve the goal, teaching the members what they need to know to reach their goal, finding a goal that interests all members, requiring them to substitute an assertive statement such as, "I feel angry when people tease me" for an aggressive, attacking, "You teased me, you rat!" and asking group members to paraphrase others' comments in order to decrease distortion of communication messages.

When group members appear not to understand the group goal, frequently disagree, and show strong positive or negative feeling and signs of impatience, you will probably not want to interfere, since these are signs of conflict arising from involvement in the task.

Conflict is best viewed as a challenge and an inevitable part of human interaction. Conflict is not likely to surface until members begin to feel relatively comfortable with one another; prior to that, they are more concerned about what others may think of them. As politeness fades in importance, squabbles or subsystem grouping may occur as human differences and disagreements are noticed and addressed. You can assist groups to learn to deal with conflict by:

- Teaching and encouraging the use of assertiveness and feedback skills
- Increasing openness
- Reinforcing and commenting on *any* positive group action
- Testing for *true* consensus
- Identifying hidden agendas
- Facilitating win-win solutions
- Changing seating arrangement
- Using negotiation skills

Teaching Assertiveness and Feedback Skills

The language of conflict can elicit feelings of threat or defensiveness; group members can close off from one another. The language of assertiveness is one of problem solving that elicits trust and positive regard for openness and directness (Sandy & Susan, 2000). Parts of group members unknown to themselves can be opened and released for constructive work when feedback is given. Novice group members may refrain from giving feedback because they are fearful of hurting or angering recipient. Constructive feedback will minimize hurt and a and open the person to discovery of information that was viously unknown.

Many nonconstructive group patterns can be successfully resolved if all group members practice assertive communication. Learning to take responsibility for one's own thoughts, feelings, and actions takes the attack out of confrontation. Group members will be more likely to remain nondefensive when assertive comments such as, "I feel angry about what is happening," or "I want to give you feedback about your nonverbal messages, Sarah," are made than when aggressive comments are: "I feel you are manipulative," or "You're always disrupting the group by groaning." By teaching group members to take the blame out of their comments, refrain from unfair fighting by bringing up past issues, focus on observed behaviors, and clearly state the issues, you can teach communication skills useful not only in the group at hand but in many other interpersonal situations as well.

You can make a pact with the group that the leader or any group member can interrupt the conversation whenever a nonassertive message is heard. This will assist all group members to be aware of nonassertiveness. At these times, the person who used a nonassertive message can be asked to "Say that again, only this time use an 'I' message." With repetition, group members will begin catching their own nonassertive messages midway through their statement and correcting themselves (Clark, 2003).

One method for describing the language of problem solving was developed by Eric Berne (1964) and Thomas Harris (1969). Their method of describing communication processes is called *Transactional Analysis* (TA). A *transaction* occurs when. one person says something to another and the second person responds verbally or nonverbally.

Transactions are categorized by Berne as *The Parent, The Adult,* and *The Child.* Parent and Child developed unconsciously or without much control by the individual. The Child is composed of recorded memories of feelings and fantasies; rage, sadness, or fear occur when the Child portion takes over. The Parent is composed of recorded memories or messages remembered from parental speeches; messages concern how to eat. dress, behave acceptably, what one "should" and "should not" do, what is good and what is bad. The Parent is the judgmental part of oneself.

Although TA, has been called simplistic, it does provide an easily teachable framework for group communication. The idea is Adult to Adult communication in which problem solving occurs through getting and giving descriptive (rather than judgmental) information.

When a group member says, "You are frightening," a Parent statement and a judgment has been made; when a group member says, "I feel frightened when you look menacing," an Adult statement has been made. By teaching group members to identify Parent, Child, and Adult messages, problem solving will be enhanced; much of what bogs down problem-solving processes is the occurrence of judgmental and helpless statements.

Problem solving is facilitated when all group members have the same information. Preparation for problem solving requires establishing an openness among group members. Just as individual group members can learn to deal at the adult level of transaction, individuals can learn to give feedback in a manner that minimizes judgment, fear, threat, and defensiveness. Some rules to teach group members to use are:

1. *Be descriptive rather than judgmental.* For example, when a nursing supervisor tells her supervisees, "You're not providing quality care," they are likely to be pained or angry. If the nursing supervisor tells her supervisees, "I noticed W. Smith's light has been on continually; let's talk about how to help him rest comfortably," then the staff can focus on a specific problem and will be more receptive.
2. *Be specific rather than general.* Saying, "I don't like your attitude," gives far less help to the person than "I get the impression I'm not being listened to."
3. *Give feedback when it can be used.* Check with the recipient to find out whether the individual wants the feedback and can use it at that time. If a group member is anxious or depressed, feedback can add more stress to a stressful situation. Ask the group member when feedback can be given or check back later that session or at the next meeting to agree on a time for feedback.
4. *Give feedback at the time the behavior* occurs. If a nurse leader says to a staff member, "I observed you talking with Mr. Jones last week and I didn't like what I heard," the details of the incident are likely to have been forgotten.
5. *Give feedback when its accuracy can be checked with others.* The group is the best place to give group members

feedback. Avoid waiting until after a group meeting to have a private chat with a group member.

6. *Use assertive "I" messages when conveying criticism or feeling.* Saying, "Don't argue with the physicians, you'll get me in trouble" is far more threatening than, "I feel uncomfortable when I hear you argue with Dr. Gonzales; let's do some role playing so you can discuss and not argue with him."

McKay, Davis, and Fanning (1985) describe *rules of fair fighting* that can be used by group leaders to teach group members how to discuss disagreements, grievances, and gripes:

1. *Hit above the belt.* Group members must learn to become attuned to criticism that is too painful for other group members to hear and that which can be heard, accepted, and acted upon. The best way to identify what is too painful is to validate with the group member whether a subject is too painful to be discussed at that moment and to respect the individual's decision. Topics that require discussion are not avoided, merely put on hold until the group member is ready to discuss them; group leaders are generally responsible for picking up the topic at a later time.

2. *Practice good timing.* Avoid storing grievances and attacking them all at once, or bringing up a "hot" topic just as the group is about to end.

3. *Be clear.* State the grievance simply using "I" statements that make it clear that "this is my feeling, not your fault."

4. *Focus on behavior, not attitudes.* Demanding respect, warmth, or any subjective, spontaneous attitude is doomed to failure. Doomed comments ("I feel you don't respect my opinions and I want you to") can be turned into successful conflict resolution statements by focusing on behavior. ("I feel left out of important decisions that affect me; I want to go shopping with you and pick out the gift.")

5. *Focus on the here and now.* Leave past disagreements or hurts out of the discussion. Fight about one specific issue at a time.

6. *Focus on one individual at a time.* Avoid raging at group members who are absent at the time or at other groups, institutions, religions, ideas, etc.

7. *Listen attentively* to the other person's gripes and avoid rehearsing a retort, hearing only what you want *to hear, blowing up or walking away, anticipating* what the other person means or will say next, or judging what is said.

Increasing Openness

Sometimes conflict can be decreased by increasing openness. Some strategies for increasing openness are self-disclosure, nonverbal and verbal mirroring, using open-ended questions, and checking out perceptions.

When the group leader discloses feelings and opinions, group members often feel more comfortable doing so themselves. Group leaders must walk the fine line between burdening the group with personal problems and showing humanness. A useful rule is to think through whether the self-disclosure is being used to make the group leader feel better or whether it is being used to facilitate group movement.

Nonverbal and verbal mirroring can reduce conflict. In one group, the leader purposefully changed her breathing pattern, gestures, and eye movements to mirror the behavior of a hostile group member; later in the session, that group member became less verbal and mentioned feeling closer to the leader.

Hover (1983) discusses using *Neuro-Linguistic Programming* methods to enhance communication in the family group. Neurolinguistic programmers have noted that individuals have & primary representational system for their inner experience. Those using a visual representational system use words such as see, observe, my point of view, my perception, and my focus. Those using an auditory representational system use words such as I hear, I like loud sounds, I enjoy soft noises, and I harmonize well with others. Those using a kinesthetic representational system use words such as I feel, I sense, I touch, I'm aware of . . . Those using an olfactory-gustatory representational system use words such as I can almost smell . . . , I enjoy the flavor of. . . . I taste, and I eat . . .

Group leaders can open communication with group members by "speaking their language."

The following example shows what happens when the group leader *does not* speak the group members' language:

> LEADER: How are you *feeling?"*
>
> GROUP MEMBER: "It *looks* like the day may brighten."
>
> LEADER: "But tell me your feelings."
>
> GROUP MEMBER: "I just did!"

The next example shows what happens when the group leader identifies and uses the same representational system as the group member:

> LEADER: "How are you feeling?"
> GROUP MEMBER: "It *looks* like the day may brighten."
> LEADER: "So that's how things *look* to you today."
> GROUP MEMBER: "Yes, you're right."

Merely by matching the verbal predicates, the leader and group member were able to communicate at a higher level of understanding. Many group members describe the experience of verbal and nonverbal mirroring by saying, "All of a sudden we were on the same wavelength. I felt more understood."

Using open-ended questions can encourage group members to describe and understand conflict. The following are open-ended questions:

"What are we arguing about now?"
"What do you think is preventing us from moving along?"
"What is your opinion?"

When the leader or any group member *assumes* what is meant by another person, conflict and negative feelings can result. To ensure conflict is not the result of assumption, it is wise to check out perceptions with questions such as,* "I hear you saying. . . . Is that what you mean to convey?" "If I hear you correctly, you're saying . . .

Reinforcing Positive Group Action

Group members may become discouraged as they struggle to become a working, constructive system. You can reinforce and encourage group action by pointing out *any* progress toward the goal. Some comments exemplifying this are: "I realize you are feeling frustrated with making this decision, but we are showing progress by discussing alternatives," and "Conflict is a normal happening in groups; I think we should congratulate ourselves on our courage in attempting to resolve it!"

Testing for True Consensus

It is not unusual for group leaders to take a cursory hand count to settle an issue. Group members may feel pressured to respond as the majority does, despite feelings to the contrary; this can result in resentment, lowered self-esteem, and conflict. You can assist the group toward true consensus by using the following behaviors:

1. Refraining from calling for a vote until all group members have had their say.
2. Continuing to ask, "Who else has a comment?" or repeating, "We haven't heard everyone's ideas yet," until all have spoken.
3. Restating that all members' viewpoints are needed in order to attain a true consensus.

Identifying Hidden Agendas

Hidden agendas are operating goals that influence group process even though they are not openly acknowledged. McKay, Davis, and Fanning (1985, pp. 77–84) list eight major hidden agendas that disrupt clear, open communication:

1. *I'm Good.* The theme of how honest, hard-working, courageous, loyal, generous, successful, powerful, or self-sacrificing one is may be used by group members who have this hidden agenda. Group leaders can be helpful to group members using this agenda as a life tune by assisting them to accept the position: "I'm a mixture of strengths and weaknesses."
2. *I'm Good, But You're* Not. Group members who use this agenda may be heard to say, "Everyone's stupid, incompetent, selfish, unreasonable, lazy, frightened, or insensitive but me." Eric Berne (1964) has identified versions of this agenda, including (a) *Courtroom* (spouses try to prove how awful the other is; in groups, group members can make statements discounting other group members' involvement or contribution to group goals), (b) *If It Weren't For You* (spouses or group members blame each other for restricted, joyless lives or sessions). A healthier position to teach group members is: "I'm no longer in the business of comparing."
3. *You're Good, But I'm Not.* A simple version of this agenda is flattery; more complex forms involve worship of smart, beautiful, or strong people. This agenda is often used to ward off rejection or anger or as an excuse for not changing. Group leaders can teach group members to accept the position: "I don't need to make excuses; I can get attention with my strengths and abilities."
4. *I'm Helpless, I Suffer.* This is the agenda of victims who refuse to be responsible for what happens to them. *Ain't It Awful* is a variation played by those who want to complain

about their spouses. Group leaders can identify the game, *Why Don't You. . . . Yes, But,* when they hear group members constantly asking for advice and help and then not taking it. This version is very good for maintaining helplessness. Teaching group members to say, "My life is a balance of pleasure and pain, hope and sadness," can give them a less helpless view of their lives.

5. *I'm Blameless* is used by group members who use excuses for their failures. *See What You Made Me Do* is used by group members who ask for suggestions or advice, follow the advice, and then blame the group leader or group member who suggested it.

6. *I'm Fragile* is used by group members who present themselves as vulnerable, in need of protection, and unable to hear the truth from others. Group members choosing the I'm Fragile agenda can learn to accept "It scares me a little when someone is honest, but I can listen to it."

7. *I'm Tough* is the agenda of group members who list all the harrowing things they do daily and still survive. The message is they are stronger; work harder, faster, and longer than anyone else. I'm Tough is also the message of the dangerous and violent who are saying, "don't attack me or I'll hurt you." I'm Tough hides the vulnerability and fear of rejection inside. A healthier message to learn is: "I can take care of myself while relaxing and without scaring others."

8. *I Know It All* is the agenda of the teacher/lecturer. Moralizing, constant teaching, or preaching keeps others away from intimacy and protects one from the shame of not knowing and not being adequate. A healthier message is: "I can learn from others by listening and watching."

Group members can learn to identify their own agendas by counting the number of times they use an agenda, verbalizing the fact that an agenda is used. ("I know I'm sounding helpless, but it's not so" or "I'm sounding down on everyone and everything, but I know it's not that bad.")

Group leaders can share information on the basic eight agendas and point out instances of use during group conversation. (e.g., "We seem to be playing, Why don't you. . . . Yes, but" or "I'm hearing a hidden agenda; does anyone else hear it?") Group members can be encouraged to write down their new life positions on three-by-five cards and carry them with them, complete a sign to hang in their room, or say them over and over as affirmations or mottos.

Facilitating Win-Win Solutions

Win-win solutions are focused on ends or goals. In win-lose and lose-lose methods of conflict resolution, the following commonalities can be identified (McKay, Davis, & Fanning, 1995, pp. 135–145):

1. There is a clear we–they distinction between group members or groups rather than a we-versus-the problem.
2. Energy is focused on total victory or total defeat.
3. Each sees the issue from its own point of view, not in terms of mutual needs.
4. Emphasis is on attaining a solution, rather than upon defining goals, values, or motives to be attained with the solution.
5. Conflicts are personalized rather than depersonalized via an objective focus on facts and issues.
6. There is no planned sequence of conflict-resolving activities or a differentiation of them from other group processes.
7. The parties are conflict-oriented, emphasizing the immediate disagreement, rather than relationship-oriented, emphasizing long-term effects of differences and how to resolve them.

To facilitate win–win solutions, you can suggest that participants (1) focus on defeating the problem, not each other; (2) avoid voting, trading, or averaging; (3) seek facts to resolve dilemmas; (4) view conflict as helpful; (5) avoid self-oriented behavior and focus on others' needs or positions; (6) seek solutions that are not unacceptable to anyone either falls in *the* category of "don't care" or "support"); and (7) agree that the leader controls the process by which the group arrives at agreement but does not dictate the content.

Confrontation (win-win solutions) leads to higher performance in organizations than either force (resorting to authority or coercion) or smoothing (agreeing on an intellectual level). Whenever possible, the group leader should attempt to teach group members conflict-resolution skills that lead to win-win solutions.

Sometimes conflict occurs because of subsystem formation or *pairing*. Prior to intervening, it is wise to observe if the seating arrangement may be contributing to subsystem formation; if this is the case, the leader can separate group members who seem to be splintering off from the group. Depending on the maturity of the members and the type of group, several methods can be used to achieve the same purpose.

In a supportive or therapeutic group, the leader can "call process" and say to the group, "It seems we're not all talking together; what do you think that is about?" Through discussion, the group may identify the problem; if not, the leader can suggest a seating change or another method of assisting group members to talk to the entire group.

Sitting in a circle is the most conducive to discussion. If a task or teaching group is not arranged in a circle, arranging chairs in that manner can promote discussion. Asking all group members to sit next to someone different is a tactic useful for breaking up subgroupings. If the group leader introduces chair changes in a neutral manner the group is likely to comply (e.g., "Let's try sitting in different chairs today; this will give you a different perspective on what happens and also may be a positive factor in promoting discussion").

The group leader can also arrange to sit between group members who are pairing or subgrouping; this will break up the subgroup. Sometimes subgrouping is due to feeling alienated from or competitive with the leader; by sitting next to the subgroup members, the leader will seem less formidable and less competitive.

By sitting next to an anxious, hostile, or new group member, the leader also signals a wish to be closer and more supportive. This may be useful in therapeutic and supportive groups, especially when other group members signal nonverbally that they are fearful of the group member. The physical presence of the designated leader can provide a calming influence on the group and also signals that the group leader is not fearful or rejecting of the group member.

The following situation describes a successful solution to subgrouping:

A group of students in a program taking a group leadership course was composed of seven members who did not know one another and two who worked in the same health care facility. The two who knew one another previously always sat together, whispered when others were talking, and talked about one another to the group. When the leader noticed the pattern, she suggested everyone take a seat next to someone different at the next session. At the end of the class, the leader asked what effect the change of seating arrangement made. A number of group members stated they were surprised how different the group seemed; one group member said, "It's because Barbara and Jennie weren't sitting together!" Jennie commented, "When I made my presentation it was easier because I didn't feel I had to speak only to Barbara." The leader then used the incident to discuss the pros and cons of changing seating arrangements in the groups the group members were currently leading.

Using Negotiation Skills

Anytime the leader or group members want something from each other, a potential negotiable situation exists. Negotiation skills assist individuals in getting what they want from others without alienating them. *Negotiation* is a process through which people with different or even opposing needs arrive at a fair agreement by generating a mutually acceptable option.

McKay, Davis, and Fanning (1995, pp. 147–148) say the process can be broken down into four stages:

1. *Preparation.* Before meeting with those involved, each person decides what outcome is desired and what would be less satisfactory but still acceptable. During this phase, gathering of information to bolster your case, strategic planning, and brainstorming occur. During *brainstorming,* all possible ideas are written down, avoiding judging the merit of each; one idea often sets off another idea, and judging merit interferes with the process. Once all possible ideas are compiled, they are ranked in order of usability.
2. *Discussion.* During this stage, each. person asks for the other's interests and elaborates on his or her own point of view. Each person describes the facts of the situation and thoughts and feelings about the situation. Discussion is the major means of resolving deadlocks.
3. *Proposal/Counterproposal.* One person makes an offer or request, the other(s) make counteroffers. This cycle is repeated until a compromise is reached; there may be time-outs for a return to Stages 1 and 2.
4. *Agreement/Disagreement.* Disagreement is a natural step in negotiation; it signals the need to try again by returning to earlier stages. Eventually a mutually acceptable option will be reached.

The following example describes how one group negotiated with its leader:

Preparation: One of the group members was going to be absent for the next meeting and asked that the session be tape-recorded. The leader asked the group to decide, but gave information on the pros and cons of taping the session, such as it will help the absent group member to stay on track with the movement of the group, the tape can be saved and used by the group to study its own behavior, taping the group may inhibit some group members from speaking (at least initially), procedures for ensuring the group session is taped and confidentiality is preserved must be developed. The leader then asked the group to brainstorm about how to deal with the group member's request.

Discussion: The group members asked why the person would be absent and elaborated on why it was important to be at each session. Feelings of hurt, resentment, and envy surfaced.

Proposal/Counterproposal. The group member who was to be absent proposed that she leave her tape recorder and *several tapes with* the group leader and asked for a volunteer to be responsible for taping the session and meeting her the following day to deliver the tapes, Several group members remained unsure about being taped and suggested a group member call the absent member during the week to fill her in on what had happened. One group member pointed out that much of the detail of the session may be forgotten and one group member's perception of the group session may be inaccurate.

Discussion: The group continued to discuss the merits of recording and not recording.

Agreement. The group finally agreed to allow the session to be taped under the condition that the group member guard the tape from others' ears and return the tape to the group at the following session. The group would have access to the information on the tape for that session, and then the tape would be erased.

The following rules for principled negotiation can be used by group leaders:

1. Keep position separate from self-worth, so that an attack on a position is not perceived as a personal attack.
2. Avoid entering negotiations with a single, rock-solid position. Instead, begin negotiations with a comment such as, "We're here to discuss how we can. . . . When you hear our requests, we think you'll agree they are reasonable and will probably want to make some suggestions of your own."
3. Use active listening to elicit others' feelings, thoughts, and needs. "The way I understand it is that you're *afraid* some-

one might hear what you said. You *think* the information might be used against you. You *need* to feel secure and nonthreatened here."

4. Share feelings, thoughts, and needs honestly. "I have mixed *feelings* about being here next week without Dorothy here too. I think *taping* is a good idea because we can use the tape to learn more about how we are doing. It will provide another source of feedback." 161 would *need* a volunteer to be responsible for the safe use of the tape to agree to the idea."

5. Uncover the interests behind an opponent's position; be sensitive to basic human needs for security, trust, intimacy, and self-esteem (Maslow, 1987).

6. Help others save face by labeling compromise as generosity (e.g., "I appreciate your generous offer to compromise on this issue.").

7. Explore trade-offs such as time for money, flexible hours for money, free overtime for future salary increase, etc.

8. Turn options into proposals by using "yesables": a yesable proposal is an acceptable option stated as a direct question to which "yes" is an easy answer. The following are deniable proposals: "I want this report and I want it by 10 o'clock!" and "No matter what you say you're assigned to Mr. Jones." Turning the proposals into yesable proposals would mean saying, "Would you rather finish the report now or give it to me after lunch?" or "If I assign you to Mr. Amos today, will you work with Mr. Jones tomorrow?" If you have trouble getting a "yes" from the person, check to be sure that that person has the power to make the requested decision.

Negotiating with an Opponent Who Has All the Power (Bosses and So Forth)

When faced with an opponent who has all the power, odds are tipped toward losing unless the other person(s) "plays fair." If the best alternative is a strong, realistic one, the proposal can be stated as an ultimatum: "If I don't get this promotion, I plan to leave institutional nursing and start my own private practice." If leaving is not possible, the best alternative is to come down hard on objective criteria: "What is it I'm doing that is keeping me from getting this promotion?" Appeal to an opponent's sense of fair play; drum up support among like-minded people; form a committee to study salary increases; or hold meetings, rallies, and press conferences. Become an expert on what other hospitals are paying and shine the harsh light of publicity on an opponent's unfairness.

Negotiating with Hard-Liners Who Will Not Cooperate

When management refuses to consider a position, look behind their position for underlying interests. Make a list of all the reasons they might have for refusing. When prepared, make an appointment with management and ask, "Why do you refuse to consider my proposal?" Sit back and wait out the silence for an answer. If you get a non-answer like, "It's against hospital policy" ask, "Why is it against hospital policy?" Also, try more specific questions: "Is it too expensive?" "How expensive do you think it would be to implement my proposal?" "Are you afraid others will try to take advantage of you if you give in to me?"

When management comes on strong with personal attacks, redefine them as attacks on the problem. For example, if accused of stirring up trouble, stifle impulses to call the boss a stooge for stupid management; instead, reframe the attack by saying, "You're right, nurses are very stirred up about staffing, and I appreciate the fact that you feel strongly about it too. It's a serious problem that deserves the attention of all responsible leaders at this hospital." By reframing attacks as shared problems, hostility can be defused and hardliners have a graceful way to start cooperating.

If there is too much feeling on both sides, the "one-text" procedure has been known to work. A text of a possible agreement is drawn up and presented to both sides; if both turn it down, another text is drafted and another, until an agreement is reached. The success of this method is due to the lack of direct confrontation or argument in the face of extremely high feeling states.

Negotiating with Opponents Who Play Dirty

There are many dirty negotiating tactics including lies, deceptions, bribery, blackmail, and psychological warfare. The best way to handle opponents who use these tactics is to "call process"; that is, stop talking about the subject at hand and talk about the process that is occurring, (e.g., "Before we go on, I'm having trouble concentrating on what you're saying because you're shaking your finger in my face. Let's move to the sofa instead of sitting across from each other at this desk."). If necessary, indicate an understanding of the temptation to take every possible advantage and that such attempts are not taken personally. Invite your opponent to help look for options that benefit everyone. Suggest some objective criteria for judging the agreed-upon options.

When this approach does not work, call in a neutral mediator. There are some conflicts that just cannot be negotiated. These occur when one or more individuals want the conflict more than the resolution. For example, unions may want to keep feelings high until a contract deadline closes; management may want to prolong negotiations until the union's funds are exhausted; students may want to prolong grading reform to keep high visibility through publicity. Hidden agendas must be uncovered before conflict can be negotiated in these cases (McKay, Davis, & Fanning, 1995, pp. 147–158).

GROUP APATHY

When group members show indifference to the task, appear bored, and seem unable to mobilize their energies or to persevere, they may be using *apathy* to deal with high anxiety. An apathetic response is a withdrawal reaction; it can be used as a disguise for tension and discomfort.

Intervene whenever the following signs of apathy are noted: tardiness, absenteeism, attempts to end meetings early, minimal participation by group members, frequent yawns, dragging conversation, loss of the point of a discussion, reluctance to assume responsibility for group functioning, precipitous decisions, failure to carry through on decisions, or lack of preparation for coming meetings.

Determine the source of apathy before intervening. Group members can be asked such questions as:

- What do you think about the group goal?
- Is the group goal relevant to you?
- What meaning does the goal have for you?
- What do you think will happen if you attain the goal?
- Do you think the group atmosphere lends itself to sharing and cooperation?
- Do you have the skills you need to communicate easily with one another?

- Is effort toward achieving the group goal clearly organized and coordinated?
- Have you been asked to make decisions you think will not be acted upon?
- Do you think I make unilateral decisions?
- Does conflict between a few members overshadow group movement toward the goal?

Once the source of apathy has been identified, you can act to overcome it. If the task goal was imposed by others or by you, the group can be helped to decide on a goal that the members consider more relevant. If group members fear punishment, you can help the group to explore whether this fear is realistic; if it is, perhaps the leader's expectations need to be reexamined. If group atmosphere is too tense, or if the room is crowded, noisy, poorly ventilated, or otherwise not conducive to effective group interaction, action can be taken to modify the milieu. If the group lacks communication skills, these can be taught through the use of the simulated group exercises at the ends of the chapters of this book and by role modeling effective communication behavior. If efforts toward achievement of the group goal are not clearly organized or coordinated, the leader may wish to rethink approaches and/or seek supervision from a more experienced group leader If decision making leads to meaningless or unilateral decisions, the leader needs to teach the group more effective ways of arriving at meaningful decisions. If conflict overshadows group movement toward its goal, the leader must determine the sources of the conflict and intervene appropriately.

NORMS AND COHESIVENESS

Norms are rules for behavior within the group. Members will bring to the group their own ideas about appropriate behavior with others. If group members are drawn from highly divergent social, economic, educational, or cultural groups, it may take quite a while for them to agree on appropriate group behavior.

Despite the attitudes the individual members contribute, certain norms will be developed spontaneously within the group. Because norms refer to expected behavior, they carry a "should" or "ought to" quality, and some beliefs may be carryovers from childhood experiences. You may set a rule for behavior, but the group will accept it only when the behavior it calls for is rewarded and enforced by other group members.

You can use several techniques in establishing norms. They can look for the presence of already existing norms and for norms that seem to be developing. Norms can be initiated by leaders who may suggest, "I think we should share our thoughts and feelings now." Leaders can have an even stronger influence on group norms by demonstrating, through their own behavior, what appropriate group behavior is. Instead of merely suggesting that others share their thoughts and feelings, the group leaders might share their own. This would allow others to see that it is safe to express themselves and would also serve as a model for expressing oneself in the group context. You can share feelings when it seems to be helpful to group process and refrain from doing so when the expression would simply serve to meet your needs for attention, sympathy, or retaliation.

Norms can work in favor of or against group cohesion. *Cohesiveness* is the attraction of the group members for each other. Highly cohesive groups are motivated to work effectively toward group goals and to satisfy all members' interpersonal needs. The more favorable the expectations are that members have about group membership, the more attractive will the idea of group membership be. You can influence attraction to the group by making sure that everyone has the same goals in mind, that group goals are relevant and clearly stated, that paths to goal attainment are known and rewarded, and that cooperation among members is promoted.

Some *measures of cohesiveness* are arrival on time, full attendance at group meetings, a high trust and support level within the group, the ability of the group to tolerate individuality and have fun, the ability to work cooperatively with other group members to enforce agreed-upon norms, and ease in making statements of liking for the group or for group members.

Groups cannot become highly cohesive unless all members, including the leader, interact on an equal basis. You can increase cohesiveness by helping group members to feel part of and equal within the group, by controlling group functioning effectively, and by teaching members how to give and get satisfaction or affection from working with each other. Try to include all group members in the discussions by asking for everyone's opinion and by seeing withdrawn or silent members individually between meetings to discover their reasons for nonparticipation. The more frequently group members interact with each other, the more likely it is that the group will become cohesive. To promote group interaction, deflect some of the questions from yourself to a group member. Frequency of group meetings can also affect cohesiveness, since the more frequently a group meets, the higher the potential for interaction; consider increasing the frequency of the meetings if other attempts to promote cohesiveness fail. Another way to influence cohesiveness is to help the group to identify similarities that exist between members; this technique increases a sense of community in group members.

Group cohesiveness is strongly influenced by the balance between members' needs to control others in the group. This need ranges from wanting to control all aspects of everyone else's behavior to abdicating control entirely because the situation is unsafe or unhealthy. When leadership is shared by all group members, all will learn to control some aspects of group functioning and to accept control in others. You can demonstrate appropriate control levels by structuring the group, yet allowing it to assume responsibility for some decisions. .

You can increase affection among group members and feelings of satisfaction or pride in accomplishment by planning meetings so that the potential for success is high. To do this, do not place group members "on the spot" by requiring them to answer after they have stated that they do not feel like talking at that time, and do not allow others to do so. Group members are rewarded for cooperation and goal attainment by receiving comments on goals reached and not by receiving comments on poor performance except, perhaps, to suggest additional ways of attaining the goal (Tomasulo, 1998).

Allowing group members to express hostility and conflict will also increase cohesiveness. Unless anger and resentment are openly expressed, they will go underground and impede member cooperation and interaction. Convey the idea, directly and indirectly, that it is "O.K. to talk about anger and differences here."

THEMES

Although many topics may be discussed by a given group or even in one group session, one predominant *theme* can usually be identified. At first, it may seem that group meetings are disconnected and that the subjects discussed or the activities pursued are unrelated. Yet a pervading theme can often be identified. It may not necessarily be logical or overt; it may be implied through association, symbolic meaning, or feeling tone. For example, one group of nursing home residents kept returning to the topic of exploitation of nursing home patients for the financial benefit of the government, and how change was needed; all the group members became animatedly involved in the discussion whenever this topic came up. On one level, a discussion of this kind could be taken at its surface value; on another level, the leader in this instance became aware that nursing home residents felt exploited and used by society and even perhaps by the nursing home staff.

The feeling of being exploited, mistreated, and used is a common theme in group sessions in long-term institutions such as psychiatric hospitals and prisons. The feeling of being different occurs as a theme in group sessions when all members have the same illness or handicap. Prenatal discussion groups may have themes of fear of pain and of the birth experience. Groups composed of people who are all at a particular stage of growth and development may exhibit themes characteristic of that period; for example, 4– to 6–year-olds in a group may have a theme of competition, while an 8– to 11–year-old group may have a theme of industry.

Not every group will have one of these common themes. Be attuned to the possible linkages and underlying consistent meaning of what is expressed in group interaction that may imply a theme or ongoing group concern.

SIMULATED EXERCISES

Each of the two simulated exercises that follow includes an experiential and a discussion section. If the group is large, it should be divided into subgroups of not more than 15 members. Following the simulation, the entire group reconvenes for a discussion period. If an exercise is completed without an instructor or supervisor present, participants should plan to share difficulties and insights with an experienced group leader following completion of the exercise.

EXERCISE 1 Sharing with Others

This exercise gives learners the opportunity to practice sharing information about themselves in a nonthreatening environment and to learn to listen to other group members who also share information about themselves. It also provides an opportunity for learners to observe how sharing can influence group cohesiveness.

Objectives
1. To develop skill in sharing information about self with others.
2. To develop a recognition of safe levels of self-disclosure.
3. To learn to listen to what others wish to say without prodding or debating.
4. To enhance group cohesiveness.

Procedure

1. The group decides the time limits for each section of the exercise.
2. The group or the instructor appoints a timekeeper, who makes sure that time limits for each section are observed. The timekeeper also reminds the group at appropriate intervals how much time remains.
3. The group or the instructor appoints a leader for each subgroup.

10 minutes per person maximum

4. The subgroup leaders ask group members to write down three questions they would like to be asked by others. Questions should deal with interests, hobbies, family, friends, beliefs, hopes, goals in life, or activities. All members write down three questions, sign their name, and pass the paper to the subgroup leader, who asks members to answer their own three questions. The leader makes sure that personal information is shared and discussed on a voluntary basis. Whenever group members feel like going on to another question, they are free to do so. There is to be no argument or debate. All are free to state their position without argument from others.

15–30 minutes

5. When all group members have been asked their three questions, the subgroup leader asks each group member to tell one new thing learned about every other group member.

(continued)

EXERCISE 1 (*continued*)

Discussion
15–30   6. The entire group then meets to discuss the following
minutes   points:
           a.   What was easy and what was difficult about this ex-
                ercise?
           b.   How did this exercise affect how group members feel
                about one another?
           c.   How did group members decide how much to tell oth-
                ers about themselves and how much to withhold?
           d.   What prevented group members from listening ac-
                tively to one another?
           e.   What was learned from this exercise that can be ap-
                plied in other group situations?

EXERCISE 2 Giving and Receiving Help and Feedback

This exercise requires two individuals to help a third solve an interpersonal problem through taking on the roles of consultant and observer.

Objectives
1. To gain skills in defining a problem and helping another person solve a problem.
2. To practice feedback skills.
3. To identify Parent, Adult, and Child statements and the effect of each on communication.

Procedure

	1. Divide the group into subgroups of three people.
5–10 minutes	2. Distribute materials so that each subgroup has one copy of: Presenter Instructions, Consultant Instructions, and Observer Instructions (see pp. 58–59).
	3. Each group decides who will play which role.
	4. Each member reads his or her instructions.
15 minutes	5. The Presenter presents his or her problem to the Consultant. The Observer remains silent during the presentation.
5–10 minutes	6. The Observer gives feedback to both Presenter and Consultant, including behavior that helped or hindered the consultation process.
25 minutes	7. Group members trade roles and proceed with Steps 5 and 6 above.
25 minutes	8. Group members trade roles and proceed with Steps 5 and 6 above. (At the end of this round, each person should have played all three roles.)
15–45 minutes	9. All group members assemble and discuss the following:

      a. Which role was easiest for you to play? Give ideas why this is so.

      b. What feedback skills do you need to polish?

      c. What presenter skills do you need to hone?

      d. What do you need to practice more to be a more astute observer?

      e. What problems did consultants encounter?

      f. What problems did presenters encounter?

      g. What problems did observers encounter?

      h. How can these problems be overcome?

(continued)

EXERCISE 2 (*continued*)

Presenter Instructions
1. Your task is to consider a problem which you are presently experiencing. Make sure it is a problem you feel strongly about and one you need help with.
2. Take a few moments now to think about some specific problem you are directly involved with. Make sure it is a problem that: is unresolved, that you are ready to do something about, that involves you and at least one other person, and that is very important to you.
3. Once you have selected the problem:
   a. Describe the problem in detail, specifying what the problem is, who is involved, and the specifics of what is involved. When describing the problem to the consultant be sure to describe the facts (your thoughts, feelings, and actions and what was said or done by others). Do not judge or comment on what you did or plan to do.
   b. Describe the factors or situations that led up to the problem, and why you think the problem persists.
   c. Describe how you could solve the problem. Describe things you could do and any difficulties you think might arise if you try to implement your solution.
   d. Describe how solving the problem might affect you and the other(s) involved.
4. When you are ready, signal the others and prepare to describe your problem using 3a, 3b, and 3c above.

Consultant Instructions
1. Your task is to help the presenter define or redefine the problem and the relationships involved in *specific* terms so that steps toward solving the problem can occur.
2. Some questions you may want to ask the presenter are:
   a. "How do you see yourself in this situation in terms of personal responsibility for what occurs?"
   b. "What is the fundamental difficulty in the situation?"
   c. "Who does or says what in the situation to create a problem?" (You may want to break this down into specifics: "What was said first?" "What was said next?" etc.)
   d. "What does not occur that could help resolve the problem?"
   e. "What seems to prevent it from occurring?"
   f. "What solutions have been tried?"
   g. "How have the things you tried worked?"
   h. "What do you plan to try for your next solution?"
   i. "In what way can I be of help to you?"

3. When discussing the problem with the presenter:
   a. Avoid taking over the problem by saying, "You should . . ." "The real problem seems to be . . ." Instead, ask the presenter, "How do you see what is happening?" If you see things entirely differently, say, "I wonder if it could be that . . ." (and then let the person know your perspective).
   b. Avoid minimizing the problem. Resist making comments such as, "We had that problem, and it was easy to solve," or "That's not such a problem, you can solve it."
   c. Ask questions beginning with what, where, how, and who.
   d. Help the presenter focus on what he or she can do, not on what others in the situation can do.

Observer Instructions
1. Your task is to watch and listen to the presenter and consultant very carefully. Remain silent. Take notes so you will remember exact words said, gestures, and postures.
2. While observing ask yourself:
   a. What is going on between the consultant and presenter? Are they warring; not listening to each other; trying to convince, judge, talk down, or understand? Write down anything said or done to support your conclusion.
   b. What does the consultant do to help the presenter speak freely?
   c. What does the consultant avoid doing that could help the presenter speak freely?
   d. Does the presenter stay with defining the problem before trying to solve it?
   e. Does the consultant stay with defining the problem before trying to solve it?
   f. What specific examples can I provide of the presenter using parent, adult, or child language or behavior?
   g. What specific examples can I provide of the consultant using parent, adult, or child language or behavior?
3. Use the rules for feedback when making your report to consultant and presenter. (You may wish to write down your feedback comments for later use or you may want to make copies of your feedback comments and give them to each person.)

REFERENCES

Aviram, R. B., & Rosenfeld, S. (2002). Application of social identity theory in group therapy with stigmatized adults. *International Journal of Group Psychotherapy, 52*(1), 121–130.

Bach, G. (1954). *Intensive group psychotherapy.* New York: Ronald.

Bales R. (1950). *Interaction process analysis: A method for the study of small groups.* Cambridge, MA: Addison-Wesley.

_____ (1953). Group equilibria. In T. Parson, R. Bales, & E. A. Shils (Eds.), *Papers in the theory of action.* Glencoe, IL: Free Press.

Berne, E. (1964). *Games people play.* New York: Grove.

Bion, W. R. (1952). Group dynamics: A review. *International Journal of Group Psychotherapy, 33,* 235–247.

Campbell, R. (1999, November). The psychology of groups: Why quality and impartial leadership is critical to a group's success. *Proceedings of the 13th Annual International Conference on outdoor recreation & education.* Jackson Hole, WY.

Chambers, C. (1966). A comparison of patterns of interaction among group members in hospitalized and non-hospitalized psychotherapy groups. Unpublished master's thesis Graduate School of Rutgers, the State University of New Jersey.

Clark, C. C. (in press). *Empower yourself! (and others): Holistic and assertive strategies for nurses.* New York: Springer Publishing Co.

Coleman, P. T. (2000). Fostering ripeness in seemingly intractable conflict: An experiments study. *International Journal of Conflict Management, 11*(4), 300–317.

Ezriel, H. (1956). Experimentation within the psychoanalytic session. *British Journal for the Philosophy of Science, 7,* 29–48.

Geller, J. (1951). Concerning the size of therapy groups. *International Journal of Group Psychotherapy, 1*(2), 12–20.

Geller, J. (1962). Parataxic distortions in the initial stages of group relationships. *International Journal of Group Psychotherapy, 7*(1), 27–34.

Gross, M. A., & Guerrero, L. K. (2000). Managing conflict appropriately and effectively: An application of the competence model of Rahim's organizational conflict styles. *International Journal of Conflict Management, 11*(3), 200–226.

Haley, J. (1964). Research on family patterns: An instrument measurement. *Family Process, 3*(1), 41–65.

Hare, P. (1952). A study of interaction and consensus in different sized groups. *American Sociological Review, 17,* 261–267.

Hare, P., Borgatta, E., & Bales, R. (Eds.). (1955). *Small groups: Studies in social interaction.* New York: Knopf.

Harris, T. (1969). *I'm OK, you're OK: A practical guide to transactional analysis.* New York: Harper & Row.

Hover, D. (1983). Enhancing family communication using neurolinguistic programming. In I. Clements & F. Roberts (Eds.), *Family health: a theoretical approach to nursing care* (pp. 83–92). New York: Wiley.

Hunter, G. C. (1996). *Cohesion and self-disclosure stage development in group therapy leadership training: Potential limitations of a common teaching model.* East Lansing, MI: National Center for Research on Teacher Learning. (ERIC Document Reproduction Service No. ED401276)

Lamoureux, P., & Debbane, E. G. (1997). The psychoanalytic group situation. *International Journal of Group Therapy, 47*(1), 47–70.

Lewin, K. (1947). Frontiers in group dynamics: Concept, method and reality in social science: Social equilibria and social change. *Human Relations, 1,* 5–41.

Martin, E. A., & Hill, W. (1957). Toward a theory of group development. *International Journal of Group Psychotherapy, 7,* 20–30.

Maslow, A. (1987). *Motivation and personality* (3rd ed.). New York: HarperCollins.

McKay, M., Davis, M., & Fanning, P. (1995). *Messages: The communication book.* Oakland, CA: New Harbinger.

Nasmith, L. (1995). Long-term impact of faculty development workshops. East Lansing: MI: National Center for Research on Teacher Learning. (ERIC Document Reproduction Service No. ED400729)

Rosen, D., Stukenberg, K.W., & Sacks, S. (2001). The groups-as-a-whole-object relations model of group psychotherapy. *Bulletin of the Menninger Clinic, 65*(4), 471–488.

Ruesch, J. (1957). *Disturbed communication.* New York: Norton.

Sandy, S. V., & Susan, K. (2000). The peaceful kids conflict resolution program. *International Journal of Conflict Management 11*(4), 337–357.

Steinzor, B. (1950). The spatial factor in face to face discussion groups. *Journal of Abnormal and Social Psychology, 65,* 552–555.

Strodtbeck, F., & Hare P. (1954). Bibliography of small group research: 1900–1953. *Sociometry, 17,* 104–178.

Tomasulo, D. J. (1998). *Action methods in group psychotherapy: practical aspects.* Philadelphia: Taylor & Francis.

Whitaker, D. (2001). *Using groups to help people* (2nd ed.). Florence, KY: Brunner-Routledge.

Whitaker, D., & Lieberman, M. (1964). *Psychotherapy through group process.* New York: Atherton.

3
Working to Achieve Group Goals

PHASES OF GROUP MOVEMENT

The phases of group movement may be classified according to several systems. Perhaps the simplest system divides the group into three phases: orientation, working, and termination. During the *orientation phase,* group members are seeking to be accepted in the group and to find out how they are similar to and different from the other members. Their expectations for outcomes of group experiences -are often unrealistic. For example, it is highly unlikely that long-term behaviors will be changed by four to six sessions of a supportive group. And certainly expecting to be cured of cancer in a supportive group is totally unrealistic. Anxiety is high during this phase, and there are frequent bids for the leader to perform unreasonable feats and to be all things to all group members. The leader may have to be quite verbal in the first few meetings in order to teach group members how to relate to one another and how to move toward the group goal. As the group proceeds, members may directly or indirectly express anger toward the leader for not being able to meet all their needs. It is important that the leader stick to realistic goals, while at the same time assisting group members to express their thoughts and feelings regarding what happens in the group.

Given time and appropriate leadership, groups will evolve into mature or working-stage groups. Groups may proceed from the orientation stage to the working stage without completely finishing the tasks of the former; in this case, the group may need to go back at a later date to complete them. Some groups end before arriving at the working or mature group stage.

Uncertainty and insecurity are characteristic of groups in the orientation phase. Group leaders should be aware that they also may experience these feelings during this phase; awareness may help leaders move through the stage focusing on assisting the group to achieve the tasks of the phase without hurrying the group to relieve leader anxiety and discomfort. In the orientation phase, group members are polite and formal with one another. Safe topics are discussed. Members maneuver to keep others at a safe distance and prevent confrontation, retaliation, and rejection. As the orientation phase proceeds, nurse leaders can assist the group to move to the working phase by being a positive role model and engaging in more open communication than other group members. Other group members will follow once they see it is safe to be more open. Referring to the group by name, for example, "our staff group," will help group members identify with the group. Referring to group behavior as "*we* are . . ." "*we* seem to be . . ." will also help group members begin to think of themselves as an entity.

In the orientation phase, group leaders may have to summarize group sessions and ask what topics group members want to discuss the next time. A signal that the group is moving into working phase is that group members summarize and volunteer ideas for *upcoming meetings*. *Group* leaders who are too rigid or too unstructured during this phase may prevent the group from feeling support, having a clear purpose, and being guided to complete individual and group goals. The two examples that follow demonstrate ineffective and effective leader behavior.

Example 1: Ineffective Leader Behavior
A cutback in funds at City Hospital upset many staff members. The staff met with the administrator to express their concern and to demand action be taken to obtain needed funds for supplies.

The administrator spent most of the meeting reading a memo from the Board of Directors. The administrator was worried that the staff would blame her for what had happened and she was apprehensive during the meeting. When the memo had been read, the administrator spent time trying to explain to the staff why the funds had been cut back. The staff took turns asking questions about why the cutback had occurred and how it would be handled. They gradually realized that the new administrator was cutting back funds from all services. No more time for discussion was available and the meeting broke up at that point.

The administrator was more concerned about her feelings than group functioning. She controlled the flow of group interaction too rigidly, allowing insufficient time for discussion and problem solving.

Example 2: Effective Leader Behavior

The head nurse on unit C was told by the director of nursing that within 2 years all units would be converted to primary nursing. Each head nurse was to prepare her staff and tell LPNs that they would no longer be eligible to work on the unit. The head nurse felt anxious about meeting with her staff, but prepared by learning relaxation techniques and using role playing to practice responses to anticipated staff hostility with two supportive head nurses from other units. The head nurse's two peers gave her helpful feedback on her defensive nonverbal behavior.

When the head nurse met with her staff, she gave a very short introduction about implementing primary nursing and then asked for their reactions. After some expressions of anxiety, hostility, and insecurity, the group settled down to discuss the meaning of this decision to each of them. The group decided to explore alternative ways of upgrading the education of the LPNs, bring in other LPNs from hospitals where primary nursing had been implemented, and set shortterm goals for implementing the long-term goal of primary nursing.

The head nurse was aware of her feelings of anxiety and insecurity, but she took constructive steps to deal with them. By opening up discussion to allow expression of feelings, this group was able to move to problem solving.

By assisting group members to use assertive, confrontive communication, group leaders can assist groups in moving away from the angry, tension-filled stage of the orientation phase. Group leaders can ask that group members discuss their feelings rather than act them out by walking out of the group or hollering at one another.

During the *working phase,* when the group has learned to work together cooperatively, you will need to intervene less frequently. Leadership functions are shared. Positive and negative feelings may be expressed, control issues are worked out to the satisfaction of all, cohesiveness increases, norms are solidified and reinforced, and progress is made toward attaining the group goal.

Teach group members how to provide needed leadership functions in the working phase. When feasible, instructions for various group leadership roles can be given to group members and they can provide the needed functions (see Simulated Exercises for group role assignments, pp. 92–96).

As the group enters the working phase, decisions are more apt to be made by consensus than by vote. Problem solving is common. Frustration and discouragement about the group are replaced with cautious optimism. Group members turn less often to the leader for help. You function most effectively in this stage by helping the group from getting sidetracked, encouraging problem solving and consensus decision making. There is less need to reinforce ground rules or provide support for group members. A measure of group maturity is the ability of the group to confront one another directly (rather than talking about one another outside the group or avoiding discussion altogether). Cooperation replaces conflict in a mature group. Differences are still there, but the group handles them by adapting and problem solving. Disagreements are verbalized and dealt with openly. Group members provide constructive feedback for one another, and feedback is heard and used to change behavior. An overprotective or overcontrolling group leader can influence whether a group is able to fully mature or not.

Effective leaders act very much like group members and effective group members act like group leaders in this phase. Contributions are evaluated on merit, not on the prestige of the contributor. From this perspective, group leaders do not solve problems in the working phase, but see that problems get solved.

The focus in the *termination phase* is on evaluating and summarizing the group experience. Feelings of sadness, satisfaction, frustration or anger, guilt, and rejection or denial of feeling may occur. The longer the group has been together, the more intense and extended will be the termination phase. In any one session, groups may show behavior characteristic of all three phases. For example, the group may show some anxiety upon reconvening after a break of a week or more, until they reorient themselves to one another. A relatively mature group will then move into shared leadership. At the end of each session, especially productive ones, group members may show termination behaviors indicating sadness or reluctance to end the group, or satisfaction with their work.

The leader elicits group members' summary and evaluative comments at the end of each session and at the end of the group. Some comments you can use are: "This is our last meeting; let's evaluate our progress. I'm feeling sad that this is our last meeting; what are your feelings?" "What do you think we've accomplished as a group (today)?" "Let's evaluate our progress today."

This chapter will concentrate on group skills needed during the working phase of a group—the stage at which a group either will or will not achieve its purpose.

DECISION MAKING AND PROBLEM SOLVING

Decision making and problem solving are often the same process. There are two approaches to decision making: prescriptive (how groups *should* make decisions) and descriptive (how groups *do* make decisions). Prescriptive methods usually outline an agenda of various steps a group goes through to make decisions. The most commonly used method of this type is John Dewey's (1910) "reflective thinking" model. Briefly summarized, the steps are:

1. A felt need or difficulty is expressed.
2. The problem is defined.
3. All facets of the problem are analyzed.
4. All possible solutions are brainstormed.
5. Each solution is tested against selected criteria.
6. The best solution is chosen.
7. The best solution is put into action.

If you are leading a group and hoping for a decision using Dewey's prescriptive model, you would follow each step and make sure it is completed before going on to the next one. This method assumes that a rational model is the best and overlooks any social or emotional needs.

The most used descriptive model is the three-phase model Interaction Process Analysis (IPA) developed by Bales (1950) and Bales and Strodtbeck (1951). The IPA also separates group task and social emotional dimensions. Task areas include giving or asking for suggestion, opinion, or orientation. Social emotional areas include agreeing/disagreeing, showing tension/releasing tension, shows solidarity/shows antagonism.

There are many methods of understanding group decision-making, but the easiest way to look at the process is to think of four phases. The first phase is an orientation phase during which the group clarifies and agrees on what the problem is or what decision is to be made. The second phase is a conflict phase during which there is dispute and ideational conflict over decision proposals. The third phase is an emergent phase during which ambiguity about decision proposals occurs again, followed by favorable opinions of the decision. The final phase is the reinforcement phase during which dissent has all but vanished and a spirit of unity prevails (Fisher, 1974).

The best way to learn about the process of decision making is to sit in on a task group that is going to make a decision. Agendas usually give a clue to whether decisions will be made or not or you can consult the leader of a particular group to see if a decision is imminent. Use the Decision-Making Observation Guide on page 94 to jot down examples of decision-making behaviors in the group you observe.

If you are leading a group, your role in decision making may include:

1. *Initiating.* Keep the group moving by suggesting an action step (e.g., "Let's poll the group"), pointing out a goal (e.g., "As I remember, our goal is to make this decision today"), proposing a procedure (e.g., "Let's role play to see if that helps us"), or clarifying what may be an obstacle (e.g., "I'm wondering if pushing too hard to come to consensus is becoming an obstacle for us").

2. *Regulating.* Summarize what's happened so far (e.g., "So far we've listed some alternative solutions"), point out time limits (e.g., "We have ten minutes left today"), and restate the agreed-upon goal (e.g., "We agreed to set priorities in the next 15 minutes").

3. *Informing.* Bring information or opinion to the group (e.g., "I brought these summaries of possible solutions based on what we discussed last time").

4. *Supporting.* Create an emotional climate that makes it easy for group members to get along, stay calm, and voice and encourage their feelings (e.g., "Let's try a relaxation exercise to keep us calm," or "It's okay to share your feelings").

5. *Evaluating.* Help the group evaluate its decisions by noting group process that is either helping or hindering from a decision and testing for a consensus (e.g., "I'm wondering if polling the group so soon is preventing us from considering alternatives" and, "Are we ready to test for a consensus?").

Decisions about when, where, and how often the group will meet, how long meetings will last, and what the behavior limits will be are the responsibility of the designated leader. If you lead a group as a private practitioner you must also decide on the fee-for-service. It is not usually feasible to open such decisions to group decision making, although the wise leader does allow group members to express their reactions to these decisions. Whichever decisions are nonnegotiable should be stated clearly by the leader.

Decision making by the group members occurs most frequently in task groups. Some decisions with which a task group might become involved include planning group activities; deciding whether to allow more—or less—time for a specific topic or problem to be discussed; deciding on the topic for the next week's discussion; and deciding how to handle group members who monopolize the conversation, pick on other group members, are silent, are new to the group, or are leaving the group.

Many groups will need to learn from you how to make effective group decisions by consensus. The first step in this process is for you to state the overall problem in clear and easily understandable terms. Next, you clarify and elaborate on the various aspects of the problem. Group members are encouraged to develop alternate solutions to the problem and even seek out differences of opinion, since disagreement can assist the group to arrive at an effective decision when a wide range of information is presented. Throughout the decision-making process, you help to keep the discussion relevant by making statements such as, "We're off the track now," or "Let's get back to suggesting solutions," or "We are discussing . . . now." Another step in effective decision making is to summarize the alternative solutions; this can be done verbally, or the suggested solutions can be written on a chalkboard or recorded by a group secretary or recorder. After summarizing the possible solutions, the group can test them out verbally and/or through action. As a decision -emerges, the leader queries group members' commitment to it; for example, "It seems that the logical solution is. . . . What do each of you think of it?" The final step in the process is for the group to reach a consensus on the decision. Admittedly, arriving at decisions by this process is an ideal to be striven for; rarely will it be completely realized. However, one important result is that the group members are introduced to the process and the skills used to make effective decisions by consensus.

Sometimes groups become bogged down when attempting to solve a problem or make a decision. Koberg and Bagnall (1972) provided *guidelines for problem solving, creativity, and goal attainment*. Methods discussed include: brainstorming, manipulative verbs, synectics, tell me stranger, games to develop belief in self, games to develop constructive discontent, games for developing wholeness, criticizing painlessly, and methods of acceptance.

Brainstorming

Gather together a group of 4 to 12 persons. Restrict the session to about 15 minutes and be sure everyone follows these rules: Defer judgment, ask everyone to suggest as many ideas as possible during the time allotted without criticizing anything presented. Avoid waiting for a new idea; as soon as one is presented, develop another one out of the last one given by changing it in some way. Avoid holding back; quantity is important. A follow-up session, using the same participants on the following day is a good way to pick up some afterthoughts.

Manipulative Verbs

This method uses a series of words to force the group to visualize the problem in unique ways. Some verbs used are: magnify, minify, rearrange, alter, adapt, modify, substitute, reverse, combine, multiply, eliminate, invert, separate, transpose, unify, flatten, complement, bypass, stretch, repel, protect, integrate, and symbolize. For example, if the problem is "inadequate staffing," the group might discuss how to magnify the problem (so administration will notice it), rearrange employees by trying different patterns, teach floating staff sufficient skills to be of use on many units, and so forth.

Synectics

Synectics is a method of analysis, ideation, and implementation in which users find relationships between apparently different and irrelevant objects (Koberg & Bagnall, 1972). When using this method, the group follows three stages: in Stage 1, existing viewpoints are stated, the problem is analyzed, preconceptions are purged from the mind, and viewpoints are clarified. In Stage 2, direct analogy, personal analogy, and compressed conflict strategies are used to move away from the real problem and look at it from a new perspective.

In the *direct analogy strategy,* the group discusses how the subject is like other things. Questions such as, "How is the problem like an artichoke?" "How is the problem like flying on radar?" "What are the attributes or characteristics of this problem?" "What alternate characteristics could solve the problem?" For example, suppose a group is trying to improve a care plan form currently in use. The group would first define the at-

tributes of the current form: 10 pages, paper, typed, 81/2" x 11."
Alternate attributes might be fewer or more pages, erasable
boards, computer-generated, 81/2" x 14."

In the *personal analogy strategy,* group members role play in
various human, animal, vegetable, mineral, and abstract contexts. Each person imagines being transformed into some object, event, or abstraction. For example, becoming the client,
the physician, intravenous tubing, restraints, siderails on a bed,
a conference room, or a wheelchair. Becoming a linen room or
linen in the room takes concentration, but it forces a different
perspective on the problem.

In the *compressed conflict strategy* there is a search for problems within the problem; a problem is always made up of a
number of little problems. Individuals often decide one of the
particular subproblems is more important than any of the others; by identifying the other subproblems, a different perspective is gained. In Stage 3, new perspectives are brought back
into relationship with the original problem and a new viewpoint and solution are designed. For more information on Gordon's Synectics, write: Synectics, Education Systems, 121 Brattle
Street, Cambridge, MA 02138.

Tell Me Stranger

It is always easier to see the solution to someone else's problem; solutions to our problems often escape us. To use this
method, ask strangers or acquaintances how they would solve
the problem. Avoid asking close friends and, family members
because they assume nearly the same personal feeling toward
the problem. For example, if the group is composed of nurses,
ask physicians, physical therapists, pharmacists, or lab technicians how they would solve the problem and then bring their
ideas back to the group for discussion.

Games to Develop Belief in Self

Sometimes a group gets bogged down because its members feel
they are not making progress. Some games to develop belief in
the group include (1) having the group write a column for the
local paper describing how well the group solved some problem
or worked together during one session, (2) having the group
imagine it has won the prize for Most Improved Group, and (3)
having the group members compose letters to their families

describing their thoughts and feelings about winning the Most Improved Group prize.

Games to Develop Constructive Discontent

Group members often do not act because they fear "rocking the boat." The following strategies can be used to develop constructive discontent; the energy released can then be used to act: (1) Imagine your boss has accused you of participating in the overthrow of the administration (an untrue accusation). She offers her regrets for having to fire you, pays you your salary, and immediately leaves on a 2–month vacation. What will you do? (2) Suppose your brain was transplanted into the body of your pet bird. You are the first and only bird who knows and knows she knows. What now?

Games for Developing Wholeness

Group members often feel cut off from their senses, and torn by various demands. Games for developing wholeness can produce a more integrated, whole approach to problem solving and decision making. Some suggestions are: (1) Blindfold the group and have each member identify three objects by touch, three objects by taste, and three objects by sound. (2) Have group members describe multisensory experiences such as walking on the beach, peeling and eating an apple, or taking a shower. (3) Have group members think of their left hand as their senses and their right hand as their knowledge; one hand feels and the other knows. Ask the group to write with each hand while concentrating on knowing and sensing. After several minutes, reverse, using the right hand to write and the left to know. (Lefthanders reverse the sequence.) Alternating back and forth will give practice in being manually whole.

Criticizing Painlessly

As group members make decisions and problem solve, they are likely to run into snags as they disagree with others' solutions. Have group members agree that whenever they are about to criticize one another's ideas they are to begin with two positive statements, state their criticism, add another positive statement, and finish with a ray of hope. For example, "You really have presented some good ideas. I like working with you. I wish we could stay on each other's team. I notice you can adapt well when given directions. Maybe tomorrow we'll be able to stay on track together."

Methods of Acceptance

Accepting responsibility for a problem and a decision is sometimes hard to do. It took courage for the signers of the Declaration of Independence to sign their names to a document that changed their existing government. Group members can write their own Declaration of Independence by writing down why they believe that solving the problem is important. The declaration is written like a long motto. It can be copied and presented to 10 interested persons.

Another method of enhancing acceptance is to imagine becoming the victim of all the worst things that could happen if the situation were not solved. Suppose the group wants to accept the problem of solving understaffing. Imagine that a plane crashes near the hospital and 600 accident victims are rushed to your hospital. Imagine that food suppliers go on strike and nursing is forced to bring in food and prepare it for residents. Have the group keep on this line of thinking until a very strong case for immediate action is built.

LEADERSHIP SKILLS

At one time, leadership was thought to be an attribute that, like charisma, was possessed naturally by certain special individuals. This approach to understanding leadership was studied as early as 1948 (Stogdill) when it was found that personal traits (initiative, neatness, courage, warmth, intelligence) made no difference in leadership in most or all situations. The evidence accumulated by this study and one by Allport and Odbert (1936) suggest that leadership is a relationship that exists between persons in a social situation. Leaders in one situation may not necessarily be leaders in other situations.

After that, study of leadership focused on a functional approach and styles of leadership were examined. Three leadership styles were discussed previously (see chapter 2, p. 21): laissez-faire, autocratic, and democratic.

Other styles of leadership include *bargaining*. Using this style, the leader agrees to meet members' personal needs if they work on the official group task. A *paternalistic leader* supplies nearly all group functions benevolently and does not allow members to perform leadership acts. A leader who uses a *cooperative problem-solving* style teaches group members to identify and supply missing functions (Miles, 1959).

Despite the style chosen, here are some criteria for judging leadership (Miles, 1959, pp. 18–19):

- The leader facilitates the group's goals and avoids threatening people with punishment if they don't perform in accordance with the leader's goals.
- The leader helps the group to do its job effectively (rapidly and well) as well as efficiently (improves working relationships) and avoids evoking a poor result, low morale, and antagonism.
- Group members grow in their knowledge, achievement of learning and ability to contribute to the group.

Taking a functional approach instead of labeling a leader by style can help you avoid the issue of the appointed leader versus the emergent leader and the issue of "leader in name only." The approach used in this book is that both the official leader and group members can be leaders as long as they provide with the right function at the right time. It seems more useful to think of group leadership in terms of a number of functions that need to be performed by some member in the group; the designated leader may, in fact, fulfill some, all, or none of these functions. From this viewpoint, you can be seen as a group leader whenever you fulfill needed group functions.

Leadership functions are of two types: task functions and *maintenance functions.* Regardless of the type of group, both types of functions must be fulfilled in order for the group to work at its highest possible level of performance.

Task functions are directly related to the accomplishment of group goals; they include the following leader behaviors:

1. Getting the group going.
   (e.g., "Let's get started.")
2. Keeping the group moving toward its goal.
   (e.g., "Let's get on with our discussion of . . .
3. Clarifying unclear statements or behaviors.
   (e.g., "I'm not sure I understood your idea, could you tell us in another way?")

4. Suggesting ways to move toward the goal.
   (e.g., "We could spend a few minutes sorting this out before we move on to another topic.")
5. Pointing out movement toward or away from the goal.
   (e.g., "So far we've finished . . . but still need to tackle the problem of . . . ")
6. Restating more clearly what others have said.
   (e.g., "Let me summarize what I heard you saying. . . .")
7. Refocusing discussion on the task or on a small step toward the goal.
   (e.g., "First let's work on . . ., then . . ., the next step of . . .")
8. Giving information.
   (e.g., "The group will meet from 8 to 9 p.m.")

Maintenance functions are directly related to improving interpersonal relationships within the group and may include the following leader behaviors:

1. Giving support to group members who are unsure or anxious.
   (e.g., "I guess you're upset about this, but give it a try.")
2. Relieving extreme tension levels.
   (e.g., "Let's role play this situation.")
3. Encouraging direct communication.
   (e.g., "Tell Mr. West what you were telling me, Mrs. Swanson.")
4. Voicing group feeling.
   (e.g., "I sense the group is worried about this.")
5. Agreeing or accepting.
   (e.g., "That's a good point.")
6. Helping the group to evaluate itself.
   (e.g., "Let's all tell what we've gotten from this group experience.")

In general, leadership skills are enhanced by using certain communication techniques. For example, *paraphrasing,* which involves restating what another person has said, gives the message "I care about what you said so I want to make sure I understand your idea." It is useful to preface one's remarks with a statement such as, "If I understood you, you said . . ." or "Did I read you right? Your idea is. . . . "

Behavior description involves stating only what was observed without commenting on the meaning or motive for the behavior. Behavior descriptions include statements such as, "Everyone talked today," "You interrupted Jane three times today," and "You already told us about your opinions today, John." Statements such as, "You must be angry," or "Why don't you listen to me?" or "You're just like my sister," are not behavioral descriptions and they are likely to create discomfort and defensiveness in others.

Feeling description involves a direct statement of how one feels. One who uses this communication technique must feel safe and secure in the group, since sharing feelings implies a risk. Direct expressions of feeling include such comments as, "I'm nervous," "I'm angry .. .. I feel happy," and "I like you." Indirect expression of feelings is open to misinterpretation by others and should be avoided by group leaders. Some indirect feeling expressions are blushing when embarrassed, saying nothing or attacking a group member when angry or anxious, and changing the subject or the rules when irritated.

Validating is a technique that includes checking with others in a tentative way to see whether one's perceptions are correct. Paraphrasing has to do with verbal statements, while validating has more to do with hunches, feelings, and nonverbal processes. When attempting to validate, the leader avoids showing approval or disapproval of behavior and merely checks out perceptions. Validating statements include such comments as, "You seem nervous; are you?" and "I sense you're angry with me; am I right?" Effective leaders never assume that their perceptions are correct without checking them out; statements such as, "Why are you angry. " and "Why didn't you . . . "I" should not be used before validating that the person is angry or did not follow through.

Feedback refers to letting group members know how they affect each other. Feedback is most helpful when it is specific, concrete, and based on empathy rather than on the leader's need to appear in charge. Examples of this technique are, "You've talked a lot today; let someone else talk," and "You've asked that question four times; what's that all about?"

TEAM BUILDING AND COHESIVENESS

Effective teams are the result of specific skill, knowledge, and hard work. Although it is not always possible to choose the people on a team, there is often an opportunity to influence the selection. Leaders who want effective teams become part of the hiring and personnel selection process. Using a method for identifying individual differences and skills among team members is important. One system, the *SELF Profile* helps identify how team members learn, add to team functioning, and are motivated to work with the team (Jacobsen-Webb, 1985).

The SELF system identifies four behavioral types: (1) *Self-reliant* (this type may appear cool and distant, is precise about time use, willing to take interpersonal risks, prefers telling others what to do, is task-oriented, and uses few voice changes or gestures); (2) *Enthusiast* (this type is verbal, quick-acting, shows feelings and concerns easily, loses interest quickly, prefers to tell others what they *feel,* and is people-oriented); (3) *Loyal* (this type is more concerned about feelings than facts, is flexible about time use, is people-oriented, prefers to ask others what they are feeling, is cooperative, and appears warm and close in interpersonal relationships); (4) *Factual* (this type is cooperative, nonverbal, and low risk-taking; he or she may seem cool and distant when trying to remain precise about the use of time; prefers to work with facts and figures rather than feelings and intuition; needs time to study facts and make a decision; and tends to ask others what they are doing). When building a team, it is helpful to have at least one of each type on the team. The self-reliant person can help conclude discussion, set the timetable, and push for decisions; the enthusiast will bring creativity to the group's work; the loyal person will make the work pleasant; and the factual person will supply the data and facts for decisions. Note that the same person may play different roles in different group situations. The categories are meant to be used to show which one usually dominates when in a nonthreatening situation (Jacobsen-Webb, 1985).

Cohesiveness in a team is developed by increasing the quantity of connections among team members. Holding regular team meetings increases cohesiveness because interacting with each other as members of the same team strengthens the sense of being a part of that team. Nurse leaders can increase the sense of "team" by: pointing out how cooperation between team members contributed to its success, asking team members to help each other out, helping team members solve problems by using team time and energy, and asking team members to share their experiences with one another. A feeling of enthusiasm for the team can be enhanced by setting some worthwhile but attainable goals with the team; success in meeting the goals will increase team spirit. Even failure in attaining goals can be used to demonstrate the need to work together to overcome failure. Although useful in some situations, negative approaches such as identifying a common enemy and competing against other teams should be used sparingly because they set up win-lose situations.

An example of how employee competition at the worksite among teams can produce positive results was reported by Klesges, Basey, and Glasgow (1986). Four worksites were used; all were financial institutions. The bank presidents challenged each other at a press conference to see which institution could produce the greatest reductions in smoking among employees. The bank with the highest participation rate received a $100 prize; the bank with the greatest carbon monoxide reductions (assessed by breath samples) received a $150 prize. The bank with the greatest carbon monoxide reductions at 6–month follow-up received a $200 prize. The "grand prize" was awarded to the bank with the highest cessation rate at follow-up. A catered meal was served to the employees of the winning bank by the executives of the losing banks. To keep the competition going, employees wore buttons stating, "I'm in the Healthy Competition." A higher percentage of employees quit smoking in the competition condition (16%) compared with the noncompetition group (7%). There were no differences between the two groups in terms of age, sex, socioeconomic status, or percentage of employees who smoked.

As with other groups, team leaders must clearly define and negotiate their purposes, objectives, and member roles. Team leaders must also consider *delegation of responsibility* and criteria for assignment making. The two most important criteria are the ability of the team member to carry out the task and the fairness of the assignment. Nurse leaders may have difficulty in delegating responsibility; signs of this include: always being very busy, needing to be in three places at once, rushing from crisis to crisis, difficulty making and scheduling appointments with team members, team breakdown (i.e., the team falls apart when the leader is not there because team members have not been taught how to handle the team's regular functions), and verbal statements from the leader such as, "I'm so busy, I don't have time to do what I need to do."

Team leaders must ask themselves: "Do I have difficulty delegating responsibility?" "Do I really trust others to do the job right?" "Do I have a need to retain control and dominate others that is keeping me from running an efficient, growth-enhancing team?" "Do I withhold information from team members as a way of maintaining control?" The following example demonstrates a team leader who had difficulty delegating responsibility.

> The team leader was frequently seen running around the halls. She cancelled appointments with her team and was always complaining about how much work she had to do; she frequently asked team members who were sitting at the desk, "Get busy, don't you have anything to do?"
>
> When the team leader called meetings, she told the team, "I'm interested in your ideas, please tell me what you think." At first, team members volunteered their ideas; however, when they learned she never let them carry out their ideas, they became more silent in meetings, and stopped volunteering suggestions.
>
> When a specialist was assigned to the unit, she started to work with the team to teach them to share responsibility. A power struggle soon developed between the and the clinical specialist. When the two sat down to find out what had gone wrong, team leader realized she had been limiting the effectiveness of her team and increasing her stress level as well. They developed a plan to gradually let team members assume responsibilities for team functioning based on their abilities and performance in new roles. As team members were given more responsibility, they began to offer creative suggestions in team meetings and were able to grow and function at a higher level.

Inadequate staffing is a common and chronic problem in many institutions. Effective teams must confront this issue directly. Team leaders are responsible for pointing out to administration the inadequacy and the effects on care, reduced efficiency, poor public relations, failure to meet legal and accreditation standards, and inability to expand operations. If the administration does not respond, the team may go public and make appropriate regulatory agencies and the media aware of the problem.

To take such steps requires a team that will support one another and not back off from pressure. Team leaders ensure such support by using the team-building measures mentioned.

Team and group building is a process during which cohesiveness develops. A working group does not just come into being because of regular meetings. As leader, you can help build the group or team by helping members take responsibility. Every activity that is shared by all members, whether it is a business meeting, a supportive or therapeutic session, or a teaching session, contributes to the group's sense of history and identity. As the group evolves toward open communication, cooperation, mutual trust, and respect, consensus and decision making gets easier.

Here are some tips for building groups or teams (Avery, Auvine, Streibel, & Weiss, 1981):

1. *Take the group's work seriously.* Take time to help the group seriously consider its goals, membership, and rules for making decisions.
2. *Say "hello" to new members and "good bye" when members leave.* Develop a formal procedure for integrating new members into the group or team. For example, introduce new members to the group; provide each member with a buddy to ask questions of; bring in new members in bunches of two or three so new members can support each other; bring in new members as interns without full group responsibility until they feel comfortable accepting it; devote a portion of the first group to exploring with new members their goals, expectations and any anticipated problems; schedule check-ins or updates with new members to ask them how they are feeling about their role in the group and what they need from others to make things easier.
3. *Set aside some time during or after the group to talk about (or write about) how the meeting went.* Evaluations help foster "groupness" by affirming what members like about a group and each other, giving a voice to dissatisfied members, providing a time to plan improvements in the process, and reinforcing the fact that group membership is important and meetings are not just to complete tasks.
4. *Build in a way for all group members to share responsibility, even if you have to assign tasks.* Better yet, ask the members to put their heads together and come up with a procedure for sharing responsibility. They'll be more likely to follow this procedure because they'll own it.
5. *Balance participation in group tasks.* Don't allow just a few members to carry the group. analyze what leads to this pattern with the group (do they have more information, more experience, more contacts, or a need to be in charge?), and come up with a way to redistribute tasks.
6. *Balance participation at meetings.* Rotate note taker, facilitator, or other roles in your group and limit speaking time. Try passing a token to the speaker, using an egg timer, or giving each person a pile of match sticks in return for turning one in each speaking time. Use a "round

robin," giving each member a turn to speak with an option to pass. Try having the last person who spoke call on the next person to speak.

Help build your group or team by using a postmeeting reaction form. If trust has not been established, you may want to consider an anonymous response. An example of this kind of reaction form appears below. If you prefer, ask the group or team members to develop their own reaction form. Either way, tabulate responses, analyze them, and provide feedback to them.

POSTMEETING REACTION FORM

Directions: Take 10 minutes to answer the following questions. Please place your completed responses on the table on your way out.

1. How did you feel about this meeting? (check)
   □ Very Dissatisfied □ Somewhat Dissatisfied □ Neutral
   □ Quite Satisfied □ Very Satisfied
2. Why did you feel this way?

3. Were there times you wanted to contribute but didn't?
   □ Never □ A Few Times □ Often □ Very Often □ Nearly Always
4. What kinds of things *helped* you speak up?

5. What things *prevented* you from speaking up?

6. What do you suggest we do to improve our meetings?

PLANNED CHANGE

There are many models for planned change. Despite the model chosen, it is wise to remember that in a *systems framework*, change in one part of the system will affect the whole system. Thus, it is not always necessary to work directly with the target person in order to effect change. Leaders who effect change will also be changed in the process.

It is common to hear employees complain, "Nothing ever changes here. It was this way when I came and it will be this way when I leave." From a systems framework, change is inevitable; it may not be large-scale, sweeping change, but all open systems change. Change is repatterning of behavior. Some changes are barely perceptible; others are large-scale alterations in organization and patterning. All systems have the potential for change; it is this thought that leaders must keep in the forefront of their minds when planning change.

Systems have a tendency to resist change and to maintain integrity and identity. Bureaucracies have built-in resistance to change, but even these systems change over time. Change is neither inherently good nor bad; some changes have positive effects on systems, others have negative effects. Resistance to change can often be a healthy response. The following example demonstrates how resistance can be healthy:

> University Hospital had developed plans for a new nuclear medicine laboratory. Staff in the hospital picketed, protested, and wrote letters to the administrator describing the negative effects such a change might have on the health of clients and staff. They saw this change as a threat to their own and others' health and opposed it.

An *open system* responds to change according to the many factors influencing the system. Known positive effects of a proposed change is only one of the factors affecting acceptance of the change. This is why having only one change model at hand may result in refusal of individual or group systems to change. The following example illustrates how knowledge alone is often not sufficient to change behavior:

> Jerry, age 45, has emphysema due to heavy cigarette smoking. He recently had a lung removed. Despite the evidence to the contrary, Jerry insists he must continue to smoke because it is the only pleasure he has left. Attempts to convince Jerry of the dangers of smoking have resulted in resistance and lack of acceptance of smoking cessation.

Another factor affecting acceptance of change is the rate of change. Leaders who expect their staff to incorporate a change rapidly, even when given sufficient preparation, are in for a rude awakening. Any change that occurs too rapidly is apt to elicit system resistance. Some of the factors that can affect system response to change include: the perceived importance of the change; the rate of change; and the needs, values, and coping abilities of individuals involved in the change.

Often, including those involved in the change in the *early* planning stages prior to implementing the change will reduce resistance to change. Evaluating the system's probable response to change and choosing a model that will be most apt to influence positive change are two skills leaders must have in their repertoires.

There are many models for planned change. Four that will be discussed are the rational model, normative model, power-coercive model, and paradoxical model. It behooves leaders to be familiar with all four models. The model chosen will depend on the circumstances and system involved. It is helpful to have more than one model to use in the event the first choice is not successful.

Rational Model for Planned Change

You are probably most familiar with the rational model for change. Assumptions underlying this model are: people are logical and behave rationally; ignorance and superstition are the main blocks to change; once people become informed, they will adopt the change willingly.

One of the best known examples of this model is Rogers' "diffusion of innovation' (Rogers & Shoemaker, 1971). This model is frequently used in health education. Rogers' model has three steps: invention of the change, diffusion or communication of information about the change, and adoption or rejection of the change.

The rational model is the method of choice when there is almost universal readiness for the change within the system. The following example illustrates a system ready for change for which the rational model is a good choice:

Sarah, a nurse practitioner in an HMO, has been asked by several of her clients for assistance with selecting foods that will lower their cholesterol. Sarah consulted references for the latest information on cholesterol and developed an outline and several handouts on cholesterol (invention of change). Next, Sarah contacted all the clients who had asked for information, surveyed records for other possible candidates, and announced in the HMO's regular newsletter and on a spot radio announcement (use of mass media for diffusion) that there would be a workshop on the subject in 2 weeks. Sarah also hung a poster and distributed fliers to her clients in the clinic for the next 2 weeks. Sarah did a 1–month and 6–month follow-up on all workshop attendees to find out if they had made changes in their daily eating habits as a result of the workshop (adoption or rejection of the change).

You can encounter a great deal of resistance to change when you choose the rational model for use with a system that is not ready to change. Sarah found change occurred in the clients who asked for information and were motivated to change; workshop attendees who attended because a family member or boss asked them to showed little if any change on follow-up.

Normative Model for Planned Change

A more holistic approach to change is provided by the normative model. It recognizes and deals with the influence of needs, feelings, attitudes, and values on efforts to change. Assumptions underlying this model are: all members of the system are active participants in the change process, rationality is only one of the many factors influencing change, the system can resist or modify change, education alone is not enough to implement change.

Two types of normative models are of particular interest the *Change Process Model* and the *Change Agent Model*.

Change Process Model

The Change Process Model was developed by Lewin (1951) and further developed by Schein and Bennis (1975). The Change Process Model is divided into three phases: freezing, changing, and refreezing. Lewin (1951) recommends an analysis of the system be made to identify forces for and against change prior to implementing the change process. For example, in attempting to assist group members to reduce stress, the leader identified the following forces for change: participation in learning about stress management procedures, lip service to the importance of role modeling, and group members' ability to learn stress management procedures. An identification of forces against change included: potential threat to group members when giving up_ their old methods of dealing with stress, little or no previous knowledge of stress management methods, refusal of participants to complete between class stress management tasks due to "lack of time," and lack of group participation in selection of class materials or topics covered.

Groups often need a push to begin the change process. There are specific procedures used to *unfreeze* the system so it will be ready to change; these include creating disconfirmation, inducing guilt and anxiety, and providing psychological safety. In the example above, participants had already come together as a group of teachers who planned to teach their students stress management methods; the leader had yet to convince them to become appropriate role models in stress reduction methods, although they gave lip service to the idea.

The group leader brought research findings to the group detailing how role modeling was a powerful teaching tool (disconfirmation), indicated group members may not be doing the best job possible if they did not role model stress management (induce guilt and anxiety), and assured group members they would have ample time and opportunity to learn how to use the procedures in their own lives prior to teaching them to their students (provide psychological safety).

During the *change phase* of the process, the group leader encouraged group members to practice and experiment with stress management procedures (so they would become part of the system's regular patterns), provided a supportive climate (to reduce resistance to change); provided opportunities to ventilate guilt, anxiety, and/or anger aroused by the change process (reduce resistance to change); provided feedback on progress and clarified goals (reinforce change and keep the group on its task); preserved confidentiality (reduce resistance to change); acted as an energizer; and returned to unfreezing tactics when resistance arose.

The purpose of the *refreezing phase* is to make sure the change becomes part of the everyday functioning of the system. If you provide continuing education experiences for groups you must pay particular attention to this phase to ensure participants do not return to their work settings and revert to previous patterns of behavior. Providing follow-up workshops, interviews, letters, phone discussions, or peer partners with specific reinforcement skills will assist with refreezing in these instances.

When working with ongoing groups, complete the following functions during the refreezing phase: providing continued interest and support in moving toward integrating the behavior; delegating responsibility to group members; keeping the change visible by stating observed change, providing charts, letters, memos, newsletter items, and other concrete measures of change; intervening when problems in implementation of new behavior occur; designating specific group members as peer helpers whom other group members can use as resources when the group is not in session.

Change Agent Model

Havelock (1973) developed a model with specific steps focused on communication skills and a good working relationship with the leader; steps in the Change Agent Model include: building a relationship of trust, diagnosing the problem through a consensus of opinion, assessing resources for change, setting goals, selecting strategies, and reinforcing change.

Normative models work best where there is little resistance to change and participants are open to being persuaded and can problem solve. Often, bosses or others may not be open to persuasion; at other times, normative models will not work well because there are conflicting values that preclude consensus, or when those in power resist sharing it with others.

The example that follows shows how one leader used the Change Agent Model to implement planned change:

Tom, a counselor who worked with groups of high school students to prevent drug abuse, spent time meeting with interested students (build a relationship). He listened as they told him about drug use on campus. All agreed that something had to be done to prevent junior high students from beginning to take drugs (diagnose the problem). The group discussed the need for specific times to meet with the junior high students to discuss the problem, provide handouts needed about drug use, and disseminate knowledge on how to prevent drug use (assess resources). 'Tom shared the peer support model he had used successfully when teaching nursing students to support one another in implementing a fitness goal. He said he would be happy to teach the senior high students the peer support process. Tom suggested they look for a *leverage point*—a point where it is most easy to get movement toward change. The group decided to hold a Saturday workshop the first week of school to offer junior high students help with resisting drugs (set goals and select strategies). One hundred junior high students attended the Saturday workshop; most were eager to speak and ask questions about how the senior high students could help. Prior to the workshop Thin had met with the senior high "peer" group and helped them learn the peer support process; although he attended the workshop, the senior high students were in charge. By the end of the workshop, 50 student-peer pairs had been formed and goals for each pair had been established. Some students worked on learning assertiveness responses to being offered drugs, others wanted to obtain more information about types of drugs and their effects. Each pair had established a weekly meeting date and place (stabilize, consolidate, and reinforce the change). Tom also continued to meet weekly with the senior high peer support group to provide direction and support.

Power Coercive Model for Planned Change

The Power Coercive Model for change is focused on overcoming resistance to change. People's needs, feelings, attitudes, and values are recognized but not always respected. Assumptions underlying the model are: consensus cannot be reached through persuasive methods; when change is needed and the target system is resistant, power must be seized.

There are many different kinds of power that can be used including physical force, public embarrassment, loss of prestige or popularity (or threat of), money, practice acts (legal power), public recognition and support, establishing oneself as an expert in the eyes of the public, using an idea or symbol that has meaning (i.e., Gandhi used the power of passive resistance effectively), strength in numbers (if all employees united in one hospital, the strength of their power would be felt), control of access to resources (if a group of employees seized access to money, communications, or information in a health care agency, they would have a great deal of power).

The basic steps in the Power Coercive Model are: define the issue and identify the opponent, organize a following, build a power base, begin an action phase, keep the pressure on, and force a decision through struggle. These *steps* are derived from Haley's (1973) and Alinsky's (1972) work. Both concentrate on the use of power by the "have nots" who do not have the advantage of holding high positions, great wealth, or other vast resources. The Power Coercive Model uses the sources of power most available to the have nots.

The example that follows illustrates use of the Power Coercive Model (Tappan, 1983, pp. 311–317):

The chief of the medical staff was being pressured by two traditional obstetricians and an oncologist not to allow nurses to teach their clients postpartum exercises or to talk with them about impending death-one client had been found weeping after a talk with a nurse. The Chief of Medicine took his complaints to the hospital administrator who asked the Director of Nursing to ask all nurses to cease client teaching and counseling; the Director of Nursing refused and showed him a copy of the Nurse Practice Act. The administrator sent out his own memo ordering the nurses to cease teaching and practicing. The head nurse on one unit was infuriated and decided the issue was nurses' rights and the opponent was the administrator (define the issue and the opponent). The head nurse met with two of her nurse friends; they decided to collect signatures and send a reasonable letter stating their position to the administrator (organize a following). Signatures were collected and key people who signed met with the head nurse to plan their next move. They identified their power by the many nurses who had signed the letter (strength in numbers); the Nurse Practice Act (legal power); support of clients, most physicians, and staff for client teaching (public support); the fact that nurses were good at their work (expert power); and the potential to refuse to work and paralyze the hospital (threat of harm). Four nurses launched a campaign to publicize their fight and build support; buttons were distributed to nurses that said, "Nurses' Rights" (begin action phase). The nurses asked clients, physicians, and other nurses to call or stop by the administrator's office to tell him they thought he was susceptible to physician influence (keeping the pressure on), and to refer to the administrator as "Chicken Chuck." By using ridicule, the nurses hoped to keep the pressure on. The four nurses met with the Director of Nursing and asked for more direct support from her. Their next attack focused on making the administrator look foolish by obeying his rules and bringing pressure from outside the hospital. They stopped talking to clients. The Director of Nursing cancelled all prenatal classes and asked the local newspaper and radio stations to announce the cancellations. The president of the board called the administrator demanding to know why they were going to be the only hospital in the city without "those popular prenatal classes" and ordered the administrator to stop the public announcements. The chief of staff told the administrator to let the nurses get on with their work and stop being ridiculous so physicians could get on with theirs.

The nurses celebrated their victory with their following. They were asked to serve on a Nursing Advisory Committee to make recommendations about any policies affecting nursing. The Director of Nursing strengthened her position in relation to the administrator so that future policies affecting nursing came only from her office.

Paradoxical Model of Planned Change

The Paradoxical Model is based on the Brief Therapy techniques of Haley (1973), and Watzlawick, Weakland, and Fisch (1974). Some assumptions underlying the model are:

1. There are two kinds of change. *First order change* is one that occurs within a given system. The individual exhibiting the behavior may change, or a variation of the behavior may change, but the system remains the same. For example, a disturbed family may exhibit disturbance through a child getting low grades in school and high absenteeism. When the child is given individual therapy, he or she may stop the behavior, but the mother may then start drinking heavily. Both these behaviors are symptoms of an underlying problem in the family system. Only the disturbance has moved from one family member to another one.
2. First order change does not alter behavior patterns, but may reinforce them.
3. *Second order change* is change of change. The system changes due to taking on a new perspective on the problem or situation. *Reframing* is used to see the problem from a different angle and approach it from a new perspective. By using the client's language and perceptual system, the problem and solution are reframed or restated so the client can change.
4. System change is produced by dealing with the effects and not the causes of the problem.
5. Insight is not necessary to effect change.

Steps in the Paradoxical Model for change are:

1. Forget trying to understand the cause of the problem.
2. Determine the symptom-solution cycle.
3. Encourage resistance.
4. Define goal behavior.
5. Secure a commitment to change.
6. Set a time limit.
7. Prescribe the symptom.
8. Include a variation.
9. Reframe in the client's language.
10. Secure agreement to follow instructions.
11. Predict a relapse.
12. Demystify or disengage.

The example that follows illustrates one use of the Paradoxical Model in a group setting:

A group of students had decided to discuss their fears of speaking up in interdisciplinary conferences. The group leader omitted exploring the past history of their speaking up and did not try to help the students understand the underlying causes of their nervousness in groups (forget understanding).

The group leader spent 15 minutes helping group members describe exactly what happened before they attempted speaking up in a group or in an interdisciplinary group. They described feeling a rush of anxiety, tightness in their stomachs, dry throats, pounding hearts, and cracking voices, culminating in remaining silent (determine the symptom-solution cycle).

One student said she would rather not talk about the problem and asked if she could just listen. The group leader told the student, "Sure, hold back until it seems all right for you to speak. Don't reveal anything until you're ready." (Encourage resistance. This gives group members two messages: It is all right to withhold, and that a time will come when they will feel all right to tell more.) The group leader then helped the group members define a behavioral goal of "Being able to speak up in an interdisciplinary meeting." (Define goal behavior.)

The group leader asked the group to think for a while about their willingness to try a new solution to the problem, and said, "I have a solution in mind, but I will only tell you if you promise to carry out the instructions to the letter." (Secure a commitment to change.) The group agreed unanimously. Next, the group leader said, "Do you want the slow or fast method?" The group replied in unison, "Fast!" (Set a time limit. By setting up an either/or question about time, the group leader secures group agreement that change will take place—their only choice is whether it will occur sooner or later.)

The group leader continued, "First of all, I want you to go ahead and be nervous when you walk into the next interdisciplinary meeting. As you walk in, notice how dry your throat is, how hard your heart is pounding, and how your voice is ready to crack." (Prescribe the symptom.) "Then, instead of the thing you plan to say, announce, 'I'm so nervous I'll probably blow this, but here goes.' Then you go into what you had planned to say." (Include a variation.) Next, the group leader said, "When you try to hide your nervousness from the group, you are lying to them. By telling them up front you are nervous, you will be able to continue because your anxiety will decrease." (Reframe in the client's language.) Several group members had indicated the importance of honesty in dealing with others so the group leader reframed the prescription stressing honesty and truthfulness. The group leader then reminded the group that they had agreed to try out the solution. (Secure agreement to follow instructions.) The next week, several group members reported speaking up in interdisciplinary meetings without difficulty. The group leader warned them that a relapse was possible, and not to worry if they were occasionally anxious in future meetings, and to stammer and squeak a bit in the next one to show they were nervous. "You don't want them to think your opening statement is a lie, so make a point of showing your nervousness just to keep in touch with the feeling," said the group leader. When the class ended, one of the group members was heard to say, "I guess my problem speaking in interdisciplinary meetings just cleared up by itself." The group leader then explained the process of Paradoxical Intention to the group. (Demystify and or disengage.)

Use of the Paradoxical Model requires a group leader and group members who are highly motivated, willing to carry out or develop a seemingly absurd strategy, are creative, and who have a sense of humor. Since the model is so different from the usual way most leaders deal with situations, it may be the last to be tried, despite its usefulness.

Choosing an Appropriate Change Model

In addition to keying change models to knowledge, attitudes, beliefs, and values, Haffer (1986) suggests using an adaptation of Hersey and Blanchard's *situational leadership* styles to choose an appropriate change model. This model shows the relationship between the amount of support and direction the group leader provides and the degree of ability and willingness to change exhibited by group members. There are four group leader styles from which to choose: telling, selling, participating, and delegating.

Telling is for low ability and low willingness to change. Directions are spelled out clearly and direct supervision, including what to do, when, and how is articulated. Power-coercive rational models work best in these cases.

Selling is for low to moderate willingness and ability to change, take responsibility, and/or problem solve. Group members are willing to change but do not know procedures for changing. They are searching for models and will often go along with a change if reasons for changing are spelled out and there is some direction given. Rational methods are more likely to succeed.

Participating is for moderate to high ability and willingness to change. Lack of confidence or motivation at this level may lead to unwillingness to change. The need for direction is low and collaboration is high. Normative and educative models are most appropriate. A supportive, participative, nondirective style is highly correlated with success.

Delegating is useful when there is high ability and willingness to change. Group members are capable of independent action. Consistency and internal motivation are characteristic of behaviors. Little direction or support is needed. Group members can determine direction, goals, and motivation. When group members operate at this level, telling or directing is apt to meet with resistance.

SIMULATED EXERCISES

Each of the two simulated exercises includes an experiential and a discussion section. The suggestions for the exercises on pages 16 and 54 should be followed here as well.

EXERCISE 1 Decision Making and Conflict

This exercise gives the learner the opportunity to practice group decision making and to assess conflict within a group,

Objectives

1. To develop skill in group decision making.
2. To develop skill in assessing symptoms of conflict within a group.

Procedure

	1.	The group or the instructor appoints a leader.
5–15	2.	The leader appoints a timekeeper, whose duty is to
minutes		assure that the task is finished in 20 minutes.
	3.	The leader locates two group members who agree to be observers for this simulation and gives them an instruction sheet to follow. (See pp. 93–94.)
20–45	4.	When the observers signal the leader that they are
minutes		ready to begin, the leader reads the following task aloud: "We are to take 20 minutes to decide on five criteria for mercy killing. When the timekeeper calls time, our observers will report to us what they have observed. Let's try to use brainstorming, manipulative verbs, synectics, games, and methods of acceptance." (Refer to text for ideas.)

Alternate procedure: The group chooses its own controversial topic.

5. The timekeeper calls time at the end of 20 minutes.
6. The leader asks the observers to report their observations.

15–45 7. The leader then asks the group to discuss the fol-
minutes lowing points:

a. What could the leader have done to reduce conflict?

b. What techniques could the leader have used to assist the decision-making process?

c. What was learned from this exercise that can be applied in other group situations?

Observer 1

Your function is to look for conflict in the group. Record verbatim examples of conflict as they occur, using the observation blank below. When you are sure that you understand the items listed on the observation blank, signal the group leader that you are ready to begin. When the group discussion is over, you will be asked to report your recorded observations to the entire group.

(continued)

EXERCISE 1 *(continued)*

Conflict Observation Guide

Symptoms	*Examples*
members are impatient with each other	
ideas are attacked before being completely expressed	
members take sides and refuse to compromise	
members disagree subtly	
comments are made with strong feeling	
members attack each other personally	
members accuse others of not understanding	
members hear distorted parts of others' speeches	
members insist the group does not have the skill to solve the problem	
members feel the group is too large or too small to work effectively	

Conclusions: an impossible task; conflicting loyalties; status seeking; personal dislikes; appropriate involvement in working toward the goal

(continued)

EXERCISE 1 *(continued)*

Observer 2
Your function is to look for decision making in the group Record verbatim examples of decision making as they occur, using the observation blank below. When you are sure that you understand the items listed on the observation blank, signal the group leader that you are ready to begin. When the group discussion is over, you will be asked to report your recorded observations to the entire group.

Decision Making Observation Guide

Steps in Decision Making   *Examples*

states the problem

clarifies and elaborates

develops alternative solutions

keeps the discussion relevant

tests commitment to the emerging
decision

summarizes

agrees to the decision

tests the consequences of solutions

EXERCISE 2   Shared Leadership

This exercise gives team members practice in assessing and changing leadership patterns.

Objectives
1. To assess leadership functions.
2. To determine alternate ways of carrying out leadership functions.

Procedure
1. A copy of the Leadership Functions Checklist is circulated to group members, preferably a few days before the next team meeting.
2. Each group member, including the leader, completes the checklist prior to a group meeting. The group decides whether responses shall remain anonymous or whether group members sign their names.
3. The group leader or a designated group member tallies the responses for each checklist and reports the responses to the entire group at the beginning of the chosen meeting.
4. The group discusses each item, identifying areas where change is needed. Items suggested for change are reviewed by the group until a consensus is reached.
5. The group fills out the checklist in a week or two and repeats Steps 2–4. This procedure can be completed periodically until the group is satisfied with its ability to share leadership.

Leadership Functions Checklist

	No One	Designated Leader	Group Member (Name)
1. Who begins our meetings?			
2. Who makes sure objectives are set?			
3. Who supports group members during difficult situations?			
4. Who helps the team make decisions?			

(continued)

EXERCISE 2 (*continued*)

	No One	Designated Leader	Group Member (Name)
5. Who brings in data to help our work stay relevant?			
6. Who helps the group break down the problem into workable small problems/issues?			
7. Who helps group members speak clearly and clarifies unclear comments?			
8. Who makes sure the group keeps on track?			
9. Who summarizes what has been said?			
10. Who points out our progress?			
11. Who voices group feeling?			
12. Who calls "process" so the group will examine what is happening?			
13. Who helps the group relieve tension?			
14. Who agrees, accepts, and provides reinforcement?			
15. Who helps the group evaluate itself?			

REFERENCES

Alinsky, S. (1972). *Rules for radicals: A practical primer for realistic radicals.* New York: Vintage.

Allport, G. W., & Odbert, H. S. (1936) Trait-names: a psycho-lexical study. *Psychological Monographs, 211,* 20–30.

Avery, M., Auvine, B., Streibel, B., & Weiss, L. (1981). *Building united judgment: A handbook for consensus decision making.* Madison, WI: Center for Conflict Resolution.

Bales, R. F. (1950). A set of categories for the analysis of small group interaction. *American Sociological Review, 15,* 257–263.

Bales, R. F., & Strodtbeck, F. L. (1951). Phases in group problem-solving. *Journal of Abnormal and Social Psychology, 46,* 485–495.

Dewey, J. (1910). *How we think.* New York: Heath.

Fisher, B. A. (1974). *Small group decision making: Communication and the group process.* New York: McGraw-Hill.

Haffer, A. (1996). Facilitating change: Choosing the appropriate strategy. *Journal of Nursing Administration, 16*(4), 18–22.

Haley, J. (1973). *Uncommon therapy: The psychiatric techniques of Milton H. Erickson.* New York: Norton.

Havelock, R. (1973). *The change agent's guide to innovation in education.* Englewood Cliffs, NJ: Educational Technology Publications.

Jacobsen-Webb, M. (1985). Team building: Key to executive success. *Journal of Nursing Administration, 15*(2), 16–19.

Klesges, R. C., Basey, M. M. & Glasgow, R. E. (1986). Worksite smoking modification. Potential for public health impact. *American Journal of Public Health, 76*(2), 198–200.

Koberg, D., & Bagnall, J. (1972). *The universal traveler: A soft-systems guide to creativity, problem-solving and the process of reaching goals.* Los Altos, CA: William Kaufman.

Lewin, K. (1951). *Field theory in social science: Selected theoretical papers.* New York: Harper & Row.

Miles, M. B. (1959). *Learning to work in groups.* New York: Teachers College, Columbia University.

Rogers, E., & Shoemaker, F. (1971). *Communication of innovations* (2nd ed.). New York: Free Press.

Schein, E., & Bennis, W. (1975). *Personal and organizational change through group method.* New York: Wiley.

Shea, C. A. (1979). The organizational environment and its constraints. In C. C. Clark and C. A. Shea (Eds.), *Management in nursing: A vital link in the health care system.* New York: McGraw-Hill.

Stogdill, R.M. (1948). Personal factors associated with leadership: A survey of the literature. *Journal of Psychology, 25,* 37–71.

Tappan, R. (1983). *Nursing leadership: Concepts and practice.* Philadelphia: Davis.

Watzlawick, P., Weakland, J., & Fisch, R. (1974). *Change: Principles of problem formation and problem resolution.* New York: Norton.

4
Special Group Problems

Among the more common group problems that you will have to deal with are monopolizing, scapegoating, silence, the new member, transference and countertransference, physical aggression, nonverbal groups or group members, absences, and manipulation.

MONOPOLIZING

Groups are likely to have one member who talks excessively. In certain situations it may be reasonable to expect one member to do most or at least a major part of the talking in a group session. For example, when a group member is presenting special information to the group, it would be expected that that person would speak more than the others. When the purpose of the group is to share ideas, to learn from one another, or to make group decisions, a member who fails to let others contribute can impede group movement. Novice group leaders tend to become irritated by the overtalkative member and often fail to consider that such behavior occurs because other group members allow it to occur. A systems framework helps the group leader to see how one group member's behavior affects group functioning and vice versa.

Monopolizing can serve as a protective device for the group. The more silent group members may be anxious or fearful, or they may lack trust, and it is somewhat comforting to them that someone else will take responsibility for what happens in the group. At the same time, others in the group may show signs of irritation with the overtalkative person but have mixed feelings about interrupting. Meanwhile, the monopolizer may also have mixed feelings about doing most of the talking. Overtalkativeness can be an effort to decrease anxiety, or an attempt to establish a special relationship with the leader. In time, the overtalkative person will no doubt feel even more uncomfortable and resentful for being the only one in the group who is talking. In fact, then, monopolizing is a group problem that arises when one group member agrees—on some level-with other group members to talk and thereby to protect them. Unfortunately, while monopolizing begins as a protective device for both the overtalkative member and the rest of the group, in the long run, resentment among the group members increases and group movement will decrease.

In such cases, the knowledgeable leader will intervene, using any of a number of interventions that have been found effective, so that group movement can occur. Which intervention you choose will be based on an assessment of the reason for the talkative behavior and also on how effective a particular intervention might be. Not every intervention is effective in every group, and the leader may have to try several before one is found that works in a specific instance. Also, your feelings about the intervention chosen must be considered. If you are not convinced that a technique can be helpful, it would be best not to use it; once negative leader expectations have been conveyed to the group, the intervention will be ineffective.

One source of monopolizing is the effort of one group member to convince others. Sometimes an overtalkative member may go on and on merely because the group does not provide feedback. In such a case, you might provide opportunity for feedback with a remark such as "What does the group think about what John has been saying?" This will often quiet the overtalkative person and stimulate other group members to speak.

Another source of overtalkativeness is the attempt of one member to interest the rest of the group in matters that are irrelevant to the purpose of the meeting. Here, you could intervene by polling for consensus about what the group considers relevant.

Yet another source is the attempt of one group member to meet a need for recognition. If you conclude that this might be the difficulty, it would be wise to assess the group atmosphere to see whether it is marked by threat and competition rather than by warmth and support; if so, several techniques are available for decreasing anxiety and tension. Also, the overtalkative member can be counseled between group sessions; individual recognition might provide sufficient support to allow relinquishment of verbal control of the group.

When you sense the support and potential strength of group members, their assistance in dealing with the problem can be elicited by saying, "I think we need to look at why one person has been given responsibility for what happens here." This may draw forth statements from the group, for example, "I don't know what to say, so I let Alice talk." The monopolizing person might also admit that silence is bothersome. If the group members are able to verbalize their feelings, the leader can then work with these with such responses as, "It's quite normal to feel at a loss for words when new to a group, but in time you'll feel more at ease here," or "Let's try to work out this problem of getting more people in the group to talk; what could we do to make the amount of talking more equal?"

Often groups are not cohesive or cooperative enough to respond effectively to this kind of intervention, otherwise monopolizing would not have developed in the first place. You may have to intervene more directly by saying, "Stop talking, Fred; let's hear what Jim and Stacey have to say," or "Everyone in this group has a right to talk; does anyone else have a comment to make?" or "Let's move on to something else now."

If none of these tactics is effective, you might consider asking the overtalkative person to leave the group for five or ten minutes whenever monopolizing occurs. The "time out" technique must be used with caution, since it can be perceived as punishment. But it does place responsibility for talking with the remaining group members, and thus has potential for changing group interactions. Such a tactic is an example of behavior modification (see chapter 7) and will probably work best when you are not overly irritated and reward the monopolizing person each time overtalking decreases.

SCAPEGOATING

Scapegoating is a process in which one or two members of the group are singled out and agree, consciously or unconsciously, to be the targets for group hostility or advice. Many times the behavior of those scapegoated has become irritating, but there are ways for the group to deal with such behavior without resorting to hostility.

The use of a scapegoat is a convenient way for the group to negate responsibility for what happens in the group. Simply by blaming someone else, the members of the group can decrease their own anxiety and ignore their responsibility. Frequently, the scapegoated member sets up situations that evoke the group's anger. Sometimes the group is really angry with the leader for not fulfilling their unrealistic expectations, but rather than displeasing you, members take out their anger on the scapegoat. They may also scapegoat one member because they themselves feel worthless or inept and can concretely focus on someone else's weaknesses as a way to feel better about themselves.

Since scapegoating hinders group movement, you need to be alert to its development in a group. The following comments may reverse the process: "We seem to be blaming Louise for our failure to progress; what is happening here?" or "Mary, you always tell Jerry he is wrong, but is it possible you have some critical feelings toward me, too?"

To deal effectively with scapegoating, you must be willing to accept anger. You need to be able to accept verbal anger, resentment, or disappointment without trying to change the subject, to comply with unrealistic group demands, or to retaliate in subtle ways. By accepting group anger appropriately, can help the group to learn that authority figures are human and should not be expected to meet everyone's needs, but that this does not necessarily mean that are punitive or nonaccepting of others' feelings.

SILENCE

The ability to use silence effectively is a learned skill. Some silences are useful to group movement, others are not. Silence can be a group or an individual phenomenon. In either case, silence can have a number of meanings. Individual silence may mean that the person is holding back information or self in order to punish the group or the leader, may fear displeasing others, is in agreement, or is trying to escape talking because he is anxious.

When silence pervades the group early, it is often used to conceal that group members are anxious and unsure of what to do. Those who are least comfortable with silence will usually speak first. Often those who break silences do so because they think they are responsible for keeping the group moving. *Sad silences* may follow discussion of separation, death, or ending of the group. *Angry silences* follow angry interchanges and may be clues to hidden hostility or resentment that can decrease group movement. *Thoughtful silences* can occur after an especially relevant interchange.

In many groups there is a tendency to assume that the leader should break silences, and this may be most comfortable for an inexperienced leader. In general, it is best not to break silences unless they appear to be building into a power struggle over who will speak first. In this case, the leader might comment, "What's all the silence about?" Thoughtful silences help group movement and should not be broken by the leader. Likewise, anxious silences should not be broken unless tension levels seem to be highly disturbing to group members. Sad silences allow the group to grieve, reminisce, or resolve feelings, and they are constructive to group movement.

In teaching or time-limited groups, you may have to decide whether it is more important to break the silence in order to convey information, or whether the group could profit from being silent. Whenever you do break a silence, it should not be done to introduce a new topic, but rather to focus the group's thinking on the meaning of the silence or what happened prior to it. If you break silences frequently, examine why this occurs. Helpful comments after a silence include: "Silence sometimes makes people uncomfortable; does anyone have any ideas why this is so?" or "What are you thinking?" or "We have a couple of people here who aren't talking. Does anyone have any thoughts about this?"

NEW MEMBERS

Highly cohesive groups will have a stronger reaction to a new group member than those that are less cohesive. Regardless of the level of cohesiveness, group members frequently have mixed feelings about the prospect of receiving a new member into the group; they may hope that the new person will contribute positively to group goals, but worry that they may upset old patterns of interaction or compete for power or leadership. The new member will also probably have mixed feelings about joining the group: fearing rejection and hoping for acceptance, and wondering whether this will be a satisfying or a threatening experience (Markus & Abernathy, 2001).

You can help by meeting new members individually before they attend the first session. This gives you an opportunity to explain the group goal, to state any standing rules for group behavior, and to tell the person when and where the group will meet and for how long. Encourage new members to ask questions and to share expectations concerning the group experience.

The group should also be prepared for the change in membership. You can ask the group for reactions to adding a new member. This tactic might reduce the potential for hostility or rejection of the new member. It would also be helpful to ask members to introduce themselves to the newcomer and to tell a little about who they are and what has transpired so far in the group.

Close observation of the group on the day the new member enters it can help you to determine whether intervention is necessary. If tension levels rise, the new member can be put at ease with a comment such as "You'll soon catch on to what happens." If the group is hostile or rejecting of the new member, say, "I guess the group is upset about having a new member. Let's take some time to talk about this." Overdisclosure can occur when a new member is anxious and uses talk to decrease anxiety. You must guard against this. Such behavior can break group norms and frighten or increase tension levels in members who have been part of the group for a longer time. The new member might also react negatively after the session and even decide not to return. For these reasons, you will find it helpful to redirect group interaction by asking other members to express their thoughts or feelings.

TRANSFERENCE AND COUNTERTRANSFERENCE

Group members tend to project aspects of former relationships onto current figures in the group setting. This transfer of feelings that were initially evoked by parents or other significant people in a person's life is called *transference*. Transference occurs when a group member reacts toward you as toward a parent, since both are identified as authority figures. If the person's parent was harsh and unloving, the group will expect you to be the same and behavior that is warm and loving will tend to be discounted. If you remind a group member of a close aunt, this member may be extremely friendly toward you—far beyond what would be expected in a brief relationship. When you are quiet, those in the group who have had the "silent treatment" from parents or significant others may react with transference of their earlier feelings of resentment. Group members may transfer onto others in the group their feelings of love, hate, competition, or even guilt that they feel (or felt) toward brothers, sisters, husbands, or other family members.

Group members frequently try to duplicate family relationships within the group. Such transference can be the start of real friendship or of arguments; they need to be considered as the distorted relationships that they are. You may feel a strong pull to act out the roles group members try to cast you in; to do so would not be a therapeutic way to relate to the persons involved.

If you respond to group members because they evoke reactions reminiscent of your own earlier relationships are engaging in *countertransference*. This occurs when a group member reminds the leader of past experiences with significant people who had acted similarly and were irritating, were menacing, showed the need to be cared for, were of a different race or cultural group (and were therefore not completely understood), or, on the other hand, who had qualities that were attractive. Because of these past experiences, you are apt to react with anxiety or a sense of immediate recognition when meeting group members who have styles of relating that tap memories of these past relationships. In such cases, you are likely to be unreasonably irritated by, fearful or overprotective of, underreactive to, or attracted by one or more group members. The effect on the group is to provoke anxiety and disruption of communication.

You need to be aware of any overreaction to group members; to neglect to do so is bound to lead to leader and group anxiety and will impede group movement. The novice leader might try to deny the existence of countertransference reactions even though they seem to be universal experiences. Rather than trying to hide the existence of such reactions, it would be useful for you to remember that countertransference is an expected reaction that frequently occurs when helping people are highly involved with patients or clients (Cohen, 2001; Motherwell, 2002; Vannicelli, 2001).

PHYSICAL AGGRESSION

The leader cannot allow any physically aggressive behavior among group members. This includes touching group members who do not wish to be touched, throwing restricted objects, and hitting or hurting oneself or others. Such behavior must be halted immediately, and firm limits must be set so that all group members will feel safe within the group setting. In many adult groups, the leader will decide before the first session that touching will not be allowed; this rule is often set so that people will be encouraged to express their feelings verbally rather than through potentially dangerous actions. Other leaders will wait until physically aggressive behavior occurs, and then set limits.

For adult groups, a number of interventions are available to the leader. At the first sign of difficulty you can say, "No touching in this group," or "Stop hitting me. I won't allow you to hurt me," or "No throwing; somebody could get hurt." The rationale behind this intervention is that the leader demonstrates respect for self and others by limiting physically destructive behavior. If this technique does not work, the leader can gently but firmly restrain the member. Or you may ask the member to leave the group and return when ready to express verbally what is felt. Another tactic is to ask the aggressive member to sit next to you; often people who are physically aggressive are frightened. But if you are very frightened, this intervention probably would not accomplish anything. Another way of intervening might be to say, "Tell us in words what you're feeling." You might also ask group members what they think and how they feel about their fellow member's behavior. This can evoke strong reactions as members recall past situations in which similar behavior occurred and can lead to fruitful discussions. When all else fails, and if you feel comfortable doing so, you can turn to the physically aggressive person and say, "I want to help you, but I can't do much about it when I'm frightened and can't use my energy to help."

Leaders in a children's group can first acknowledge the child's feelings; "You're angry and you want to hit me?" Next, clearly state the limits of behavior: "No hitting allowed here." Other channels for releasing anger can be suggested: "Here, hit this pillow instead of me," or "Tell me in words what you are feeling." Finally, the child can be asked about being restricted: "What do you think about not being able to hit me?" For younger children, you may use nonverbal methods: hovering over the child in a calm, protective manner, or using your own arms or legs to restrain the child's arms or legs gently but firmly. When relaxed, the child may be able to cry (in relief) and/or share feelings.

NONVERBAL GROUPS OR GROUP MEMBERS

Children and older adults may be less able to express their thoughts and feelings verbally in groups than are people of other ages. This does not hold true for all groups, however, since adolescents and young adults or middle-aged persons may also have difficulty expressing themselves verbally. Whenever this is a factor in group conduct, you may need to develop techniques for stimulating group interaction. Planning and implementing a group activity such as cooking a meal or taking a trip to a favorite place is one way to get group members involved in different types of interaction with one another.

When unsure of nonverbal or silent members' reactions to a group session, you can learn about their thoughts, feelings, and perceptions by asking them to write on a card or piece of paper a summary of the main things that have occurred during the session, or to respond to an incomplete sentence. Some stems for nonverbal groups include:

Today, I feel _____
Having diabetes means _____
Being in this place is _____
I wish someone would ask me about _____
The worst (best) thing that happened to me since the last
    meeting was _____
The thing I remember most about our last meeting was

_____
I like (dislike) this group because _____

Once the members have completed one of the above incomplete sentences, you can collect them, select one or more, and use the information as a focus for discussion. Merely reading them aloud may stimulate discussion. If no one responds verbally, hearing the ideas of others read aloud can be useful and may increase cohesiveness. Before reading anyone's comments aloud, however, it is best to check with the group to make sure that no one minds. Keep members' comments anonymous unless members volunteer that the remark is theirs.

To stimulate group discussion, you can ask group members to draw pictures of themselves or of their families, or bring a living or inanimate object to the group to serve as a focus for discussion and nonverbal interaction, such as a kitten, a loaf of freshly baked bread, a plant, some flowers, or a picture. Using a picture that contains one or more people, you can ask each group member to tell what the person in the picture is thinking, feeling, or doing; this may initiate discussions about attitudes, biases, and other barriers to working together or communicating with other people.

Movement and structured exercises will help to release tension, build group feeling, and teach control of impulses. One group member may be asked to start a movement, and the rest of the group is asked to imitate it. This process is repeated, until each group member has led and has followed the movements of the others.

Even though group members may be essentially nonverbal in their interactions, you can make many observations about the group when activity is their primary focus, including looking for smaller groupings within larger groupings (who plays with whom, who leads and who follows) and for changes in these patterning. Relationship to you is another area to be examined—which group members withdraw, battle, ask for help, challenge others, channel or divert the focus of activity, cry, or laugh. Group members who can express their feelings and thoughts readily will still communicate during activities as one member tries to get another to do what is wanted, makes suggestions, threatens others, or carries out the activity. You can also learn about the various group members by observing the atmosphere in the group. Is it busy, apathetic, noisy, scattered in activity, aggressive, peaceful? How do members react to support, approval, suggestion, and limit setting from others? What themes of play or work can be identified, and how do they compare with normal growth and development levels for that age group? Finally, what individual styles of relating to the materials or activity can be discerned, and how can these styles be best described—that is, are they scattered, unrelated, concerned with being enclosed or shutting out others, experimental, creative, secretive, attacking, disorganized, stereotyped in thought or action?

ABSENCES

Absences from a scheduled group session may be due to real factors such as car failure or illness, but they can also be due to anxiety and fear about what is happening in the group. Absenteeism may also be related to group size; when many members are involved, subgroups and time limits can prohibit satisfying participation. It can also be a form of testing group limits. The absent member may be indirectly asking, "Am I accepted or missed?" In other instances, absence occurs because the group takes low priority in the member's life.

When assessing the source of absenteeism, you may find there is a need to reduce anxiety. The group can be polled to ascertain goal relevance for the members, create a smaller group, evaluate leadership skills, and/or open up the problem of absenteeism for group discussion. In the latter case you may ask, "How do you think it affects the group when everyone's not here?" Try to contact absent members via phone or letter, not in order to make them feel guilty, but to convey concern. Members need to know that their presence is desired, that they have been missed, and that the leader is concerned about them. In highly cohesive groups, a group member may volunteer to contact an absent member.

MANIPULATION

Group members may try to manipulate other group members, including you, to meet their own special needs. One member may be especially charming and helpful to you in the hope of being recognized as a favored child with special privileges; you may fall prey to this kind of seduction and, by rewarding compliant behavior, hope to get the group moving. Another member may try to put someone else on the "hot seat." Guard against rewarding or punishing the member who attempts to manipulate the group and say, "I notice that some of the members seem to be taking advantage of others in the group; has anyone else noticed this?" No names need be called; rather, the topic is introduced to help the group to understand how the group can be manipulated for one member's benefit.

SIMULATED EXERCISES

The two simulated exercises that follow each include an experiential and a discussion section. If the group is large, it should be divided for the simulation into equal-sized groups of not more than 15 members. The entire group can reconvene for the discussion.

EXERCISE 1 Nonverbal Communication

This exercise is designed to give the leader practical experience in observing and using nonverbal communication modes. Gestures, facial expression, eye contact, body movements, touch, physical distance and proximity, posture, clothes and their arrangement, sign language, silence, vocal and body sounds, and objects all can be used to convey an array of messages to others. Nonverbal communication can be as influential as verbal communication. When nonverbal communication contradicts verbal language, a mixed message results, which is confusing to the observer. For this reason, your wish to be awre of your own body language as well as that of other group members. Because this exercise allows participants to focus on nonverbal messages only, it encourages a deeper understanding of an aspect of communication that is often not examined in real-life work, supportive, and teaching groups.

Objectives
1. To practice conveying common feelings without the use of words.
2. To receive feedback regarding nonverbal communication ability.
3. To learn to teach others to be more effective in expressing themselves nonverbally.

Procedure

1. The group or the instructor appoints a timekeeper, who is instructed to make sure that time limits for each section are observed. The timekeeper is directed to warn the group when ten minutes remain to complete the task.
2. A leader is chosen by the group or the instructor for each subgroup.

15–45 minutes

3. The leader asks each person in the group to portray the following feelings, using only nonverbal communication:
   a. tension
   b. anger
   c. love
   d. acceptance
   e. fear
4. The leader intervenes only when a group member is having difficulty expressing the feeling. In that case, the leader asks the group, "Give some feedback about showing the feeling more clearly." The leader coaches the group to help each one express nonverbal messages. The group can be told to draw from experiences in charades, drama, dance, or film. Feelings should be expressed one by one, with time for feedback from group members concerning what is effective and ineffective in the member's presentation of feeling.

(continued)

EXERCISE 1 *(continued)*

15–30 minutes	5.	The leader asks the entire group to discuss the following points:

a. What is difficult about using nonverbal communication exclusively?

b. Which nonverbal mode does each member feel most comfortable using, and why?

c. What ideas does the group have about the reason for some modes of communication being used more frequently than others? How could more modes be used by each person?

d. What was learned from this exercise that can be applied in other group situations?

EXERCISE 2 Stating the Purpose

This exercise gives participants skill in formulating, verbalizing, and assessing others' presentations of group purposes or goals. By formulating and actually putting into words the purpose of the group within which the nurse will be working, goal clarification can be increased, and hesitancy in presenting the group purpose to the real-life group can be decreased.

Objectives
1. To practice stating group purposes or goals to a group.
2. To assess strengths and weaknesses of group purpose presentations.
3. To list important points to be considered when stating a group purpose.

Procedure
1. The group or the instructor appoints a timekeeper, who makes sure that the time limits for each section are observed.
2. The group or the instructor appoints a leader for each subgroup.
3. The leader appoints a recorder to jot down important points to consider when stating a group purpose or goal.
4. The leader asks each member in turn to state the group purpose for the group each is to lead (or be a participant in), as if each was the actual group leader speaking to the group. If some or all participants do not know the purpose of the group or even the group to which they will belong, the following hypothetical groups can be assigned: a postoperative teaching group, the family of an individual who will return home after a long hospitalization, a supportive group for the severely burned, a consciousness-raising group for men, a supportive group for people with epilepsy, a teaching group for new parents, a nutrition group for prison inmates, a teaching group for individuals with congestive heart failure, an orientation group for new nursing staff members, a supportive group for families whose children are dying, a supportive group for people with quadriplegia, a play group for preschoolers, an activity group for senior citizens, a social group for nursing home residents, an exercise group for psychiatric clients.
5. When each group member has stated a purpose, each of the other group members points out at least one thing that was good about the way the person stated the purpose and one thing that could be improved; then that group member restates the purpose, using the group's suggestions for improvement.
6. The whole group convenes for 15 to 30 minutes to list important points to consider when stating a group purpose.

REFERENCES

Cohen, P. F. (2001). The practice of modern group psychotherapy: Working with past trauma in the present. *International Journal of Group Psychotherapy, 51*, 489–503.

Markus, H. E., & Abernathy, A. D. (2001). Joining with resistance: Addressing reluctance to engage in group therapy training. *International Journal of Group Psychotherapy, 51*, 191–204.

Motherwell, L. (2002). Women, money and psychodynamic group psychotherapy. *International Journal of Group Psychotherapy, 52*(1), 49–66.

Vannicelli, M. (2001). Leader dilemmas and countertransference considerations in group psychotherapy with substance abusers. *International Journal of Group Psychotherapy, 51*(1), 43–62.

5
Beginning, Guiding, and Terminating the Group

PREMEETING PREPARATION

Much of the preparation needed should be done by you before the first group meeting. Three major preparatory tasks leader are: handling administrative details and relationships, making structural decisions about the group, and interviewing or notifying prospective group members.

Administrative Issues

Novice group leaders may think that the client or work group will be the largest system with which they will need to be concerned (Ojanen and Keski-Luopa, 1995). In reality, group members will be greatly influenced by other systems such as family, community agency, hospital, and other institutional systems. Highly organized bureaucratic institutions such as prisons, long-term hospitals and even schools may present the greatest resistance to innovative suggestions to start a group within their walls. Your first task in such a setting may be simply to locate the appropriate administrator who can grant access to a group population. It is important to note that although highly organized institutions may present the most resistance to groups, smaller community agencies can also be resistant to change.

You may have to educate administrators about how you can function in task, supportive, and teaching groups. Resistance may be decreased if you can clearly spell out objectives for the group experience and potential group content during planning sessions. The clearer expectations and plans, the less likelihood there will be later that administrators may directly or indirectly undermine group movement. Group experiences should be presented as a joint venture, and it is especially important for the leader to help administrators to specify their expectations of how she will function. Points that need to be agreed upon include deciding on whether administrators will receive feedback about group functioning and exactly how this will be done; deciding who will be involved in the mechanics of setting the time, length, and place for group meetings; and deciding who will enlist, convene, and retrieve group members, and how this will be accomplished.

In summary, when you are about to start a new group consider the following factors:

1. The larger systems within which the group population exists
2. The appropriate administrator or authority figure who can give permission for the group to begin
3. The administrator's knowledge regarding how you function as a group leader
4. An appropriate way to communicate the leader's expectations and plans for a group experience, including objectives or goals and a potential agenda or list of possible topics to be discussed
5. The administrator's expectations about the group experience
6. How to collaborate with the administrator in deciding how information will be shared once the group starts
7. Ways to agree on a method to ensure smooth handling of the mechanics of group operation

Decisions About the Group

The first decision to be made is the makeup of the group to be led. In some cases this will be determined by the needs and availability of client or staff populations, or by your job description or assignment. In other situations, you may have developed an interest in a certain problem area and may wish to lead a group of other interested people. If, for example, you are interested in emotional reactions to the physical illness process, you may decide to start a group for people—either clients or families of clients—who are involved with such illnesses. At some point, you will have to decide whether the group is to consist of people with acute or chronic illness or with only one certain illness, whether it should be limited to clients of a certain age, and whether to include family members or friends who might be involved in care. Yet another point to think about is the way potential group members may relate to each other. If you suspect that most of the candidates will be withdrawn and monosyllabic, it will be more difficult to stimulate group interaction; if members who are likely to be more verbal are added, there is a risk of having these members dominate the group.

One guideline for deciding on group membership is that close friends and relatives should probably not be included in the same group, since they may tend to reinforce old behavioral patterns. All members of children's groups should be of the same developmental level; when exercise or skill is the focus of the group, the children should be of approximately the same ability so as to eliminate feelings of failure or the scapegoating of less skilled members.

At times, you will have few options as to choice of members. Perhaps only six or eight people who meet the requirements of the group will be available. If the group is to be made up of nursing aides, membership will be predetermined by the number of available aides on the unit. An inservice educator who plans to lead an orientation group for nurses may find that the group membership will be determined largely by decisions made in the personnel and nursing offices.

Regardless of how group membership is determined, you need to consider the aspect of group size. Groups of 4 to 12 members are the optimal size when frequent interaction and group cohesiveness are objectives. When you are inexperienced, or when children or highly verbal or active adults compose the group, it may be advisable to limit groups to four to five members. Groups of six or seven, or even more, can be formed when there is more than one group leader, when group members are primarily nonverbal, when the leader is more experienced, or when structured exercises or learning situations are used. Remember that as groups become larger, the potential for cohesiveness decreases since there is less opportunity for members to interact with one another.

You will also make the important decision regarding how often the group should meet. Again, more frequent meetings are likely to lead to greater cohesiveness. In a busy hospital unit, however, meeting more than once a week or once every other week may become a problem in terms of scheduling.

The decision about the length of group meetings is dependent on several factors—your time and energy level, the group's attention level, the purpose of the group, and the group's need for a warming-up period. You may feel quite drained physically after a 40-minute session if you are not yet skilled enough to cope with the highly complex and stimulating atmosphere of group interaction. It would seem wise to limit group sessions to 40 minutes until the leader has developed the skill and supervisory abilities needed to deal with longer sessions. Children's groups may also meet for less than an hour, depending on the members' attention span. Some groups seem to require a warming-up period of 10 to 15 minutes for chatting and socializing before work starts. This may be a useful device, and you may need to decide whether the meeting time should be expanded to 1½ hours so that more work toward the group goal can be accomplished.

Once a time limit is set, it should not be changed whimsically or without discussion of the pros and cons with both the supervisor and the group members. This is important for several reasons. First, by structuring the group and keeping the time and frequency of meetings the same, consistency is maintained: Over time, it can demonstrate to the group that the leader is trustworthy, responsible, and able to stick to limits. Second, short-term groups are likely to accomplish more if they know the time limits of their existence. Groups in which the prevailing philosophy is "This group will go on forever, so why rush into anything?" will accomplish little. The leader who runs a shortterm group can encourage more efficient movement toward the group goal by stating at the beginning and end of each meeting, "We have x meetings left to accomplish the goal." Lastly, a consistent time structure is important if members tend to try to make it necessary for the group leader to extend a session by bringing up an important issue at the end of the time allotted; in these cases, it is better not to extend the session, because it teaches the group to work within limits without waiting until the last moment to bring up important matters. To assist in this teaching effort, remind the group at intervals, "We have 30 minutes left today" or "We have 10 minutes left for talking today."

The total number of group sessions may be predetermined by the agency or the availability of group members. Groups that continually take on new members and lose old ones, such as orientation groups in professional agencies, or about-to-be-discharged client groups, may be ongoing. Planning or supportive groups, on the other hand, may be circumscribed and only exist until group goals can be attained.

Whether groups are ongoing or not, decide whether they will be open or closed. *Open groups* are those to which new members may be added. When the open group system is used, you will need to identify a population pool from which to draw additional group members. *Closed groups* are those that do not add new members, despite the fact that some may leave the group before it officially terminates. Neither is the better system, but deciding on this point is another matter for you to weigh and evaluate. In doing this evaluation, consider whether the potential population is large enough to support an open group, how and when this potential population could be oriented about possible group membership, whether introducing new members would slow movement of the group toward its goal, and whether the group could exist and work with only two or three members.

Group sessions should always be held in the same place, if possible. The meeting room should be private, uncluttered, well ventilated, have comfortable seating arrangements (preferably circular to encourage interaction), and be readily accessible in terms of transportation. Smoking is now prohibited in most public places. Since health concerns are being discussed, it is important to consider whether smoking (and/or allowing others to smoke) provides a useful role model of healthful behavior. Likewise, furnishing high-calorie, low-nutrition foods such as cookies and ice cream to poorly nourished group members is a consideration to be balanced off against the reward factor of offering sweets as an inducement to participate. Such a trade-off may be more easily resolved if you decide to offer fruit juice and a nut-and-fruit bread or some other sweet but nutritive combination.

You can't force group members to attend the group meetings. (However, in some institutional settings, staff members often bring people to meetings in wheelchairs or make special privileges contingent upon group attendance.) Staff are usually expected to attend scheduled meetings, but client care may interfere. The most you can do is to stress the idea that a group experience has potential usefulness and that for the group to be of the most benefit to all the members, all sessions should be attended by the complete membership.

The goals or objectives that you formulate for the group experience depend on the type of group and its duration and the agency constraints. Some agencies become quite involved and influential in constructing group goals; others leave this task almost entirely up to the leader. For some groups, the leader's purpose may be to help clients to formulate their own goals. Group goals are best stated in behavioral terms using action verbs that connote observable behaviors. When goals are stated in this way, both leader and group members know when goals have been attained. Some group goals that have been stated in behavioral terms include:

To role play job interviews
To practice colostomy irrigation
To prepare an ethnic meal
To state four purposes of breast feeding
To plan health care for residents on unit 6C
To practice three alternative ways To express anger
To demonstrate effective breathing techniques for each stage of labor
To share thoughts and feelings about having diabetes
To develop alternative ways to handle other people's reactions to disability
To prepare staff for primary care nursing

When choosing a probable group goal, consider how to state the goal in clear terms, and specify the tasks that must be performed to accomplish the goal and some interaction processes that probably will occur or be encouraged among group members. Most groups have a number of goals; some are short-term goals, others are medium- or long-term. The importance of specifying goals is that they guide group action and motivate members to work in a specific direction. Some variables that can affect whether groups meet their goals are: (a) the extent to which goals are defined in clear, observable behaviors, (b) whether members see the goals as meaningful, (c) a cooperative group atmosphere, (d) consistency between individual and group goals, (e) small risk of failure, (f) availability of resources to meet goals, and (g) the allowance of enough time and flexibility to modify and attain goals.

Preparing Prospective Group Members

When selecting participants for a group, it is best to speak with each potential member individually. This interview may be ei-

TABLE 5–1 Written Group Contract

I agree to attend ten sessions with a group of other new parents to learn parenting skills. I realize that the group will meet every Monday evening from 7 p.m. to 8 p.m. and that I will be expected to attend each meeting at the University Center. I know that anecdotes of individual parents are confidential, and not to be shared outside the group. I understand that a nursing student will record what is said in the group as part of a learning experience in group dynamics, but that the recordings will only be shared with her instructor for learning purposes.

_____

Group member's signature and date

_____

Leader's signature and date

ther brief or extensive, depending on the purpose of the group. Conduct more extensive interviews when you are concerned about balancing the composition of the group, or if the group experience needs to be explained fully to the prospective member. For example, prospective members of a supportive group for those with cancer may need time to learn more about the proposed experience and to react to the idea of being in a discussion group with others who have the same condition. Providing potential members with a sample experience in group may stimulate them to proceed with a longer-term group experience (Peluso, Baruzzi, & Blay, 2001).

A short lecture or summary of learning content can be given to those being considered for a teaching group. Written or recorded materials can also be used to give potential group members a better idea of what to expect.

Factual information about how the group will operate is given to prospective members before the first meeting of the group. "Group contract" is the term used to refer to the basic operating agreement between you and group members (see Table 5-1). This contract can be either written or verbal; either way, it is intended as a statement of group structure and expected group behavior. Statements in the contract cover such data as number of sessions; time and frequency of meetings; whether the group will accept new members if some leave; member and leader responsibilities for confidentiality; how recording equipment will be used by the leader; limits of behavior such as attendance and physical aggression; specific expectations about participation, goals, and (if applicable) fees. The contract can provide both structure and safety for group members. People frequently enter a group with many misconceptions about what will happen during the sessions. The more time you spend discussing the contract before the first meeting, the better the chances that a climate of collaboration will be created. Avoid presenting too much information regarding the contract in a short period of time, because prospective members who are highly anxious may distort or selectively fail to hear specific aspects of what is being said. No matter how detailed or how general the group contract, it is wise to give members an opportunity to express their ideas and feelings about the items. While preparing group members, encourage them to state-what they hope to learn from the group experience or how they will benefit from it.

The group contract may not necessarily be used for a working or task group. However, it is useful to invite reactions and, if possible, to orient prospective members to the group goals, frequency and duration of meetings, and to limits and expectations for member behavior within the group.

Checklist for Beginning a Group

Use the checklist that follows to ensure you have considered all important areas before beginning a group (Tomasulo, 1998):

___ Talk with administrators and cofacilitators and agree on the purpose and function of the group and how it can contribute to the agency's mission.

___ Choose the meeting place for the group, keeping in mind safety, comfort, and ease of transport.

___ Limit the first group you run to no more than six members.

___ Choose members who are highly motivated to work with you.

___ Consider working with a coleader who is more experienced and who is willing to critique your work and teach you in a helpful way.

___ To prevent burnout and enhance the status of the group, run your group in a facility in which you don't work.

___ Review your work regularly to identify problems, strengths, and focus.

___ Videotape your initial groups and review them with a more experienced leader and/or your facilitator.

__ Meet at least once a month to discuss problems and successes with a peer support or supervision group containing people who are experienced in group work with the population you've chosen and who know group process.

__ Attend classes, read articles, and review training videos on group process.

EARLY GROUP MEETINGS

Warming Up the Group

Warm-ups can help you and the group relax. It is best to have a couple of warm-ups in mind in case the group votes against the one you wish to use. Here are a few ideas (Clark, 1997):

1. *Group Back Rub.* Ask participants to rate themselves on a scale from 1–10 with 1 being bored, distracted, or stressed out and 10 being calm, energized, and ready to learn. Tell the group that tension can lead to tense muscles and an uncomfortable body. Ask every other person in the group to give a back rub to the person to his or her right. After 3–5 minutes, ask participants to switch roles, then record their second rating. Conclude with a discussion of how back rubs might be used to reduce tension at other times of the day.

2. *Soothe the Savage Beast.* Choose some soothing music or sound (running water, ocean waves, etc.) and play it, asking group participants to draw whatever images are brought forth. After 5 minutes, lead a discussion about what images and feelings they had while listening to the music.

3. *Relaxation Exercise.* Read aloud from pages 30–31 or play a relaxation tape at the beginning and end of each group session.

Working with Large Groups

You may be forced to or choose to work with large groups. One of the most difficult things about this kind of work is getting peoples' attention once you get them moving around. Use a bell or whistle to keep group members on the task. Use one of the following exercises or adapt it for use with your large group.

1. *Spectrogram Technique* (Tomasulo, 1998). A spectrogram can help you get people interacting, and help group members of like minds to talk to each other.

Choose two opposite ends of the room to begin and end your spectrum. Stand on one end of the spectrogram and say, "Everyone who is feeling great stand down here." Allow a few minutes for group members to space themselves. Move to the other end of the spectrum and say, "Stand down here if this is a very bad day for you." Wait until people find their spots, then say, "The rest of you please stand in a spot that fits your feelings at this moment." After everyone is standing, say, "Chat with your neighbors and see if you're in the correct spot or whether you need to move to another place." You can use any alternative statements, such as novice group member vs. experienced group member, or just out of the hospital to been home for months, and so on. Devise your own spectrum endpoints depending on the kind of group you're leading. The spectrogram can also be used to enhanced cohesiveness and self-disclosure and to form smaller, homogeneous groups. Come with at least three different questions to ask the group in case the first two bomb. In groups, as in other aspects of life, it's always better to be over-prepared.

2. *Face of the Clock.* This technique, developed by Robert Siroka of the Psychodrama Institute in New York City, helps group members gather and share information in a relatively safe way.

Use chairs or some other objects, or use masking tape to exemplify the face of a clock, or ask participants to imagine a clock with 12 o'clock as north, 3 as east, 6 as south, and 9 as west. Ask participants to stand by the time of day they feel most happy (in pain, sad, spiritual, lonely, ill, or whatever is closest to the purpose of the group).

3. *Group by sociometry.* Once you have the large group warmed up, you can break them into smaller groups by using sociometry (Tomasulo, 1998). To do that, say, "Choose someone who looks easy to talk with (would be a safe person to talk with, you would feel comfortable revealing one thing about how you're feeling at this moment to, etc.), and put your hand on that person's shoulder. If you choose more than one person, travel with that person to your next choice." Once choices have been made, say, "Tell the person you chose why you chose him or her." After two minutes, say, "Ask the person you chose to share what it felt like to be chosen." Now, ask group members to form groups they would feel comfortable in. By letting the participants decide which group they feel comfortable in, you maximize group feelings and the potential for a successful small group.

Introductions

After warm-ups, you will probably begin your first session by explaining why you're all there and presenting the main focus of the group. Here are some introductions. Choose one that would work for you or change it to fit the group with which you'll be working. Think about whether you want to use your given name or a title and what effect each may have on the group's functioning. Also, decide what you will call group participants. It is wise to ask them how they wish to be addressed. In some cases, agency policy may dictate these choices, but if it doesn't, use the group process to empower the group in their own decisions.

1. *Introduction to a Caregiver Group.* "My name is Carolyn and I'm a nurse practitioner and the leader of this group. Everyone here is looking after a relative or friend. We'll be meeting Tuesday nights from seven to eight-thirty for six weeks to share experiences and ideas. At the end of six weeks, we'll decide if we want to continue the group. Who has an experience they'd like to share?

2. *Introduction to a Parenting Group.* "My name is Carolyn Clark and I'm a nurse practitioner. I'll be facilitator for the group. Everyone here is a new parent. We'll be meeting Thursday mornings from ten to eleven-thirty for ten weeks to share experiences and ideas. Who would like to start?"

3. *Introduction to a Post-Heart Attack Group.* "My name is Carolyn Chambers Clark and I'm going to be facilitating these sessions. You're all recovering from a heart attack. We're going to be meeting for a month on Saturday afternoons from two to four to talk about the best ways to cope with your situation. Who'd like to start?

4. *Introduction to a Remotivation Therapy Group.* "I'm Dr. Clark and I'm the group leader. We're going to be meeting every Friday from two to two-thirty for twelve weeks. Each time we meet, we'll focus on a different topic. This week's topic is animals. Who has had a pet?

Tuning in to Group Process

Even after warm-ups, groups can feel chaotic. Everything seems to be happening at once. Group members change the subject, interrupt, become irritated, get upset, make jokes or act silly, pair off and whisper, won't talk, and so on. Alliances build, then shift. People express positive feelings, then get angry or attack in a passive-aggressive way, or express positive and negative feelings at the same time. The conversation seems to make sense, then suddenly shifts to halting words, agitated words, or silence. Topics shift unexpectedly. Group members don't always stick to the agenda that's been set. You may suggest an activity only to find group members resist or ignore you. You may find your feelings jumping quickly from pleased, to angry and frustrated, to despairing, to excited, sad, approving or disapproving. If you work with a coleader, you may find you are being undermined or ridiculed and become irritated or impatient with your coleader (Whitaker, 2001).

The group may jump right in and start talking about the topic you've suggested or everyone may just sit and stare at you. If the group is silent, you might ask a question, such as "What is making it difficult to speak up in this group?" Or "Is it hard to get started?" This will make it possible for group members to tell you they don't know where or how to start or that they expect you to talk.

You might respond with, "We're all a little anxious and that's normal. You can begin anywhere you like." If that brings no takers, be more directive, for example, "It's understandable that you feel unsure. We could go around the group counterclockwise and introduce ourselves and talk about why we're here." This kind of comment gives guidance, but not direction. If this brings no takers, you might try, "I'll start."

How are you to make sense of the hodgepodge of events? Once you become more relaxed, you will begin to form hypotheses about why group members are doing what they're doing. As group members begin to interact, they offer factual information, but they also play out parts of their personalities.

Restrain yourself from interviewing group members in front of the group to find out what motivates them. Undesirable consequences often follow. Other group members will become bored, quiet and frustrated. They may even feel envy and set up a situation for others to hide behind your interviews. Instead, address your questions to the group. If you are patient, members will show you through their behavior what they're like. They will send you messages about them by the words they choose (attacking, apologizing, making themselves look good, and so on), and their nonverbal behavior (looking at the floor so you won't press them, waving their arms to show you how upset they are, falling asleep to show you how bored they are).

Don't come to conclusions too fast about how group members are or act. They may surprise you. Hold tentative hypotheses, then listen for more information to back up your hunches.

Focus on taking in the group as whole and trying to figure out just what's happening. Granted, this is not an easy task, but with practice, it will become easier. Remember, it is the interaction of group members, not the individual group member's behavior, that is important to group process.

You will notice moods and atmospheres by slowness or quickness of words said, the tone of voice and choice of words. Sometimes you may even pick up and react to the feeling of the group: sad, glad, mad, or bored. Notice your own countertransference and how it is different from realistic anger. Realistic anger doesn't have roots in shame or unrealistic expectations of yourself as countertransference does. If you're not sure which is operating, ask the group, "Have you noticed any change in the group?" If they have, you might want to ask, "Do you think it has anything to do with what I said or did?" (Whitaker, 2001).

You may find that group members do talk, but they talk in the abstract about the plight of being alone and having a heart attack or about single moms who are alone without anyone to help them with child care. In a supportive group, you might try to specify the feeling, for example, "We have been talking about being alone in a difficult situation. What would happen if we all talked about our feelings of being alone?" or "We've been talking about being alone in broad terms, but we need to ensure our discussion has meaning for each of us. How will we do that?"

If you are recording the session, group members may raise issues about that. Comments you can make are: "Only my supervisor and I will hear the tapes, but I can understand your concern. It think it's important for each of you to decide what you feel comfortable divulging in this group." This often reassures participants because you have sided with the resistance to recording.

Sometimes group members will question your credentials. Be prepared to give an honest and simple answer, such as, "This is the first group I've led at this facility." Quickly move into finding out "In what way is this important?" If questions about your competence continue, you can ask, "What sorts of concerns does the group have?" The aim is to get group fears out into the open and examine them. Avoid being defensive and remember that it is their fears, not your competence that raised the question in the first place.

Hidden Agendas

During the first meeting of a group, it often becomes apparent that individual members have some goals that are at cross-purposes to the group goals. These individual goals are referred to as *hidden agendas*. Leaders, too, may have hidden agendas. For example, you may say it is up to the group to decide what its goals are, while having already decided on the direction in which the group should go. Or the group goal may be to share thoughts and feelings about having cancer, but one of the individual members may hope for a cure. Hidden agendas in supportive or therapeutic groups often reflect the expectation that the leader will provide special safety, protection, advice, or knowledge. Whatever the items on the hidden agenda, they can be detrimental to effective group work, and the leader needs to act to decrease this potential. During the first meeting of the group, the agreed-upon goal should be stated and the group given a chance to discuss it thoroughly in order to clarify misunderstandings any of the members may have about how to reach the goal. Hidden agendas that are unrealistic and discordant with group goals need to be examined by the whole group. You may say, "I wonder if we've said everything about this goal? Perhaps we could go around the group so everyone can have a chance to react to it." Although it may seem that undue stress is being placed on this point, you can often trace later group problems to insufficient clarification of the group goal.

Once the goal has been clarified, you might restate it for emphasis, for example, "This group is for kids with diabetes to share with one another experiences they have had with others who do not have diabetes." In addition, start the group off by having them tell, in turn, what it was like when they found out they had diabetes.

Signs of Anxiety

Especially in supportive groups, but also in task and teaching groups, the ambiguity of the situation often causes a certain amount of anxiety. To reduce it, members will use their usual means of coping with anxiety. Some will attempt to seek structure and reassurance by demonstrating dependency on the leader or on other group members; to prompt the leader to care for them, they will ask many questions, seek advice, or behave ineptly. Others may pair off to provide mutual support. Still others may deal with their anxiety by acting as assistant leader or teacher.

The communication in early group sessions is often stereotyped, intellectual, and rational, following norms for usual social conversation. This early communication structure allows members to get to know one another slowly; too high (as well as too low) levels of self-disclosure inhibit early group movement. Some common themes in early group meetings are trust, safety, and dependency.

Attempt to create a climate of acceptance and comfort, and stay away from the role of the all-knowing, all-giving parent or "expert." Group members will repeatedly try to cast you in that role. This is a form of dependency. When the leader persistently refuses to be the "authority," group members will probably become angry. Some anger, directed at the leader, is an expected part of the group process and needs to occur in order to enable high-level cohesiveness and relatedness to emerge. If anger is not expressed directly ("You're the leader, do something!"), it will often emerge indirectly. ("The staff here is not doing its job," or "The staff mistreats us.") This particular form of attack may often startle you and you may jump in defensively or try to be the ultimate authority. Neither of these responses is particularly helpful. Instead, use your reactions of frustration, an-ger, anxiety, or guilt to "hear" and understand what is going on in the group. In supportive groups, comment, "I wonder if the group is irritated with me because I don't have all the answers?" By helping participants to understand and verbalize their concerns, you can help the group move toward its goals.

You can perform three important functions during early group meetings:

1. Develop a sense of cohesion and connectedness in the group.
2. Provide sufficient structure for group interaction in order to keep anxiety at a tolerable level.
3. Identify the basic norms for group behavior.

Promoting Interaction

It is to be expected that group members will talk to you more often than they talk to one another. Very early in group sessions, you can begin to promote interaction and connectedness by assisting members to talk to one another by saying, "I don't know. Who in the group has a thought about that?" or "Ask Jimmy that one," or "Tell Mrs. Lane what you just told me." In teaching or activity groups, you can promote group interaction by saying, "Show Sarah how to draw up the medication, Andy," or "Toss the ball once to every member in the group; you start, Wayne," or "Perhaps Mr. Edwards can tell us how he handles that problem." By not providing all the answers or doing all the tasks, you can give the message that the members are capable of taking some responsibility for what happens in their group.

Another tactic to use to increase group interaction is to reward participation through verbal and nonverbal communication. For example, you might say, "You seemed unsure about sharing with us, but you were able to do it!" or "Learning to breathe efficiently in preparation for labor is difficult, but you've made progress today." Nonverbal communications such as head nods and eye contact can be used to reward members when they speak or participate.

In the supportive group, the focus is on encouraging group members to share their thoughts, feelings, and reactions to crises, health conditions, or interpersonal relationships. A discussion or teaching group has a different kind of focus and structure. Since there must be a shared understanding of the language that is to be used, terms and concepts may need to be defined. Ask members to draw up a list of words or concepts they do not fully understand. Part of the session can then be devoted to clarifying the meanings of the words and to checking to see that all members understand the terms.

As in other groups, the goals and objectives for teaching and discussion groups should be clearly stated. Since there may be new goals for each session, you should state the goal at the beginning of each meeting. Time should be set aside for discussion of each topic or agenda item. You may appoint a timekeeper to see that sufficient time is- spent on each topic. The group is encouraged to help decide the priority of items to be discussed. Help members to integrate new information by relating material to previous topics, by comparing and contrasting new and old information, and by summarizing and reviewing. Time needs to be allowed for application of new learnings or decisions. Depending on the type of group, members can be asked to identify the implications of the day's session for their lives, work, and/or their relationships with others. At the end of a session, group members can be asked to tell how or whether the session has been useful and to suggest topics for the next session.

Regardless of the stated purpose of the group, encourage members to share their common problems or interests. One of the major benefits of any group experience is learning that others are struggling with the same difficulties or decisions. You can point out common issues or problems and suggest that "these are important things for us to discuss at some point." In beginning groups, the members may not be ready to discuss the issues, but by merely indicating their importance, the leader opens the door for discussion at a later date.

GUIDING THE GROUP

As the group progresses, you continue to be a role model for clear, effective communication (see chapter 2): being adept at revising goals as work progresses or as circumstances within the group change, teaching group members to share leadership. By summarizing what occurs in the group sessions, you can teach group members how to organize group experiences in a meaningful way, for example: "Today we've covered how to sterilize syringes," and "We're moving closer to a decision," and "I wonder if we haven't been talking about feeling angry because several members have left the group." As the group begins to take more responsibility, you can ask one member to summarize what happened in a particular session. Teach the group how to clarify thoughts and feelings; for example, "Tommy, you seem to be expressing anger; am I right?" or "I think you're both making the same point about disliking overtalkativeness."

Problem Solving

The group can also be taught to solve problems, using clarification of the problem as the first step. "The problem seems to be that we need to decide on a topic for next week," or "Barry could use some help from the group in drawing up the medication." Once the problem has been clarified, the leader can ask the members to volunteer their ideas about how to solve the problem and then guide them in testing out or thinking through the possible results of each solution suggested.

Helping the Group Meet Its Goals

A few noisy group members can prevent the group from reaching its goals. In a supportive group, you might ask the others to deal with the problem by saying, "Jack and Franny are forming their own group; what do you think is happening there?" In a teaching group, you might ask the noisy members to demonstrate a procedure or give their suggestions about the topic being discussed. In a group of older participants, assess whether the noisy pair is temporarily disoriented; if this is the case, ask them to try to listen to what is being said, or provide them with written or verbal orientation to the focus of the group's interaction at that moment.

As the group begins to move into the working phase, members feel concern about their position in relation to the leader and other group members. Also, there is less need for control and social acceptability; this is evidenced by the use of slang, swearing, and informality; and the ability to deal with more complex issues. Depending on the type of group, observe other signs that the working phase has been entered. Often, members become more involved in sharing and intimacy issues; they seem to be testing out how much they want to reveal about themselves and how close they wish to be to others. Cohesiveness increases, along with a sense of respect and acceptance of self and others, and there is more sharing of personal data and reactions to others in the group. In testing to find the limits of interdependency, independent group members may engage in conflict with one another or in direct or indirect war with the leader. It is important that you do not take sides or make judgments about who is right or who started an argument. Be vigilant about not giving in to the tendency to retaliate when group members challenge your authority. Although at this stage there appears to be a definite shift in behavior, some of the behaviors typical of the working phase may appear in early group meetings (see Table 5–2).

Table 5–3 shows leader behaviors that can be effective in moving the group from the orientation to the working phase.

TABLE 5-2 Early and Later Group Behaviors

Orientation Phase	Working Phase
Dependency on the leader	Interdependency and shared leadership
Anger that the leader is not omniscient or omnipotent	Increased intimacy and sharing
Attempts to play assistant leader	Conflict between members and or with the leader
Stereotyped, intellectual-rational, and socially acceptable conversation	Conversation on a deeper, less superficial level
Learning about others' similarities	Increased sense of respect and acceptance of other group members
Refining group goals	Collaborative effort in identifying and dealing with group issues

TABLE 5-3 Some Effective Leader Behaviors

Techniques	Examples
Reflection	You feel . . .?"
Deflection	"What do group members think about that?"
Clarification	"I wonder if you're asking the group for assistance, Mrs. Tanner?"
Asking for group reaction	"How do group members feel about not meeting last week?"
Increasing cohesiveness	"Many of you seem to be expressing an interest in changing the group goal."
Promoting interaction	"I don't know; ask Tom."
Exploring	"Tell us more about that."
Teaching decision making	"As I see it, the problem is to decide on an activity; let's pool our ideas. Who will start?"
Summarizing	"So far we've talked about sterilizing equipment, but not about drawing up medication."

TERMINATING THE GROUP

The process of terminating a group is both a group and an individual task. The entire group may disband, or several members may leave the group at one time. When termination is handled effectively, members can learn how to deal with the separation from others that occurs in many life situations. The ability to say goodbye and move on to other relationships is a skill some people have never learned.

Early in group experiences it is not unusual for members to drop out, because they feel they do not fit in with the group, their expectations are not met, they have been scapegoated by others, they fear success or intimacy, or they have become part of a subgroup that decides to leave. Generally, you can make leaving most therapeutic by making goodbyes explicit; for example, by asking, "John is leaving the group; how do you feel about this?" When this is done, there is less chance for unfinished business concerning leave-taking and separation. Especially in supportive groups, it is important to help the leaving member and the group examine the meaning of separation. Increased understanding can reduce the possibility that both those who leave and those who are left will feel they have failed or been rejected. Instead, the leaving of individual members can be explained as being due to unfitness, poor timing, external pressures, or unreadiness for a group experience. When group members leave a group because they have benefited from and grown through the experience, the termination is less abrupt and can be dealt with in several sessions of the group.

Even when handled well, termination can be anxiety provoking when it evokes unresolved feelings about previous separations. Some people find it easier to leave the group; others are more comfortable when they are the ones being left. Hopefully, a group experience can help members to be comfortable both with leaving and with being left. Feelings that commonly occur in all types of groups when they end or when group members leave include sadness, anger, rejection, longing, relief, and accomplishment.

In some termination situations, members may attempt to continue the group experience by bringing up new problems or crises for discussion. However, setting new goals or starting new activities when termination is near is not a useful procedure. Rather, say something like, "This is our last session, and we can't begin to deal with such a complex problem now; we can make better use of our time by discussing our thoughts and feelings about the group experience we have shared." You may also wish to continue the group; in that case, reluctance to separate should be examined outside the group, preferably with a supervisor or experienced peer.

Termination can be used by the group as a time for review, just as the end of each session can be thought of as a mini-termination when thoughts, feelings, and accomplishments are summarized. Group members may also use these times to get in touch with unresolved feelings connected with past separations. They may find it difficult to share these feelings, but they should have an opportunity to do so. Take the initiative by sharing your own reflections on the ending or separation and by reviewing the group experience from your point of reference. This may give the group members encouragement to share their own reactions. You could ask for written evaluations or summaries from group members. Whatever method is used, it is your responsibility to provide direction for the group about the way to end a group experience. It is also your responsibility to explore your own reactions to the ending of a group or the leave-taking of group members; once these are identified, there is less likelihood of over- or under-reactions to terminations.

SIMULATED EXERCISES

Each of the two simulated exercises that follow simulates one session of an actual group meeting. A list of questions to be discussed following completion of the exercises can be used to tie theory to practice. Group members may wish to record on tape either or both simulations and play back the recording to help them answer the discussion questions. If the exercises are completed without an instructor or supervisor present, a later discussion session should be held with a more experienced group leader present.

Each participant should have a copy of this book, if possible, or one or more books can be passed around to enable each person to read the designated material.

EXERCISE 1 A Simulated Supportive Group for Cancer Clients and Their Families

This intermediate- to advanced-skill exercise is designed to give you a group experience that simulates some group processes that might occur during one supportive group session. In this simulation, group members role play communication skills, leadership anger, dependency, monopolizing, silence, new members, helplessness/hopelessness, and denial. The person who is the designated leader will have practice in leading this simulated group. The other participants will be able to assess how the designated leader led, how this may compare or contrast with their own group leader experiences, how it might feel to be in this type of supportive group, and what problems could be anticipated in a real-life supportive group.

Between nine and fourteen members can play in each simulated group. If more than fourteen people are available, divide learners into groups of between nine and fourteen and begin a new simulation.

Objectives
1. To provide skill practice as leader of a supportive group for one or more participants.
2. To assess communication skills, leadership, anger, dependency, monopolizing, silence the entrance of a new member, helplessness/hopelessness, and denial as they might occur in a real-life supportive group.
3. To examine alternative ways of dealing with typical group processes.

Procedure
1. Seat the group members in a circle.
2. The group appoints a timekeeper, who times the experiential supportive group to run for 20 minutes and the postmeeting discussion group to run for no more than two hours (the group should spend no more than 15 minutes on each discussion question). The timekeeper may also be assigned to run the tape recorder and/or take notes, depending on the group's decision.
3. The group or instructor appoints a leader for each group of nine to fourteen members. The leader takes the leader role in the simulation (page 000), appoints or asks for volunteers to play the following roles, and assigns each to read her role description only on the indicated pages in this book:
a. dependency role (1–2 players), page 137;
b. monopolizing role (1 player), page 136;

c. denial role (1–2 players), page 136;

d. silent role (1–2 players), page 136;

e. new member role (1 player), page 136;

f. anger role (1–2 players), page 136;

g. helplessness/hopelessness role (1–2 players) page 137.

20 minutes · 4. When group members have read their role descriptions on the designated pages, the leader starts the group by saying, "Perhaps each person could tell why they joined this group. Who would like to begin?" The group simulation then continues for 20 minutes.

5. When the timekeeper calls time, the leader or a volunteer from the group leads a group discussion about each of the behaviors enacted, focusing it on the following points:

15 minutes maximum · a. How did the role leader deal with the person who played the denial role? Was it effective? How else could the leader have handled the situation?

15 minutes maximum · b. How did the role leader deal with the person who played the anger role? Was it effective? How else could the leader have handled the situation?

15 minutes maximum · c. How did the role leader deal with the person who played the helplessness hopelessness role? Was it effective? How else could the leader have handled the situation?

15 minutes maximum · d. How did the role leader deal with the person who played the dependency role? Was it effective? How else could the leader have handled the situation?

15 minutes maximum · e. How did the role leader handle the overtalkative person? Was it effective? How else could the leader have handled the situation?

15 minutes maximum · f. How did the role leader deal with the silent person? Was it effective? How else could the leader have handled the situation?

15 minutes maximum · g. How did the role leader deal with the person who played the new member? Was it effective? How else could the leader have handled this situation?

15 minutes or more · h. How did the leader accomplish the four assigned tasks?

1. Starting the group: Think of three other ways that could have been used to start this group.

2. Keeping group members talking to one another: Describe comments a group leader might make to encourage interaction among group members

3. Drawing similarities between group members: Make three statements designed to increase cohesiveness by pointing out group members' similarities in the simulation in which you have just participated.

(continued)

EXERCISE 1 *(continued)*

---

           4. Ending the group: State one or two other ways to end a group.

Variations: 1. Group members change roles and replay the simulation.

                  2. Add the roles of personal reactions and dependency, deleting other roles you have already mastered.

Role Descriptions

A SIMULATED SUPPORTIVE GROUP FOR CANCER CLIENTS AND THEIR FAMILIES

Group Leader Role
Your role has four parts: starting the group action, keeping the members talking to one another instead of you doing all the talking ("Tell the group that" or "Ask if someone else has an answer for that question!"), summarizing what has been said ("Mr. S seems angry, while Mrs. T seems to feel hopeless"), drawing similarities ("Everyone seems to have strong feelings about this"), and terminating the group session. ("Our discussion time is up for tonight; see you Thursday night at seven.") Before you begin this simulation, decide whether the group will be composed of patients, families, or a combination of both.

Monopolizing Role
Your role is to continue talking whenever you can. Keep trying to convince the group that you know all about the cause and treatment of cancer.

Denial Role
Your role is to deny the fact that your spouse (or you) is dying of cancer. Whenever anyone in the group starts expressing anger or helplessness, make comments such as, "Don't get so upset," or "Things will get better," or "Cheer up; it's always darkest before the dawn."

Silent Role
Your role is to remain silent throughout this simulation. Observe how the others and especially the leader react to you.

New Member
Role Leave the group before the simulation begins. Come back and join the group in exactly ten minutes.

Anger Role
Your role is to be angry because you (or a family member) are dying from cancer. Whenever you speak, make sure you express irritation. Make comments such as, "How can this happen to me?!" or "How can you sit there so calmly when people are dying?" or "God is punishing me," or "That's a stupid remark."

Helplessness / Hopelessness Role
Your role is to feel helpless and hopeless. Make comments such as, "It's no use; nothing can be done," or "This group can't help me," and "What's the use of talking anyway?"

Dependency Role
Your role is to seek direction from other members in the group, especially the leader. Look at the leader frequently, and make comments such as, "We don't know what this group is for," and "Tell us what to do," or "How can we cope with this problem; it's so overwhelming?"

Variation:
Personal Reactions Role
Imagine someone in your family is dying of cancer. Play the role you think you would play if this occurred.

EXERCISE 2 A Simulation of a Health Team Meeting

This exercise is designed to give you a group experience that simulates some of the group processes that might occur during one task group session: apathy, conflict, decision making, and leadership. It gives the learner an opportunity to "get the feel" of how these group processes operate by examining and analyzing them in a relatively safe, standardized environment. At least 6 (and no more than 11) members act out this simulated exercise or those suggested as variations.

Objectives
1. To allow skill practice as leader of a task group.
2. To practice leadership skills, even though one is not the designated leader.
3. To assess the processes of apathy, conflict, decision making, and leadership as they might occur in an actual task group.
4. To examine alternative ways of dealing with the typical task group processes.

Procedure
1. Seat the group in a circular arrangement.
2. The group appoints a timekeeper, who times the experiential task group to run for 30 minutes and the postsimulation discussion to end after 20 minutes.
3. The group or instructor appoints a leader for each group of six to eleven members who use the simulation. The leader appoints members or asks for volunteers to play the following roles, assigns each to read the role description as presented in this book, and warns each not to read the others' role descriptions:
   a. apathy role (at least 2 players), page 139;
   b. conflict role (1–2 players), page 140;
   c. decision-making role (1–2 players), page 140;
   d. leadership role (1 player; designated by group or leader), page 139.
4. When the group members have read their role descriptions, the leader says, "My role is team leader for this group. We are to plan health care for 50 clients and their families. Since we've not worked together before, we might start out by deciding how we will proceed to develop health care plans for these people. Who has some ideas about how to proceed?"
5. The simulation continues until the timekeeper calls time.

6. After time has been called, the leader (or a volunteer from the group) leads the entire group in a discussion of each of the behaviors enacted, focusing on a discussion of each of the following points;
   a. How did the leader deal with the apathetic role players? Was it effective? How else could the leader have handled the situation?
   b. How did the team leader deal with the members who displayed conflict? Was it effective? How else could the leader have handled the situation?
   c. How did the leader deal with group members who tried to assist with decision making? Was it effective? How else could the leader have enlisted their help?
   d. How well did the leader lead? Did others in the group provide leadership functions? List five important leadership functions, and discuss whether they were adequately provided.
   e. Have each participant tell what she learned from this exercise and how it can be applied in other task group situations.

Variations: 1. Group members change roles and replay the simulation.

2. Add the roles of pet project, do-gooder, and/ or anticommittee, deleting other roles you have already mastered.

Role Descriptions

A SIMULATION OF A HEALTH TEAM MEETING

Leader Role

Try to fulfill both task and maintenance functions in the group. Try to keep the group moving toward its goal, clarify unclear statements, suggest ways of moving toward the goal, point out movement toward or away from the goal, summarize what others have said, give the group the information it needs to complete its task, and suggest small steps toward the task, such as writing down suggestions given today as a basis for the next meeting's agenda. In fulfilling your maintenance functions, give support to unsure group members, relieve tension, encourage direct communication, voice group feeling, accept group members' ideas, and help the group to evaluate its progress.

Apathy Role

When the simulation begins, yawn frequently, and pretend you are falling asleep. Squirm in your chair, and whisper to other group members. Make frequent suggestions to adjourn the meeting, and refuse to take any responsibility for decision making.

(continued)

EXERCISE 2 *(continued)*

Conflict Role
Express impatience with others' comments. Make derogatory comments, such as "baloney" or "that's a crock!" Insist that the group does not know what it is doing or that the group needs an expert to help figure out this planning. Disagree with the team leader whenever you can. Accuse others of not understanding your point of view. Claim that only you know the best way to care for patients and that others are "very poor nurses" and "incompetent practitioners."

Decision-Making Role
Try to restate the problem whenever you think others are off the track by saying, "Let's get back to our job," or "You're off the track." If you forget the group goal, ask the team leader to restate it. Clarify or elaborate others' comments with statements such as, "Are you saying that . . . ?" and, "I'd like to add to your idea; what about. . . ." Summarize what has happened every five or ten minutes; for example, make statements such as "Gene has an idea he wants to push, but I'm not sure it's what the rest of us are getting at" or "So far we have decided (or have not decided) to do . . ." Test to see others' commitment to emerging de cisions by saying, "How many agree with the suggestion to. . . . ?"

Variations

Pet Project Role
Imagine you have a pet project, such as consumer advocacy, clients' rights, or preventive health care. Use this team meeting to try to interest others in your pet project. Cite imaginary facts and fallacies related to your pet project. Be sure not to assist the group whose task is to plan health care for the assigned group of patients and families.

Do-Gooder Role
Imagine yourself as a do-gooder, novice leader. Make grandiose plans for health care, without considering restrictions of time, money, or energy.

Anticommittee Role
Imagine you are someone who hates committee meetings and who has had negative experiences while working with other task groups. Tell others about your previous negative experiences rather than focusing on the task at hand.

REFERENCES

Clark, C. C. (1997). *Creating a climate for power learning.* Duluth, MN: Whole Person Associates.

Ojanen, S., & Keski-Luopa, T. (1995). *The importance of forming a work group in small group teaching.* East Lansing, MI: National Center for Research on Teacher Learning (ERIC Document Reproduction Service No. ED398197).

Peluso, E. T., Baruzzi, M., & Blay, S. L. (2001). The experience of public service users with group psychotherapy: A qualitative study. *Rev Saude Publica, 35*(4), 341–348.

Tomasulo, D. J. (1998). *Action methods in group psychotherapy.* Philadelphia: Taylor & Francis.

Whitaker, D. S. (2001). *Using groups to help people* (2nd ed.). Philadelphia: Taylor & Francis.

6
Supervision of Group Leaders and Coleadership

SUPERVISION

In group work, supervision refers to the interpersonal process whereby leaders present specific data from group sessions to a supervisor in order to receive feedback about their leadership ability. Supervision of group leaders can occur in a number of different settings and in a variety of ways. Regardless of these variables, the group leader is always entirely responsible for what happens in the group. Although able to influence the group leader, the supervisor cannot be responsible for group process when not present in the group (Green, Shilts, & Bacigalupe, 2001).

Group-work supervision can occur in individual or group settings. The novice group leader may meet individually with a supervisor, expert group leader, or fellow student to receive feedback about group leadership skills. This feedback is important because all people have "blind spots" in their perception that can operate to impede group movement, but of which they are unaware. Peers who are no more experienced than the group leader can often provide more objective perceptions because they have not yet been subjected to the pressures and stresses of the group. At the student level, peer supervision involves students supervising one another in their group work, under the guidance of an instructor. By serving as supervisors for one another, they learn not only how to be leaders, but also how to supervise others. Some questions the peer supervisor needs to ask when supervising other group leaders are:

Did the leader make assumptions without having sufficient data to support them?

Were theory or concepts regarding observations applied in an
appropriate way?

Were recordings or presentations difficult to understand?

Were there noticeable gaps in presentation of observations or
thoughts?

Were enough alternative leader actions suggested?

What evidences were there of transference and countertransference?

Was the peer supervisor critical or overbearing with the supervisee?

Did the peer supervisor create an open, comfortable environment for supervision?

What needs to be included in an evaluation of the supervisee
that the peer supervisor will share with the nursing instructor or supervisor?

Figures 6–1 and 6–2 show the results of one hour of peer
supervision from both the supervisor's and the supervisee's viewpoint.

Students and graduate students who lead groups as part of
their clinical experience usually receive supervision from faculty.
Written or verbal presentations of group process recordings are
often used. In some instances, students present videotaped or
audiotaped portions of a group session that is being supervised.

Although students or novice leaders often question whether
taping a session or phoning a supervisor during the middle of
a group might interfere with group functioning, research has
shown this may not be the case. Locke and McCollum (2001)
found that clients did not object to live supervision of their
sessions as long as the supervisor's comments were helpful. In
another study (Moorehouse & Carr, 2001), clients were found to
be cooperative with the supervisory process when a quality of
collaborative behavior was shown by the therapist. In other
words, if you are comfortable with the process and have a helpful supervisor, clients are apt to go along with it and probably
will benefit.

In whatever setting supervision occurs, it must focus partly
on the supervisory process and on how it relates to group process. It is not unusual for the person being supervised to rep-
licate struggles that are occurring in the group. For example,
when the supervisee is competitive, reluctant, anxious, dependent, or angry, it is most likely that the same struggles are
occurring within the group led by that supervisee.

FIGURE 6-1 Group peer supervisee form.

Supervisors: *S.C., J.B.*   Supervisees: *C.G., S.T.*

Date of Supervision: *12/11*   Type of Group: *Sensory Motor*

Supervision of *3rd group session   Stimulation for 5-year-olds*

5 minutes   1.   Problems encountered with this session:

     a. *monopolizing by Teddy*

     b. *Tommy and Sue vie for leader's attention*

     c. *limited attention span of group*

     d. *high anxiety level of leader*

5 minutes   2.   Themes:

     a. *competition,
e.g., all trying to be first*

     b. *fantasy,
e.g., Tommy pretended the toys were real animals*

5 minutes   3.   Transferences and countertransferences:

     a. *Tommy looked at leader when crying;
Susie called him a baby;
leader said (protectively),
"He is not a baby!"
(countertransference)*

     b. *leader sees monopolizer
as a "smarty pants"
(countertransference)*

---

    c. leader angry with group
       for "abandoning me"
       by leaving 5 minutes early
       (countertransference)

5 minutes   4.   Problems we want help with:

    a. recognizing transferences and
       countertransferences when
       they occur

    b. help in using facilitating questions

    c. drawing out the silent member

    d. adjusting to a new member

Evaluation of Supervisors' assistance:

1. Helped us to organize our presentation
and told us when to move on to the next
part of our presentation.

2. Pointed out our progress in recognizing
transferences and countertransferences;
suggested we go through our recordings
to see what group events seem to evoke
our under- or overreactions.

3. Explored reasons for silence of member;
agreed new member was probably uncomfortable
and would talk when ready.

(continued)

FIGURE 6-1 (*continued*).

4. Suggested facilitative questions, e.g.,
   "What are your thoughts?" rather than,
   "Do you agree?"

5. Asked questions when they needed more information;
   put us at ease by not confronting us or
   being negative.

6. Helped us to see how we were competing
   for the group's approval.

Because you may feel quite unsure about your effectiveness as a leader, you may be hesitant to participate in the supervisory process. Presenting one's work to others is bound to create some anxiety. Also, you may be alarmed to find that you have some of the same feelings about being in the group that other group members have. For example, as the leader of a new group you may feel just as anxious in the beginning as the group members do; or you may feel anger, sadness, or guilt that parallels group members' feelings when a group experience ends. Student-group leaders often devalue their contributions to a group experience and may feel quite guilty and frustrated about their leadership accomplishments or their sense of relief that the experience is over. Anger, too, can be experienced by the group leader who feels that termination of the group also terminates a chance to learn and to experience satisfaction; these feelings of loss may be expressed as anger toward the group supervisor, school, or agency, which is viewed as depriving the student leader of a good learning experience.

Because some of these feelings may be strong and uncomfortable, the novice group leader may try to avoid them, tending to censor data or to try to escape from exposure. It is important for you to talk through your difficulties with a supervisor to lessen the potential for acting out your feelings in the group. As you become more skilled in the group leadership

FIGURE 6-2 Group peer supervisor form.

Supervisors: *S. C., J. B.*   Supervisees: *C. G., S. T.*

Date of Supervision: *12/11*   Type of Group: *Sensory Motor*

Supervision of *3rd group session*   *Stimulation for 5-year-olds*

1. Problems supervisees encountered with this session

   monopolizing
   vying for leader's attention
   limited attention span
   high leader anxiety

2. Themes supervisees identified

   competition, fantasy

3. Themes identified through supervision

   competition between coleaders
   denial of group feeling

4. Transferences and countertransferences

   leader acted protectively toward Tommy
       (countertransference)
   Tommy looked to leader as parent (transference)
   leader angry with monopolizer
       ("smarty pants")
   leader angry with group for leaving early

5. Problems supervisees want assistance with

   recognizing transferences and
       countertransferences;
   using facilitating questions;
   drawing out silent member;
   new member

(continued)

FIGURE 6-2 (*continued*).

---

6. Suggestions we made to supervisees:

*go through process recordings for evidences
of transferences and countertransferences
not to use questions that can be answered
with a "yes" or "no"
that silent member may be anxious*

7. Evaluation of supervisees' presentation:

*Needed minimal direction in presenting data;
presented clear, relevant information
in all four areas.
Showed ability to question their behavior
and listen to our ideas without using
denial.
showed ability to apply group concepts and
to identify group process.
We think they did an excellent job!*

---

role, you may progress to peer supervision or even self-supervision (Lowe, 2000).

To further develop your group leadership skills, obtain adequate clinical supervision, which should be supplied by the employing agency. If no expert group leader is available at the agency, you can ask the agency to purchase supervision from a group consultant or pay for it as part of a continuing education program. Or, the agency should provide funds and time for you to obtain supervision on a private basis. Ongoing supervision is especially important when you lead a supportive or therapeutic group; a brief course in group dynamics cannot provide you with all the skills necessary to be a proficient leader.

Regardless of your level of skill or experience, certain processes and leader signals point to the need for supervision. If you answer in the affirmative to any of the following questions you probably need supervision:

Do problems arise in beginning a new group?
Are tension or anxiety levels in the, group high?
Is conflict that is not useful proliferating?
Is the group apathetic?
Is decision making unilateral or fragmented?
Is leadership autocratic?
Is the group lacking in cohesiveness?
Does the group continue in the orientation phase for more than six sessions?
Done or more members always monopolize group sessions?
Is one group member being scapegoated?
Are silences usually broken by the leader?
Are new members about to enter the group?
Do group members leave the group abruptly?
Are members absent frequently?
Does physically aggressive behavior occur in the group? Are group members primarily nonverbal?
Is the group approaching termination?
Does the group seem unable to reach its goals no matter what is tried?

Apart from group-process signals that point to a need for supervision, other signals may also indicate a need for assistance from an experienced group leader. Many social, educational, or work factors can make you more susceptible to group pressures and precipitate countertransference reactions in both the novice and in the experienced leader. One is the presence of reality events in your life situation that may create added stress. Another is a need to be successful or to be recognized as competent; when the group members show anger or frustration rather than expressing praise or appreciation, you may have countertransference reactions. Still another factor is a past significant relationship between you and the group, which can impair your ability to see situations as the group sees them. Finally, countertransference reactions can result from the communication of individual or group anxiety to you; to prevent this, learn how to differentiate your own anxiety about the group from the anxiety transmitted by the group. Unless you learn to deal with the countertransference response adequately, you may leave a group prematurely or feel guilty, disappointed, or frightened. For this reason, take responsibility for seeking out adequate supervision. One way to do this is to share perceptions and reactions in classroom discussion with an advisor rather than discussing the exact sentence-by-sentence exchange that occurred in the group. Another way is to ask for individual appointment time with a more experienced group leader or to submit written or taped recordings and ask for assistance in analyzing the situation that brought the countertransference about.

Beginning group leaders may feel angry when their unrealistic goals for group movement are not met. Some leaders report overwhelming feelings of guilt, followed by irritation and eventual apathy when group members do not respond as the leaders had hoped they would. Sometimes the irritation and anger are forced underground, and the leader may end up being overprotective of group members or unable to stick firmly to limits for group behavior. One of the most frequent signs of countertransference is a feeling of physical illness or discomfort: diarrhea, muscular aches, headaches, or even persistent colds. Other important symptoms are an inability to focus on what is happening in the group, which can lead to a rejecting attitude toward group members, or other strong positive or negative feelings. Whatever the signs and symptoms, use them to become aware that countertransference is occurring and seek out supervision.

COLEADERSHIP

The question of whether there should be one or two (or even multiple) leaders of a group is a moot point. Some leaders prefer to work with another person; others feel that working alone is best for them. Agency requirements may dictate coleadership. In some teaching institutions, it is common practice to pair a more experienced group leader with a novice. This arrangement provides the less experienced leader with a role model to imitate. In other institutions, two trainees are paired, in the hope that they will learn from each other.

Coleading a group with another person has advantages and disadvantages that need to be considered carefully prior to starting work with the group, because this type of leadership creates a more complex situation than individual leadership. In general, it is not recommended that leaders work in teams casually; the two leaders must be as seriously committed to working on the relationship between themselves as to working on that between themselves and the group members. In addition, the supervisory process must be relentlessly focused on the coleader relationship, since teams are particularly vulnerable to transference and countertransference reactions. Having two leaders gives the group an opportunity to try to play one leader off against the other, in much the same way as a child turns to father when mother denies a request.

Another difficulty of coleading a group is that the leader who talks more, the one who has more group experience, or the one toward whom the group has more positive transference feelings may end up being perceived as the senior leader, and the other will be seen as the junior person. This situation can create tension, because the group will be uncertain about the leaders' roles. The difficulty can sometimes be dealt with to some extent by having the coleaders interview prospective group members together.

Coleading can have disadvantages when efficient use of leaders is an important factor. The group size cannot be doubled just because another leader is added. Therefore, only half the number of groups can be run as when there is only one leader per group. Coleading is also not useful in a group with very young children, because they are often unable to relate to more than one adult at a time.

Lastly, any disagreement or strain between leaders is quickly sensed by the group. This situation is analogous to another family phenomenon wherein the children of fighting parents may react by trying to mediate, by feeling guilty because they think they may be the cause of the disagreement, by withdrawing as if trying to escape the situation, or by "acting up" to direct the parents' anger toward them instead of toward each other. Any of these group reactions can be counterproductive because members use their energy in trying to help the leaders instead of working at their task. Anxiety and inhibited group functioning may be an offshoot of leader disagreement. Trying to hide a disagreement will not be helpful either, because undercover disagreement can be as destructive as open disagreement, if not more so. At the same time, coleaders need to acknowledge the probability of some disagreement, since this occurs whenever two individuals attempt to form a relationship.

Although these disadvantages of coleadership are very real, ways can be found to decrease the potential for group movement to be hampered by them. In the first place, coleaders should meet before the sessions begin for the sole purpose of becoming acquainted with each other as people. Openness and respect should prevail. Each leader could draw up a list of questions to ask the other. There is bound to be some difference in their approaches to group interventions, but the differences should not be so great that the two cannot work together. The coleaders might discuss such questions as:

What are your goals for this group?
What is your theoretical orientation to group leading?
How do you see yourself functioning in this group?
How do you see me functioning in this group?
What group-leader strengths do you think you have?
What group-leader weaknesses do you think you have?
What suggestions do you have for handling possible disagreements between us in the group?
Do you think we will try to compete with each other and, if so, how can we recognize and deal with this to keep it from interfering with group movement?
How do you feel about our seeking out supervision?
How could we present group data to a supervisor?
What are your thoughts about how we can deal with such group problems as monopolizing, scapegoating, silence, new members, transferences, physical aggression, nonverbal members, absences, and manipulation?

One or more meetings prior to the beginning of the coleadership experience can decrease the likelihood that each coleader will try to meet his or her own needs rather than the needs of the group. If the coleaders wish to continue to monitor their activities in the group, they could meet together after each session to review group process, validate one another's perceptions of group events, identify special needs of the group, and identify areas of growth and the need for supervision of the coleaders. Ideally, some of these postmeeting sessions should include a more experienced group leader.

One purpose of the postmeeting session is to give the leaders a chance to deal with any disagreement they may have about how to handle the group process. During the orientation phase it is not wise to attempt to try to settle any disagreement within the group context, since the focus at this stage of group development is on the establishment of a sense of trust in the leaders. Many coleaders continue to deal with any disagreements outside of the group even later in the group process. This approach is reminiscent of that taken by parents who discuss problems in their relationship when children are not present. On the other hand, some coleaders have begun to think that if their disagreements can take place within the group, in an atmosphere of trust and respect, they can teach group members how to disagree yet continue to work together effectively. If the leaders can manage this, the group could have powerful learning experiences in effective interpersonal relationships. However, this approach should be used with caution. It should not be attempted unless the coleaders have worked through their relationship so as to be able to disagree without becoming angry; in most cases this requires supervision and practice.

Coleading does offer several advantages over single leadership:

1. Novice group leaders can observe a more experienced leader in action, and they can gradually assume leadership functions as they become comfortable in those roles. Moving from a more structured, dependent role to a less structured, interdependent role can provide support and decrease the anxiety level of the beginning leader.

2. Inexperienced leaders who work with more experienced group observers have an opportunity to validate their perceptions of group process.

3. Coleaders can act as role models for the group by demonstrating how to communicate clearly, cooperate, collaborate, and disagree effectively.

4. The coleadership relationship re-creates the family situation of mother and father; such a re-creation can be especially useful when working with parents, families, or children. Regardless of the leaders' sex, they can be perceived as parental figures by group members, thus making transference reactions clearer and more easily identifiable.

5. Coleaders can act in complementary roles, each reinforcing the other. For example, one can act as nonverbal observer of group process for one session, while the other is verbal and directs group interaction. The nurse who acts as nonverbal observer may also serve as recorder for that session. In postmeeting sessions, the observer/ recorder can give the coleader helpful feedback on group process. For the next session, the two may reverse these roles, or

not. In the latter case, there is less need to work out the relationship within the group, but time is required to work out how continuity will be maintained when leaders do alternate roles. Even though the pair may seem to be working as a single leader, there is still a tendency to compete with each other as leaders, to compare leading styles, and to disagree about how to approach group problems. It is not unusual for group members to try to create a division between the group leaders by complimenting that day's leader, by complaining about last week's leader, or by acting in ways divisive to the leadership pair. For these reasons, postmeeting sessions can be helpful even in a complementary role arrangement.

Another way a pair of leaders can work together in a group is for one leader to focus on the group process, while the other focuses on individual members. This approach can be especially effective with individual group members who may need more structured situations. In such cases, one leader can move around the group, orienting confused group members to group events, providing physical and emotional support by sitting next to anxious or disruptive group members, and by setting limits on disruptive behavior. A final advantage of the coleadership situation is that it allows the group to continue during the absence of one of the leaders.

SIMULATED EXERCISES

Each of the two simulated exercises that follow includes an experiential and a discussion section. If either exercise is completed without an instructor or supervisor present, participants should plan to share difficulties and insights with a more experienced group leader following the completion of the exercises.

EXERCISE 1 **Assertive Behavior**

This skill exercise can be used whenever participants find it difficult to state their wishes, desires, or needs in an assertive way. Peer supervision is a component of this exercise.

The exercise helps to develop skill in "I" assertive presentations of self. Withdrawal and/or "You" aggressive responses are replaced by clear, consistent messages.

Each person is to identify one situation where she wishes she had been able to say, "This is what I think," "This is what I feel," or "This is what I want."

Objectives
1. To identify interpersonal situations in which aggressive or withdrawal behavior was used.
2. To practice giving "I" assertive messages.
3. To practice giving feedback to others about their communication.

Procedure

1. The group or the instructor appoints a timekeeper, who makes sure that agreed-upon time limits for each step are observed. The timekeeper is also responsible for warning the group when five minutes are left to accomplish the task.

10–15
minutes
2. The larger group breaks into pairs. One person in the pair briefs the other on the situation from which she withdrew or became aggressive instead of assertive. The first person then practices saying, in an assertive manner, whatever was not said in the actual situation. The second gives feedback to help bring out assertiveness: "Look me in the eye when you say that," or "Don't laugh when you say that," or "Your words say one thing but your face says another."

10–15
minutes
3. The leader asks the pairs to reverse roles and the second person in the pair briefs the other person on the situation in which she was unable to be assertive. The pairs then proceed as described in number 2 above.

15–30
minutes
4. The entire group reconvenes and discusses the simulations, focusing on the following points:
   a. How did it feel to be assertive?
   b. What prevented each person from being assertive in the original situation? Were their fears realistic?
   c. What was learned from this exercise that can be applied in other situations?

EXERCISE 2 **Peer Supervision**

This exercise is useful for developing skills as peer supervisor and peer supervisee.

Objectives
1. To learn to use supervisory time efficiently by focusing on the issues of themes, transferences, countertransferences, problems encountered in the group, and problems that cannot be solved without assistance.
2. To practice presenting group-process data verbally.
3. To practice commenting on others' data presentations in a nonthreatening way.

Procedure
1. The larger group breaks into subgroups of five; two will have the role of supervisor, two will be supervisees, and one will be timekeeper.
2. Each subgroup appoints one of its members to be the timekeeper, who is responsible for making sure that the supervisees present data for no more than 20 minutes.
3. The supervisees (or coleaders) are directed by the timekeeper to begin presenting data to the group, but first to look at the guide on page 157 of this book. Meanwhile, the timekeeper briefs the other two group members on their roles as supervisors.

5–30 minutes
4. The timekeeper tells the supervisors to follow the guide on page 157 when taking notes on the supervisee(s) presentation. The supervisors are to ensure that all four areas are covered during the 20-minute presentation period. If supervisees spend too much or too little time on any area, the supervisors (coached by the timekeeper) are to redirect the presentation with comments such as: "Let's move on to countertransferences now," "What about themes?" or "Tell us some more about the problems in the group that we might be able to help you with."

20 minutes
5. When both supervisee(s) and supervisors are ready to begin, the timekeeper begins timing the presentation, warns the group when only five minutes of presentation time remain, and calls time when 20 minutes have elapsed.

20 minutes
6. Supervisors criticize the supervisee(s)' presentation, give suggestions for handling group problems, point out omissions in data, and compliment the presenter(s) on strengths. (See pps. 147–148 for ideas.)

10–30 minutes
7. Each member of the group is asked by the timekeeper to tell what was learned from this experience and in what ways peer supervisors or supervisees could have been more effective in their roles.

(continued)

EXERCISE 2 (*continued*)

Peer Group Supervision Presentation Guide
You have 20 minutes to present data about one or more group sessions you have led. Be sure to cover all four areas below in the allotted time period.

Group themes

Group problems (monopolizing, scapegoating, anxiety, conflict, decision making, and so on)

Transferences and countertransferences

Problems the leader(s) need help with

REFERENCES

Green, S., Shilts, L., & Bacigalupe, G. (2001). When approval is not enough: Development of a supervision consultation model. *Journal of Marital and Family Therapy, 27*, 515–525.

Locke, L. D, & McCollum, E. E. (2001). Clients' view of live supervision and satisfaction with therapy. *Journal of Marital and Family Therapy, 27*, 129–133.

Lowe, R. (2000). Supervising live supervision: Constructive inquiry and embedded narratives in case consultation. *Journal of Marital and Family Therapy, 26*, 511–521.

Moorehouse, A, & Carr, A. (2001). A study of live supervisory phone-ins in collaborative family therapy: Correlates of client cooperation. *Journal of Marital and Family Therapy, 27*, 241–249.

7
Behavioral Approaches for Group Leaders

The terms "behavioral modification" or "the behavioral approach" refer to an approach that focuses on behavioral change and is based on certain principles of learning, such as reinforcement. To some extent, all communication can be said to be behaviorally oriented, since it usually represents an attempt to influence others. If you nod in approval when a group member speaks you reinforce that behavior, thus increasing the possibility that it will occur more frequently. The behavioral approach is not concerned with insight or with whether people understand why they act as they do, but it focuses on decreasing unsatisfying or disruptive behavior and on increasing satisfying, goal-directed behavior.

A behavioral approach considers the individual's present difficulties, identifies specific behaviors that must be changed, counts the frequency of each behavior (baseline data), and then uses reinforcement to increase desired behaviors. The behavioral approach can be used in a number of ways in a group setting. One way is to gather together a group of either staff members or clients in order to teach them assertive behavior. Behavioral modification techniques can also be used to help one or more group members to make more verbal statements, or to decrease disruptive behavior in others. Yet another way to use this approach is to gather together parents who are concerned about their children's behavior. Common behavioral patterns that can be dealt with by teaching parents certain behavioral approaches include complaining, soiling, teasing, truancy, temper tantrums, sulking, not picking up toys or possessions, and crying. (Hemphill & Littlefield, 2001). A behavior approach has also been used successfully for crime victims with posttraumatic stress disorder (Krakow et al., 2001).

ASSERTIVENESS

An assertive person demonstrates through words and actions that "This is what I think. This is what I feel. This is what I want." Assertive people set goals, act on achieved goals in a clear and consistent way, and take responsibility for the consequences of those actions. In contrast, aggressive behavior has a controlling or manipulating aspect that is often hidden, out of proportion to the relationships, or off the point of discussion. In assertive behavior, a person states and stands up for his rights, knowing full well that others may disagree or attempt to block his action. The assertive person gives clear and open messages about what is desired (Clark, 2003).

Giving "I" Messages

The first way a leader can help a group to become less aggressive or withdrawn and more assertive is to teach the members to give "I" messages. Such messages convey how the individual thinks or feels: "I can't help you now .. .. I don't like to be shouted at." "I believe your figures are wrong." "I want to talk this over with you . . . .. I feel angry." "I feel guilty about being late." "I feel uncomfortable." "(I) thank you." "I disagree with that." These "I"-assertive messages are definitely different from "you"-aggressive messages that place blame on the other person, who then tends to become defensive: "You know I'm busy." "Don't you shout at me!" "Can% you ever add this up right?" "You don't know what you're talking about!" "Stop meddling in my work . . . .. Why do you always start the group so early?" "Why are you always picking on me?" When increasing assertiveness is a goal, the leader should stop any member who gives a "You" message during a session and ask her to restate it in "I"-message form.

CHANGING UNWANTED HABITS

You can teach group members how to identify and change unwanted habits. Five steps are involved in developing this skill.

The first step is to express the habit in behaviors that can be counted or measured. For example, if the objective is to increase one's ability to communicate effectively with coworkers, one could count frequency of direct eye contact, loudness and firmness of the speaking voice, and whether the speaker sticks to the point or makes qualifying statements—"I'm sorry, but . . . " or "This is probably not right, but. . . ."

The next step is to count the selected behaviors over at least a week's time. This data will give the person a baseline to use in checking progress in changing the habit.

The third step is to determine what precedes the unwanted habit behavior. For example, does the person have difficulty only when speaking with coworkers in a group setting, or only when speaking to a certain coworker? Is there a beginning or midpoint at which the habitual behavior could be interrupted? At what point does it seem impossible to interrupt the habitual behavior?

The fourth step is to have the individual make a contract of intention to change the habit. In this case, group members can make contracts with other group members. Contracts may be verbal or written, but they should contain simple, attainable goals. A reasonable beginning contract might be: "I will look directly into the group leader's eyes when speaking to her." Once the objective of this contract has been met for several sessions, it can be expanded to include looking into all group members' eyes when speaking to them. Each time a contract is fulfilled, the next contract can be aimed at correcting more difficult behaviors. When all the group members' counted behaviors have been changed, the leader can set up role-playing situations in which group members describe a coworker with whom they have been unable to communicate directly. Practice sessions using tape recordings and/or videotape can give group members feedback about how well they communicate with others. The group members can then practice communicating directly, with one person playing the coworker role. Finally, the contract can be extended to include extragroup behaviors with the real coworker.

The final step in the process is to try to arrange the environmental elements so that the goal will be easy to reach. For example, approaching coworkers for discussions might be most fruitful when all concerned are neither rushed nor fatigued.

INCREASING COOPERATIVE BEHAVIORS

Group members who are unusually noisy, inattentive, or nonverbal are prime candidates for taking on the scapegoat role.

As soon as the leader notices that a group member does not sit still, leaves the group, loudly interrupts others, or does not speak clearly, this should be a signal to begin to plan an intervention, perhaps using the behavioral approach.

In this approach, your first task is to differentiate between behaviors that are deviative and those that are cooperative. For example, some deviating behaviors in a group might be getting out of one's chair, interrupting while another person is talking, and not answering when asked a question.

The second task is to record baseline data. This kind of data gives the answers to several questions. How often during a certain time unit does the group member get out of his chair? How often per time unit does he interrupt another person? How often per time unit does he fail to answer when asked a question? Several group sessions will probably be needed to establish the average frequency of each behavior. These baseline data need not be kept a secret. In fact, people are sometimes influenced to change their behavior just by knowing how frequently a certain action occurs. The noncooperative member or other group members can be enlisted in this data collecting procedure, depending on the leader's judgment.

The next step is to pinpoint the events that precede the unwanted behaviors being studied. Often the leader or other group members may be instrumental in setting off noncooperative behavior. For example, the leader may reinforce a group member's disruptive comment by paying undue attention to it; this is often a signal for the member to continue being disruptive. It may be assumed that there are some current rewarding consequences of the behavior. The leader might formulate several functional hypotheses regarding what particular reinforcement is maintaining the noncooperative behavior and then test these out through observation and experimentation. Although the leader may have hunches about what the member finds rewarding in noncooperative behavior, it is imperative that such rewards should not be removed during the baseline data-gathering period.

Many reinforcers—a smile, a nod, or a grimace—would seem to have low influence, yet they can maintain a group member's behavior. Alter the milieu so that the most powerful reinforcers will be those that strengthen cooperative behavior.

One way to find out what is reinforcing or rewarding to a group member may be to ask some or all of the following questions: "What do you like to do best?" "What would make it more pleasant for you in the group?" "Which person in the group do you feel most comfortable with?" If the group member can answer any or all of these questions, you can then begin to formulate ideas about how to elicit cooperative behavior from him. For example, if a group member says that getting up from the chair relieves tension, you might contract to exchange 1 minute of getting up for each question answered with three or more words. This contract may be verbal or written. In carrying out the contract, you may involve the group in giving support to cooperative behavior by saying, "We have a group problem to help T learn how to answer questions more effectively. I've devised a plan that may work. Wendy, will you keep track of the number of words, and make sure he gets to take his prize of being out of his chair for one minute?" When it is difficult to engage the group in assisting with the contract, the leader could try the token system, in which members who volunteer to assist with the contract may earn tokens or other privileges. Decide whether or not the tokens can be turned in later for more concrete rewards, such as candy, cake, a group termination party, or some other reward decided on by the group.

When working with a group of children or adolescents, ask parents to provide reinforcers. Allowances, television viewing, or other special privileges can be granted by the parents when they receive a note or call from the leader indicating that a reward has been earned. When working with others in providing rewards, structure the relationship so that whoever else is involved also gets rewarded for being consistent in dispensing rewards. If this facet is not considered, parents or others will not be motivated to collaborate.

Whether a contract is written or verbal, it may be to your advantage to enlist the support of other group members in helping the noncooperative member count words spoken and remind the member to get out of his chair. Thus other group members are cast in the role of helping, supportive, and cooperative persons, and they are less likely to scapegoat the noncooperative member because they will be rewarded by your comments and praise for their efforts.

Another way to involve all group members in the contract is to use charts or graphs to show progress toward the goal. Stars, checks, or other measures of progress can be used by the leader or by other group members to demonstrate and reinforce concrete movement toward a goal. You may wish "a comment to the group on a member's progress as a further reward for movement toward more appropriate behavior.

Involving the group as reinforcers will only work when several factors have been considered. First, the group must be able to dispense the reinforcers. If the noncooperative member says that the only pleasant thing is a hot fudge sundae, and he is on a diabetic diet, the reinforcer cannot be dispensed. Then, the group may have to search for other reinforcers by observing what pleases him, or by asking family members or friends what pleases him. Second, the reinforcer can only be given as stated in the contract. Also, the reward must be given each time the cooperative behavior occurs, without exception, since it is the consistency of the reinforcing response that will maintain the cooperative behavior. Additional reinforcers may also develop in time; for example, other group members will probably become more friendly toward him, and this new reinforcer will help to maintain the cooperative behavior. A third factor that needs to be considered is the way you present the contract. It must be presented in a matter-of-fact, nonpunitive style, with no verbal or nonverbal comments about noncooperative behavior, since the purpose of the contract is to reward cooperative behavior. Concentrate on changing one behavior before moving on to the next target behavior. For this reason, the most disturbing behavior is dealt with first. In the example given above, the getting-out-of-seat behavior may decrease simply due to satiation; that is, the group member may be able to get out of his seat-and in fact is encouraged to do so-whenever he wishes to answer with three words or more. At a certain point, getting out of his chair may become more of a task than a reward. Once other group members start reinforcing his verbalizations, he may learn that talking can be more pleasurable than leaving the group circle.

In addition to using reinforcers to promote wanted behaviors, you can use behavioral modification techniques to help members develop new behaviors. One such technique is called shaping. *Shaping* is the reinforcement of successive approximations toward the desired behavior. For example, if the goal is to get one member to talk to another group member, the first desirable behavior may be to look at that person. By praising or rewarding the member for first looking at another group member, you can shape behavior in the desired direction. Other desirable behaviors, such as maintaining eye contact and saying hello to the other, would also be praised. The idea of shaping is that each small step toward the goal is praised, and thus the group member slowly develops the entire repertoire needed to achieve the goal in the end.

A second behavioral modification technique is *prompting* or telling the group member how to perform one or more steps in the desired behavior pattern. For example: "Look at Sally now; look right in her eyes and say hello." The techniques of prompting and shaping are frequently combined to achieve an appropriate response.

Modeling is another useful behavioral modification technique. In modeling, the leader demonstrates the desired behaviors. For example, you might say, "Watch me as I talk with Karen." Modeling can also be used more indirectly. Group members naturally imitate significant other people; thus, as a significant person in the group, you model behavior whenever teaching the group how to interact by interacting with them. Use as role models group members who are proficient in a skill.

Another behavioral modification technique is the use of *incompatible responses* when the desired behavior is incompatible with the undesired behavior. For example, the undesired behavior in a teaching group may be classroom disruption. Therefore, the target behavior may be academic performance. The rationale for choosing to focus on academic performance is that adequate performance in this area is incompatible with classroom disruption. The initial behavior required to be eligible for a reward should be easily attainable. A beginning behavior might be to open a book or to hold learning materials. Once the disruptive member has attained this goal, a more complex goal, such as reading two paragraphs of the book or learning the purpose of one piece of equipment, will be sufficient to receive the reward. Gradually, the level of accomplishment is raised to include understanding of more complex learning material.

WORKING WITH PARENTS

Until recently, parenting was thought of as an innate skill. Now it seems an accepted fact that people do need assistance in learning to be effective parents. The group setting can be an especially productive environment for learning parenting skills, since parents can learn from one another as well as from the leader.

Some skills parents can learn in group sessions are how to praise and give reinforcers for appropriate behavior, how to ignore deviant or inappropriate behavior, and how to implement three-minute "time-out" periods. The time-out period may consist of having the child go to his room to be alone for the time specified, or removing him from a pleasurable situation such as watching television or playing with his toys.

A group of parents can be taught how to specify behaviors, collect baseline data, select reinforcers, and develop contracts. While group members are collecting data at home, one or more of the problem behaviors can be selected for the group to explore. Parents whose children do not have that specific behavioral problem can model what they would do to handle the problem. The rest of the group can give feedback to the modeling parents, ask questions, and discuss their own difficulties in handling that problem.

Subsequent group sessions might be used to discuss difficulties and successes in using various behavioral approaches in the actual parenting situation. You will probably also have to deal with family resistance to certain behavioral modification methods. Such resistance is most likely to occur when parental discord and family disorganization are ongoing and chronic. In these instances, parents habitually provide inconsistent and contradictory cues to their children. When you note that this is the case, the family can be referred for marital-pair psychotherapy, a type of therapy that deals with basic parental conflict. Another source of resistance occurs when parents insist that all children should be treated alike, without favoritism. Although parents frequently claim to practice nonfavoritism, they often individualize punishment. In such cases, try to extend behavioral modification techniques to include all the children. Another family resistance is related to the "needed family scapegoat" phenomenon. Here, the child's problem behavior serves a highly complex purpose in the family; as a result, when the behavior of this sibling improves, forms of disturbance or friction may appear in other family members. In such instances, parents should be referred to a family therapist.

A nearly universal resistance to behavioral modification is the philosophy of not wanting to control another person's life. Parents frequently wish to be friends with their children, or at least hope to be viewed as permissive, progressive parents, and the group leader may need to present oral or written material about how parents reward and punish behavior in any case. What the behavioral approach teaches is how to reward positive behavior consistently and effectively. (See chapter 10 for more information on parenting.)

SIMULATED EXERCISES

Two simulated exercises follow. Both are skill exercises, and for each a list of discussion questions is given. If the group is larger than 15, it should be divided into equal-size subgroups. When an experienced group leader is not present during the discussion session, a postexercise session should be held with a supervisor or instructor to discuss difficulties encountered.

EXERCISE 1 Preparing for Changes

This skill exercise can be used whenever a change such as termination, entrance of a new group member, or movement from one group phase to another is anticipated. It can also be used to increase flexibility to un-known change situations, since a problem-solving approach is taught.

The purpose of the exercise is to gain skill in planning for change, whether it is an anticipated or an unanticipated change. Changes are examined using a problem-solving approach that can be transferred to real-life situations.

Objectives
1. To learn a problem-solving approach to change.
2. To practice preparing for upcoming changes.

Procedure

1. The group appoints a timekeeper, who makes sure that time limits for each step are observed. Together, the group decides on what time limits will be used. The time-keeper orients the group at each step regarding how much time remains for the task.

2. The group or the instructor appoints a leader for each group.

10 minutes
3. The leader asks each group member to write down on a piece of paper a real or hypothetical change, what is to be learned from the change, what is to be produced as a result of the change, and what would be a reward or satis-faction as a result of the change.

30–60 minutes
4. The leader asks each group member in turn to tell the other group members what the change is, what is to be learned or produced, and what reward would be helpful. The leader then asks the group member what barriers there are to reaching the goal, what alternatives the per-son has what resources are available, and what further planning for change is needed. If the group member is un-able to answer any or all of these questions, the leader can ask, "Who in the group has a suggestion for this?"

15–45 minutes
5. The leader assists the group to discuss the following points:
    a. What is difficult about change?
    b. What could be rewarding about change?
    c. Is change seen by the majority of group members as satisfying? If no, why not? If yes, what opinions does the group have about this?
    d. What barriers seem to be mentioned most by group members? What ideas does the group have about why these barriers are mentioned most often? What can be done to remove barriers to change?

EXERCISE 1 (*continued*)

---

    e. What seems to prevent group members from stating alternative actions or from identifying untapped resources?

    f. What was learned from this exercise that can be applied in other situations?

EXERCISE 2 Teaching

This exercise can be used whenever skill in teaching others is needed. The purpose of the exercise is to help the leader gain skill in preparing and delivering information to others. Skill in giving feedback to others' teaching efforts is also enhanced.

This exercise requires a great deal of preparation. Prior to undertaking it, each group member must be familiar with the content of the material to be taught and must have thought about presenting a 5–minute segment of the material to the group. Source materials, as well as the reference section at the end of this chapter and other chapters, may be consulted.

Objectives
1. To identify a topic suitable to be taught in the group format.
2. To list factors that need to be considered when teaching others.
3. To practice teaching in a group format.
4. To give and receive feedback on teaching skills.

Procedure

	1. The group or instructor appoints a leader for each group.
75 minutes maximum	2. The leader asks each group member in turn to "teach" the rest of the group. The leader does not intervene in each person's teaching but allows it to go on for 5 minutes and then asks the group for helpful hints on teaching the content chosen. The leader also asks the group for feedback to the group member who taught on the following: What are important things to consider in teaching a group this material? What types of resources need to be considered? Does the teacher need to do further research on the content of her presentation? What principles of learning need to be considered further? What problems seem to be inherent in this teaching situation?
20–60 minutes	3. When every group member has finished presenting and received feedback, the leader assists the group to discuss the following questions: a. How does readiness affect learning? b. How can the teacher find out what the learner already knows? c. How does the teacher assess whether the presentation is too technical, complex, fast, or slow for the learner? d. How can anxiety affect learning? What can the leader or teacher do to decrease anxiety in the group? e. How can repetition and feedback be built into a teaching program?

   f. What kind of media and equipment could be used to teach the material most effectively?

   g. How can the teacher assist group members to share information with one another and participate in the teaching–learning experience?

   h. What was learned from this exercise that can be applied in other situations?

REFERENCES

Clark, C. C. (2003). *Empower yourself! (and others): Holistic and assertive strategies.* New York: Springer Publishing Co.

Hemphill, S. A, & Littlefield, L. (2001). Evaluation of a short-term group therapy program for children with behavior problems and their parents. *Behavior Research and Therapy, 39,* 823–841.

Krakow, B., Johnston, L., Melendrez, D,. Hollifield, M., Warner, T. O., Chavez-Kennedy, D., & Herlan, M. J. (2001). An open-label trial of evidence-based cognitive behavior therapy for nightmares with insomnia in crime victims with PTSD. *American Journal of Psychiatry, 158,* 2043–2047.

8
Recording and Analyzing Group Process

Recording group interactions for study is important for a number of reasons. First, recording the multitude of verbal and nonverbal communications as they occur in a group meeting decreases the chances of omitting important details, since recall of events decreases rapidly with time. Second, recording what happens in the group will allow you to review what happened within and across group sessions. Third, recording group interactions will help you to review group skills, to compare them with those previously demonstrated at other sessions, and to evaluate your progress. Fourth, recording will encourage you to think of what has been said or done in various group interactions, and this will increase the potential for dealing more effectively with similar situations in the future.

RECORDING METHODS

A number of methods can be utilized for recording group interactions for later study. Three of the most useful types of records are the written record, audiotape recordings, and videotape recordings.

Some group participants may become anxious when they learn that a permanent record is being made of their behavior. You can usually prevent or decrease such anxiety among group members by:

1. Stating in a positive manner that recordings will be made. (e.g., "I'd like to record what happens in this group so I can learn about how groups work. (Pause.) Any comments?" or, "I'm going to be recording this meeting so I can learn how to be of more help to all of you. Any reactions to this?")
2. Telling the group members with whom the recording will be shared. (e.g., "I will share the recordings with my in-

structor and fellow students only," or, "The only people who will hear this tape are my supervisor and your social worker.")

3. Playing back a segment of the tape or showing the written notes to participants who seem especially anxious about the recording. This can be done at the end of a meeting or at the time of establishing that recordings will be done, depending on the insistence of the group members. Much anxiety about recordings seems to be related to how participants sound on tape or to the idea that the recorder is recording more than what is actually happening. Once participants hear how they sound on tape and/or what is being recorded, anxiety is minimized.

If none of these techniques works, you may be forced either to change the method of recording to one that is more acceptable to the group, or to stop recording. But before doing either of these things, the recorder can inquire, "What is it about recording that you object to?" Sometimes a group member will voice an objection, such as concern about confidentiality, that can be dealt with without stopping the recording. Generally, the group recorder will receive group consensus to record; rarely, if ever, do groups refuse to allow recording if the suggestions given here are followed.

Written Records

To be of most use later, the written record should be made at the time the group meets. Depending on the type of group interaction, the recorder needs to spend some time receiving group consent for this. In committee meetings, where a secretary usually takes notes in any case, there may be little difficulty in receiving group consent. But in supportive groups where members may fear disclosure of their comments it may be more difficult to get their consent to make a written record of the group session.

Once it has been decided that written records will be made, practice recording before the group sessions actually begin. Experience in this skill can be gained through practice in simulated group situations. To be proficient in recording group interaction, several skills will have to be learned: a coding or symbol system for words or actions that occur frequently, a way to determine what is important to record and what is not, and the ability to observe and write at the same time. Novices at recording often complain of feeling overwhelmed ("There's too much to record"), or they worry that they are unable to tell what is important and what is not important to record ("I can't write down every sigh and frown; how do I know what to record?").

Develop a coding or symbol system for group interaction. For example, group members can be assigned numbers or initials, anxiety can be represented by a *, or silence by S. Common symbols used in nursing, such as c̄ for with, s̄ for without, can also be adopted to conserve time and space. Two advantages of the written record method are that little equipment is needed and that tapes need not be replayed after the group meeting in order to evaluate group interaction. Writing in a group may also be less intrusive and more acceptable to group members than would audio- or videotaping. A disadvantage of the written record is that nonverbal messages, such as body posture, eye contact, and gestures, may not be noted if the recorder becomes too involved in recording verbal communication. Usually, the recorder will be unable to be a vocal group participant as well, since participating and recording are both full-time functions. This can be remedied by having two recorders: verbal and nonverbal.

Audiotape Records

Audiotape recording must be done while the group is in session. It is important for the leader to be familiar with the use of the audiotape equipment before the group meets. Audiovisual, educational technology, or library and learning resources technicians can be approached for assistance in this area. The meeting room should be checked out to make sure it is suitable for recording; in very noisy settings, unwanted sounds may be picked up which can override spoken conversation. The group recorder also has to place the microphone so that it will most effectively pick up all group members' remarks.

Some advantages of audiotaping are that the group recorder is free to join in the group discussion and can then evaluate leadership skills by listening to the tape at a later date, and that portions can be replayed to teach participants or to refresh memories about what really was said. (Hearing one's own voice make a statement is much less likely to be dismissed than hearing someone read back what was apparently said.) A major disadvantage of the audiotape method is that visual cues, such as gestures or movements, are not available for study. Therefore, the leader may wish to jot down important visual cues for later study. Another disadvantage is that it takes at least twice as long to listen to and evaluate a tape as it does to record the session. However, if the group recorder, instructor, and or group supervisor is interested in hearing a tape rather than reading a written record, the audiotape may be the method of choice. Audiotapes have also been used effectively in research (Brown et al., 2000).

Videotape Records

Videotape equipment is used while the group is in session. Becoming proficient in the use of cameras and other needed equipment is mandatory and may become quite time-consuming. Consequently, the leader may need at first to request the assistance of a videotape technician or an experienced student. Lighting, noise/quietness, space, and other aspects of the environment must be adequately checked out before taping begins.

Some advantages of the videotape are that the group recorder is free to join the session, and a complete record of verbal and nonverbal communication is recorded, exactly as it occurred. Another major advantage of the videotape method is that portions can be played back to the group to demonstrate concepts, to review what was said, or to do on-the-spot teaching of participants. Teaching sessions can be recorded and used again, freeing the leader for collecting data or other activities (Dai et al., 1999; Capafons, Sosa & Vina, 1999).Disadvantages of videotape are that equipment is relatively heavy and unwieldy and not always available, and that, because of the intrusiveness of the method, it may take longer for group members to relax and participate in the group discussion.

THE GROUP RECORDING GUIDE

The Group Recording Guide, which has been tested with more than 100 beginning leaders, was developed as a means of enhancing the leader's observation and leadership skills and recording ability. It tests for all the types of information a group recorder, observer, or leader needs in order to assess group interaction.

Supplementary Data Needed for Meaningful Recording

The top half of Figure 8–1 illustrates the type of supplementary data the leader needs to collect at the beginning of each recording session, before the actual discussion begins. (This part of the form is not repeated on succeeding pages of a single recording.) Seating arrangement may be highly significant, because it can reveal information about that session as well as offer comparison with other sessions. For example, if member number 1 always sits next to the leader, looks to the leader for answers to questions, and never initiates topics for discussion, the leader may well speculate that this member is highly dependent on her. Or if the leader and group recorder always sit next to one another and group members always leave an empty chair between themselves and the "authority figures" (L and R. you may suspect that the group is not one, but is split into factions.

Another example of the significance of seating arrangement is seen when an empty chair is always left next to certain members; those group members are probably being isolated by the rest of the group. Or if all couples in a group composed of couples sit together (the norm) with the exception of one, and these two sit one on each side of the leader, what theories might the observer want to test out through observing the session? Seating arrangement may or may not be significant, but the leader, as an observant group member, will want to use all possible group data available to help in improving group function.

Dates of the meetings should be recorded, since there may be need later to trace the sequence of progress from session to session. Also, the names of the group recorder and leader can be used to trace their development of group skills. The type of group and its purpose are recorded to aid readers who are not familiar with the group composition. Table 8–1 lists other data to be collected.

A *sociogram* can be developed from the seating arrangement chart; the number of comments made by each group member to each other group member or the group as a whole is tallied. The data can be reviewed to see who dominated the conversation, who spoke to whom, who is involved in pairing, who is an isolate, etc. When a sociogram is used, the person recording may be kept very busy drawing arrows from person to person indicating the direction of a comment and tallying responses. (See p. 16)

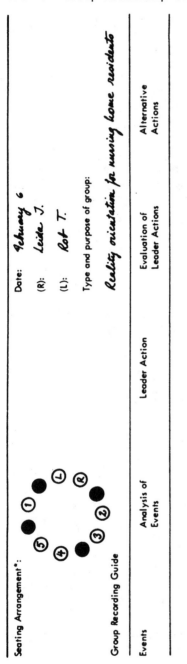

Seating Arrangement*:

Date: February 6

(R): Leila J.

(L): Rob T.

Type and purpose of group:

Reality orientation for nursing home residents

Group Recording Guide

Events	Analysis of Events	Leader Action	Evaluation of Leader Actions	Alternative Actions

*L = leader, R = recorder, ● = empty chairs.

FIGURE 8-1 Group recording guide.

TABLE 8-1 The Group Recording Guide

Events	Analysis of Events	Evaluation of Leader Action	Leader Actions	Alternative Actions
All behaviors of group members:	Hunches about what the events seemed to mean:	What the leader did, including all behaviors listed in the Events column:	All hunches about why leader action was effective or ineffective:	All *specific* statements of how the leader might more effectively:
Words spoken	Changes in group atmosphere		Introduction sufficient (insufficient)	
Who speaks to whom	Changes in cohesiveness		Group returned to focus of discussion (did not return)	
Silences	Distortions of what occurred		Tension decreased (increased)	
Gestures	Feelings revealed			
Tone of voice	Coping devices used		Leader's feelings interfered with action	
Increase or decrease in speech flow	Type and/or effect of silences		Communication skills used (not used)	
Eye contact	Dependency			
Facial expressions	Pairing		Less talkative people are (are not) talking	Give responsibility to a group
Posture	Monopolizing		Overtalkative, people are quieter (more talkative)	Increase security
Body movements	Characteristic phase behavior			Keep action moving
	Decisions reached			Restate
	Norms revealed			Give information
	Group disruption			
	Competition			

(continued)

TABLE 8–1 (continued)

Events	Analysis of Events	Evaluation of Leader Action	Leader Actions	Alternative Actions
			Apathy has decreased (increased)	Clarify
			Goals defined (need definition)	Point out
			Leader placed responsibility with group (did not)	Test for consensus
			Effective (ineffective) decision making	Summarize
			Conflict decreased (increased)	Explore
			Nonuseful (useful) silence	Get information
			Cohesion increased (decreased)	Keep to topic
			Scapegoating ends (continues)	
			Evaluation of leader actions (continued)	
			Competition ends (continues)	
			Even (uneven) balance between task and maintenance functions	
			Themes	
			Transferences	
			Countertransferences	

Events

Group events are all the behaviors of group members during a session except those of the formal or designated leader. Since informal leadership always occurs in groups to some degree, leadership behavior of informal leaders is placed in the Events column.

Words that are spoken should be placed in quotation marks, following the group member's number or initials:

EVENTS

H.G. "That's a rotten thing to say. You really don't know what you're talking about."

Q.O. "So what?"

Silence, 2 minutes.

T.Z. "Well, what else is new?"

The group recorder strives to get word-for-word quotes from each speaker, unless the speaker repeats herself; then the group recorder may enter something like,

H.G. "That's a rotten. . ." (repeats last speech).

It is suggested that novice recorders err on the side of recording everything they can, until an instructor or group process supervisor can review the recording and suggest observations that could be omitted. In general, all verbal and nonverbal interactions are relevant for understanding the ebb and flow of group interaction.

Analysis of Events

The Analysis of Events column should include all hunches about what an event seemed to mean. Not all events will have a clear meaning. However, when events are coupled, appear repeatedly, or appear to affect group interaction, guesses about their meaning can be made. For example, when each of a series of speeches by a group member is followed by a sudden, tense silence, the leader could hypothesize that the group atmosphere is changing (from cohesive to tense, or from informal to formal) in relation to that group member's behavior. Such hunches are useful because they give the leader ideas about when and how to intervene in group interaction and when to remain silent.

However, since they are only hunches about the meaning of events, question marks can be placed before the analyses that require more supporting data. Examples of comments that might be placed in the Analysis of Events column are the following:

ANALYSIS OF EVENTS

anxiety increasing rationalization
helplessness
intellectualization dependency on leader
? pairing
? scapegoating expected orientation behavior
? group moving into working phase decision reached by consensus unilateral decision
? group norm of politeness
? competition for leadership
? competition for leader approval
? theme: "We're deprived"
? theme: "We're different"
informal leader behavior-summarizing
informal leader behavior-giving feedback
informal leader behavior-clarifying
unclear-uses indefinite pronouns

Leader Action

The Leader Action column should include all verbal and non-verbal communications of the designated leader of the group. This column, then, together with column 1 (Events) should contain all the verbal and nonverbal interaction of the session. When written records are being kept, columns 1 and 3 are filled in during the group session. Columns 2, 4, and 5 are filled in after the group session is over.

Evaluation of Leader Action

Suggestions for comments that might be placed in this column indicate effective or ineffective action.

EVALUATION OF LEADER ACTION

effective—tension decreased
ineffective—? countertransference toward H. G.
effective—Q. R. started verbalizing feelings
ineffective—asked two questions at once
ineffective—asked a "yes/no" question
effective—redefined goals
effective—placed responsibility with the group ineffective-insufficient introduction
ineffective—apathy continues
effective—decision reached by consensus ineffective-conflict
ineffective—anxious silence followed effective-cohesiveness increased
ineffective—uneven balance between task and maintenance functions
ineffective—leader uses unclear pronouns

Alternative Actions

Suggestions for more effective leader behavior are placed in the Alternative Actions column. The purpose of this column is to provide a means of suggesting more concise, clear, and effective ways of intervening.

Some alternative action comments may be more concise restatements of what was said during the session. Others may be to remain silent or to provide needed actions, such as giving responsibility to the group, validating, pointing out time limits, providing support, giving feedback, keeping the group on its task, giving information, testing for consensus, summarizing, exploring, starting the group, and keeping on the topic. Examples of each of these suggestions, in the order listed here, are given below:

ALTERNATIVE ACTIONS

Remain silent.
"Several group members seemed concerned about
(to the group) "What's going on between Betty and Bob?"
"If I understand you right, you have mixed feelings about surgery."
"We have 10 minutes left to talk today."

"I guess I would feel upset, too."

"That sounds reasonable."

"Let's move on to discuss day care now."

"I'm Jan Shawn, a nurse. I'll be leading this group today."

"Are we all agreed then?"

. . . May we covered how gastritis occurs and what different people do to decrease it."

"Say more about that"

"Let's all introduce ourselves"

"We're off the track; we were discussing birth control."

Table 8–2 shows a sample recording for a group of children who have diabetes. Notice the location of comments in each column of the recording. The interactions can be numbered to enable the reader to follow the comments in the sequence in which they were made.

USING RECORDINGS

Recording group interaction is a tedious but rewarding task. Students often complain about the time and effort involved, but they also always comment on the helpfulness of recordings in learning group skills.

Recordings can be used in a number of ways. They can provide the learner with information about what happened in the group, what to observe in the future, and what would have been more effective leader action. Novice group leaders are often so busy participating in the group that they do not absorb these events and interactions unless recordings are made.

Recordings are often shared with a supervisor or instructor who can use the information about a leader's group skills to provide feedback. When this is to be done, space is left for supervisory comments to be inserted between events recorded.

Another use of recordings is to provide information to use in assessing the leader's progress in developing group skills. Table 8–3 shows a group skills checklist that can be used to evaluate leadership skills.

Some instructors or supervisors may prefer that the learner abstract recording difficulties and group problems that need to be solved. Table 8–4 shows a report sheet that group members can use to abstract information from the complete group recording.

TABLE 8-2 Sample Recording of Group Interaction for Children with Diabetes

Events	Leader Analysis	Leader Action	Evaluation	Alternative Action
M shakes head No. P has parka over head, body turned away from M.	?Anxiety; expected behavior when a new member enters the group.	"Would you like to introduce yourself, M?"	Not a good question because it can be answered with yes or no.	"This is M, a new group member."
		"Perhaps E and K could help me tell the new member what we have discussed so far."	Shares responsibility with the group.	Leader could review; could ask members how they "feel about having a new member."
E, "I forgot." K, "There's a new injector for insulin. You pull the trigger."		"Uh huh, in a few minutes we'll get K to show us the gun."	Half-heartedly acknowledges K's remembrance of the last session.	"Yes, that's right; show us the injector."
3-minute silence with group members moving in chairs.	Anxious silence.	"I know we talked about food last week. What kind of diet is everyone on?"	Perhaps leader is anxious about how to deal with new member and so breaks the silence.	
H. "What time is this over?"	Anxious: wish to get away from uncomfortable situation.	"The group is over in half an hour."	Task function of giving information.	

TABLE 8-3 Group Skills Checklist

Orientation Phase
 1. ____ Completes introductions
 2. ____ States purpose of group
 3. ____ Starts group action/keeps it moving
 4. ____ Brings information to the group
 5. ____ Gives feedback
 6. ____ Clarifies
 7. ____ Summarizes events
 8. ____ Helps group focus on task
 9. ____ Encourages clear, direct communication between members
10. ____ Diagnoses apathy and intervenes
11. ____ Diagnoses monopolizing and intervenes
12. ____ Diagnoses conflict and intervenes
13. ____ Diagnoses scapegoating and intervenes
14. ____ Places responsibility for decisions with group
15. ____ Identifies group norms
16. ____ Encourages ventilation of feelings
17. ____ Relieves tension
18. ____ Voices group feeling
19. ____ Identifies themes

Working Phase
 1. ____ Encourages description of problems or goals
 2. ____ Encourages statement of alternate actions
 3. ____ Allows group to do most of talking
 4. ____ Helps group evaluate their decisions
 5. ____ Tests for group consensus
 6. ____ Identifies transferences and countertransferences

Termination Phase
 1. ____ States length of group experience
 2. ____ Reminds members that group experience will end in 2 sessions
 3. ____ Assists group to discuss thoughts and feelings about the group ending
 4. ____ Uses last group to summarize and evaluate group experience

Still another way for you to gain group skills is to present group interaction recordings orally to an instructor and/or to a group of other learners. Entire recordings may be presented if time permits. If only 30 to 45 minutes are allowed for a presentation, you can use the brief presentation form for group interaction, as shown in Table 8–5.

SAMPLE RECORDINGS AND EVALUATIONS

Condensed examples of a session of a task and supportive group follow. Each recording is evaluated in terms of leadership skills, and suggested interventions are offered.

TABLE 8-4 Group Problems Report Sheet

Recording difficulties:

Group problems:
Describe specific examples of problems you found in the group you observed. Consider these problems in terms of the following behaviors:
  anxiety
  conflict
  apathy
  decision making
  task leadership
  maintenance leadership
  monopolizing
  scapegoating
  pairing
  cohesiveness
  silences
  dependency
  disruptions
  competition
  themes
  transferences/countertransferences

TABLE 8-5 Brief Presentation Form for Group Interaction

Divide your presentation of the following topics into four time segments:

1. Problems encountered with this group.

2. Themes (give one or two examples of each theme).

3. Transferences and countertransferences.

4. Problems (for which you need help).

A Task Group Recording

Table 8–6 presents the recording of a task group session.

Assessment of Group Leader's Effectiveness

The atmosphere of the group from beginning to end is one of casual communication; it is almost gossipy. This is not unexpected, since the participants have been classmates for two years. Perhaps because of relationships with her peers, the leader has difficulty establishing her leadership position in the group. Her very first comment indicates that she will give the group responsibility for making decisions. Unfortunately, there is no decision that is open to choice by the group, since the purpose of the group has already been established.

The casual atmosphere continues as members arrive late and share lunches. The leader makes no acknowledgment of the late-coming member. Some pairing occurs as members 7 and 9 develop a subgroup interaction. Next, the leader takes charge in an ineffective fashion. By making a unilateral decision about when decisions are to be reached and by suggesting how to proceed, the group is not encouraged to decide on how to plan its course. Perhaps as a reaction to this, member 3 states opposition to the leader's idea. At this point, member 5 shows anxiety and unsureness by questioning the recording procedure. The leader attempts to explore this query somewhat but does not clarify the group contract or elicit the member's concerns about recording. Next, tension is partially relieved by laughter and somewhat defused by returning to a topic that does not require members to take a stand against the leader and risk rejection.

The leader seems to benefit from the decrease in tension and is able to acknowledge a group member's suggestion, thereby rewarding making suggestions and promoting decision making and shared leadership. Group cohesiveness increases as member 4 joins in the task. At this point, the pairing activity of members 9 and 8 begins to interfere more seriously with group movement toward the goal. Member 7 asserts a leadership function and refocuses the group to its task. This action appears to increase cohesiveness again. The leader encourages movement toward the goal by rewarding and accepting suggestions, but fails to notice that member 2 has not participated actively in the group. Perhaps due to noninvolvement, that person leaves

TABLE 8-6 Recording of a Task Group Session

Seating Arrangement

```
  7  8  9  1
 6     5  4  3  2
```

4 = leader
1 = recorder

Date: *3/18/*

Group: *2ND Meeting*
Planning Committee for Class Follies

Events	Leader Analysis	Leader Action	Evaluation	Alternative Action
		"Do you want to talk about the Follies?"		Should not have given a choice.
7 "A skit could be made out of bedmaking."	7 Is involved and comfortable.			
9 arrives late; shares lunch with 8.	? Pairing.	"Today we're going to make definite decisions about what to include."	Task function of stating purpose.	
		"I thought we could use popular songs and have themes."		
3 "Oh, no."				
5 "Is 1 recording this?"		"Yes, is that O.K.?"		Leader could have reassured group that discussion was confidential.
Group laughs.				

(continued)

TABLE 8-6 (*continued*)

Events	Leader Analysis	Leader Action	Evaluation	Alternative Action
5 "We could impersonate faculty."	Group takes pressure off leader by returning to previous subject.	"Good idea. Some of you can do that."	Acknowledges suggestion and expands on it; part of decision-making process.	
4 "7 does; she imitates R real well!"	Becomes more active and makes first verbal comment.			
9 "I acted out a real vignette at work the other night."	9 and 8 pair off.			
8 "What happened?"				
7 "I'd like to do something like Truth is Stranger than Fiction."	Leadership function refocuses group to its task.			
9 "Oh, yes."				

TABLE 8-6 *(continued)*

Events	Leader Analyses	Leader Action	Evaluation	Alternative Action
8 "We could do our VW skit!"	?Cohesiveness increases.	"Those all sound good. Let's have them one at a time."	Maintenance function of accepting task function of suggesting.	
6 "What about . . .?"				
2 "I have to leave; see ya."				Might have asked 2 to stay.
8 "I thought of another one; well, that's irrelevant."		"Go ahead and tell us."	Leader responds to 8's enthusiasm.	Refocus.
8 relates work incident.		"Don't you wonder if that will happen to you?"	Joins unrelated topic.	
9 "It did." Group continues to discuss work incidents.		"We'll have to end soon."	Task function of giving information.	

the group. The leader then switches from pursuit of the group goal to an unrelated topic. The group takes its cue from the leader, and from this point on the group makes no movement toward its goal.

Leadership skills during this task group session can be assessed to some extent. The leader seems able to tolerate anxiety within the group, but the levels were never very high. The leader is hesitant about establishing leadership, which may be due to unsureness and to unrealistic expectations about what the role entails; in such a situation a novice leader can become quite anxious, and consequently leadership skills will diminish. The leader does not exhibit any overt hostility or confronting behavior. The only incident that might lead to a confrontation occurs when number 3 says "Oh, no" in response to the leader's suggestion. Since neither person pursues the disagreement, no hostility develops.

Because it is not possible to know inner thoughts, the only way to evaluate how well the leader organizes and understands group process is to observe responses to the process. One clue here is the leader's response to member 5, who questions the recording procedure. By responding to this comment, the leader shows recognition of anxiety in the group. In the analysis, the leader also notes when member 4 begins to participate verbally in the group. When member 9 begins to discuss irrelevant work incidents, it is not clear whether the leader remains silent attempting to force the group to take responsibility for refocusing, or is unaware of the process that is occurring. Since this is only the second session of the group, it is unlikely that the leader has already taught group members to assume responsibility for leadership functions. It is possible, however, that member 7 has developed refocusing skills through other group experiences. When the leader joins in topics unrelated to the group purpose, it becomes clear there is a lack of understanding of the group process that is occurring.

The leader does seem to have spent some time thinking about the group goal and is probably aware of its importance to group process. This is evident from the third comment, when there is a suggested direction the group might take in working toward the goal.

The leader does not ask the group to assist with group functions, or record that the supervisor's assistance is requested. However, merely by using the process recording method, areas in which assistance is needed are clarified; and by giving the record to a supervisor or instructor, feedback can be obtained.

There are no examples of the leader's use of humor in the recording. Although the group members laugh at one point, this seems to be anxious laughter used to release tension.

The leader shows several signs of prompting independence in group members: allowing them to take leadership in refocusing the discussion, and promoting independence by telling them that they can share in developing skits to impersonate faculty members and that they can help to develop skit ideas one by one.

The leader seems to have mixed feelings about being a leader with peers. The task-leader functions of getting the group going, stating the group purpose, acknowledging and promoting exploration of suggestions, and giving information are only partially fulfilled Some task functions that are not fulfilled (or not encouraged to be fulfilled) include clarifying the group task, keeping the group moving toward its goal, clarifying unclear statements, pointing out movement toward or away from the goal, restating, and teaching the group to solve problems.

The leader partially fulfills the maintenance function of acceptance by telling group members that they make good suggestions. One of the maintenance functions the leader does not fulfill (or encourage others to fulfill) is to give support to anxious or unsure members. For example, member 5 seems anxious about the recording procedure, and member 2 may have left due to anxiety. Other functions left unfilled are relieving tension, promoting attraction for the group, voicing group feeling, and helping the group to evaluate itself. This is not completely unexpected, since task group leaders often focus more intensively on the group goal and tend to ignore maintenance functions.

In the condensed group recording, the leader does not use the communication techniques of paraphrasing, behavior description, feeling description, or validating. Perhaps because the leader is so involved in the group task and work incidents, she focuses more on stating the purpose, decision making, and giving information.

The leader records no reactions to group processes. This is probably understandable in the beginning leader, who is preoccupied with directing the group and ensuring that the mechanical aspects of group structure are fulfilled. However, as leaders progress in their development of leadership skills, it is expected that they will begin to be more aware of their thoughts and feelings about what happens in the group, and of how they respond to group members' attempts to cast them in a role or to evoke under- or overreactions.

How could the leader intervene to make this task group session more constructive and fruitful? An assessment of leadership skills can serve as a guide to the supervisor or instructor in suggesting possible interventions to the leader. Some of the functions the leader of this group did not fulfill have already been discussed.

One suggested intervention in this instance might be for the leader to provide a clearer statement of the group goal or purpose. For example, the leader needs to be more specific about decisions the group is to make during that session; for example, "We're here to agree on five skits to include in the Class Follies." Another way to clarify the group goal would be to ascertain group members' reactions to the stated goal by asking outright, "What are your feelings about completing that task today?"

In these examples and in the interventions that follow, the leadership function could be provided by the designated leader or by one of the other group members. The leader might ask a group member to state (or restate) the group purpose, and to ask for feedback, or a group member might volunteer to state the group purpose and to test for group reactions. In some groups, the designated leader may not be the most skilled of the members in assuming group functions and/or may not have taught others how to assume group functions.

Although the leader notes that member 5 is concerned about the recording, no specific alternative action is suggested. One that could be used is, "This information on the recording is shared only with my supervisor for learning purposes. How do you feel about having this meeting recorded?"

The next significant event not dealt with by the leader is the leave-taking of number 2. If this person's silence is observed early in the session, the leader might try to draw the silent member into the group by saying, "What are you thinking about?" or "What is your reaction to this discussion?" Even if the leader does miss the silent member's clues, a comment when the member is about to leave can be made, such as, "Leaving?" or "We only have 15 minutes left today, and we really need your input." Sometimes just by questioning the leave-taking, or by reinforcing the members' commitment to the group, the leader can promote attraction for the group and the common good.

Another event that requires the leader's intervention is the switch in group focus from the group goal to work incidents. In this case, the leader might comment, "We're off the track," or "Tell us after the meeting," or "Let's get back to the skits for the Follies."

Some of the missing leader functions may be the result of inexperience in acting as group leader. Others may be due to the leader's inability to cope with mixed feelings about being leader in a group of peers. A suggested preventive intervention would be for the leader to examine his or her reactions to members. Although it is often useful to be liked by group members, this is not always a prerequisite to the leader's helpfulness to a group. If the need to be accepted, liked, and approved by group members exceeds or equals the wish to be helpful, the leader's need may interfere with effective leading of the group. For these reasons, leaders would be well advised to seek out supervision from a more experienced group leader until they have gained considerable experience.

Assessment of Group Recorder's Skills

The group recorder has reported seating arrangement, date of the meeting, the names of the leader and the recorder, and the purpose of the group. Events and leader actions are clearly stated. Quotation marks are used to separate verbal statements from nonverbal communications. The Analysis of Events column contains no observed behaviors; analyses that have little data to support them are preceded by question marks.

This recording could be improved by making two changes. First, observations regarding lack of leader reactions to the group could be placed in the fourth column. Examples of comments that could have been included in that column are, "Vying with group member for leadership," "Angry with group member," and "Anxious about beginning the group."

Second, specific statements or behaviors are called for in the fifth column. Instead, the suggestions found there are general in nature. Specific alternative actions that might be suggested are, "Let's talk about the Follies," "The recordings will be shared only with my supervisor," "Leaving?" and "Tell us after the meeting is over."

A Supportive Group Recording

Table 8-7 represents the recording of a supportive group or "rap session" for adolescents who have diabetes. The focus of

TABLE 8-7 Recording of a Supportive Group for Adolescents with Diabetes

Seating Arrangement

Date: 3/25   Group: Rap Session for Adolescents with Diabetes

```
   3   4   5
 2           6
   1   8   7
```

7 = leader
8 = recorder

Events	Leader Analysis	Leader Action	Evaluation	Alternative Action
All members look at leader.		Reviews group contract. Leans forward on chair with hands partially covering face.	Task function of getting group going. Mixed message via body language.	Remove hands from face.
		"Let's go around the group introducing ourselves."	Leader could encourage more disclosure.	"What else would you like us to know about you?"
Members state their names but look at leader while doing so; all deny difficulties with diabetes.	Dependency and low-level self-disclosure characteristic of orientation phase.	"I think it's interesting that no one's been hampered by diabetes."	Tries to increase cohesiveness by pointing out similarity.	"No problems at all because you have diabetes?"
6 "I had a teacher once who acted like I had a contagious disease." Group laughs.	6 Decreases group tension.	"How did you feel then?"	Could introduce doubt to decrease denial. Leader tries to explore feeling.	"Have others had a similar reaction?"

TABLE 8-7 (continued)

Events	Leader Analysis	Leader Action	Evaluation	Alternative Action
3 "I try to keep it a secret from teachers."	?Group compares leader with other authority figures.	"Sounds like some teachers could use some health teaching themselves."	Supports 3, but may be over-protective due to irritation with teachers.	"How come?"
4 "Most of my friends know. There's one teacher who refers to it as my problem."	Potential monopolizing member; may be seeking approval or recognition.		Need to try to relate 3's difficulties to others'.	"Anyone else feel as 3 does?" or "What does the group think about what 3 is saying?"
3 Proceeds with long monologue with theme of being mis-understood especially about diet.				

TABLE 8-7 (*continued*)

Transcript	Rationale	Leader Response	Function
2 "I always have food hidden in my room." 6 and 4 "Me too!" General discussion about sneaking food.	Level of self-disclosure deepens with sharing of a secret. Cohesiveness increasing in most of group members.	"You have something in common." Goes on to discuss why diet is important.	Promotes cohesiveness then tries to retain leadership by redirecting the focus; is leader anxious here?
3 Looks at leader and does not join in.		"What's your reaction to that?"	Silence.
6 "No matter what's wrong, my mother says it's due to diabetes." Looks at leader.	May be testing to see if leader will respond as mother does.	"Do you resent that?"	Labels feeling without validating it.
5 "I always know when I'm going to have a reaction."	First time 5 spoke. 3 and 1 are potential isolates in this group.	"Let's talk a little about reactions."	Seeks to explore a topic.
All but 3 and 1 join in a discussion of reactions.		"Time's up for today. See you next week." "Let's summarize what happened today."	Takes responsibility for ending group.

the group is on sharing interpersonal situations and knowledge related to the diabetic experience.

Assessment of Group Leader's Effectiveness

Of the sample recordings that have been presented, this one reveals the highest level of self-disclosure. Perhaps this finding is not completely unexpected, since supportive groups zero in on personal thoughts and feelings. However, the leader also demonstrates a level of communication skill and ease that the other two leaders did not.

The leader discharges her responsibility by reviewing the group contract and encouraging all group members to participate by sharing in introductions. Member dependency and low self-disclosure occurs when they initially look to the leader and deny difficulties with diabetes. When the leader assists group process by pointing to how similar they are in their reactions to diabetes, the potential for group cohesiveness increases, and there is greater freedom to discuss difficulties. Tension is further released through group laughter, which may be laughter of recognition; group members may have shared the experiences of being treated differently because of their diabetes.

It is not unusual for group members to perceive the group leader as a teacher. For this reason it is possible that the discussion about teachers may be an attempt to compare and contrast the leader's responses to other authority figures' behavior. Some thoughts group members may be having in this area are: Will this person be like other adults I know? Will I be understood here? Can I be safe and comfortable here so I can share my thoughts and feelings? Instead of recognizing this process, the leader sides with the students and makes a slightly derogatory comment about the teacher.

The leader shows some irritation, and a monologue concerning being misunderstood follows. It could be that the members feel that the leader misinterpreted their earlier testing behavior of comparing authority figures, and so member 3 speaks for the group and tells about feeling misunderstood. Also, member 3's behavior may be seen as monopolizing. The leader seems not to recognize or at least not to know how to deal with monopolizing as it occurs. Perhaps the leader's silence was helpful because members 2, 4, and 6 feel secure enough to share a secret. With this increase in self-disclosure, group cohesiveness increases. At the same time, member 3 continues to try to have a special relationship with the leader, as exemplified by the fact that she does not join in the secret-sharing activity and looks toward the leader instead.

Perhaps the leader becomes anxious with the level of self-disclosure shown, because no sooner has she increased cohesiveness and sharing than she increases distance in the group by taking the teacher role of information-giver. Member 6 continues testing to see if the leader is like other authority figures—in this case, his mother. The leader tries to explore the member's relationship with his mother, but she puts some words into his mouth by labeling his feeling as resentment rather than by allowing him to describe his own feeling.

Despite the leader's action, member 5, who has been silent until now, is able to assert herself as an independent person who knows as well as her mother when she is going to have a hypo- or hyperglycemic reaction. It is interesting that member 5 chooses this point at which to speak. It may be that this person has been observing the others' behavior, including the leader's, and only now feels comfortable enough to join in. Or number 6's comment may be one that number 5 can identify with. The leader makes a judgment at this time that the topic of reactions has relevance for the whole group and so tries to explore it further. In the process of this group, as in all groups, a number of events occur during the session that make it necessary for the leader to decide when and how to intervene. Part of this decisionmaking process is based on theory and timing; part of it is related to the leader's personal style and experience in handling various group events.

As the session ends, the leader introduces more structure into the group by calling attention to the end of the meeting. She also encourages its ongoing quality by stating her intention to see the members at the next session.

There are three times during this meeting when the leader's anxiety has potential for influencing group process. The first occurs at the beginning of the session, when the leader gives a mixed communication message. The verbal message is "I am open and interested," while the nonverbal message is "I am closed off and distant." It is quite likely that this mixed message is caused by the leader's anxiety. If the leader's ability to tolerate anxiety were evaluated on the basis of this message alone, the conclusion would be that the leader might have shown more tolerance for anxiety had she not given a mixed message and had she been able consciously to remove her hands from her face.

The second occurrence of anxiety is less clear. It is probable that the leader experiences some anxiety when member 6 brings up the example of being mistreated by a teacher who "acted like I had a contagious disease." The leader's anxiety then may be due to her unmet but unrealistic expectations of teachers, to the member's attempt to evoke a sympathetic response from the leader, or to some other reaction. Despite the cause, it is fairly clear that leader anxiety is converted into irritation or anger; such conversion is not unusual and is the kind that group leaders need to watch for in themselves and in other group members. If the leader had a higher tolerance for anxious feelings, she might not have to convert her discomfort into irritation or anger.

The third time the leader's anxiety is evident is when she deflects the group focus from disclosure and cohesiveness to a more neutral topic. Changing topics is a common reaction to anxiety. Again, if the leader had a greater tolerance for anxiety, she might not need to change the subject and thereby increase distance between herself and the group. Anxiety is more likely to occur in a less structured group, such as a supportive one, where guidelines for behavior are less clear and the expectations of higher levels of self-disclosure can increase discomfort. For these reasons, the leader of a supportive group needs to be especially skilled in identifying and dealing with anxiety in self and others.

There are no examples of hostility among group members; all seem to be trying to get along with one another and to impress the leader. This is expected behavior in early group sessions.

The group recorder's analyses of events and evaluation of leader action give some clues to how well the leader understands group process. There is evidence of application of group theory and of such concepts as dependency, self-disclosure, monopolizing, cohesiveness, testing, isolation, communication, and denial. The leader also demonstrates an ability to understand her own anxiety and irritation in reaction to group processes.

There is only indirect evidence that the leader had thought through how to proceed with the group session. For example, she begins the group effectively by reviewing the group contract and starting group introductions. She also has decided how to end the group. The middle part of the session seems to have been less well thought out; at one point the leader begins to teach about diabetic diets; whether this is due to insufficient preplanning or spur-of-the-moment anxiety is not clear.

The leader asks the group to share in introductions. She makes some attempt to get group members to talk to one another when she points out their similarities, but she could make more attempts to have group members ask one another questions and react to comments, rather than expecting the leader to direct and comment on what is said.

Neither the leader nor the group recorder requests any assistance. However, producing a written record is itself one way the inexperienced leader can ask for assistance.

Although there is laughter in this group, it is unclear whether humor is intended. Here, as in the task group recording (Table 8–6), laughter may be primarily tension-relieving behavior. In this case, exaggeration is a factor in the member's comments, and this could be the basis for the laughter. The leader herself makes no use of humor during the session.

The leader promotes independence by asking group members to introduce themselves and by suggesting that the group explore diabetic reactions more thoroughly, Both of these actions imply that the leader considers the group members as capable of performing these tasks.

In the Alternative Action column the leader makes further suggestions about how she could have promoted independence. She says she could have asked the group to compare and contrast their reactions ("Have others had a similar reaction?" and "Anyone else feel as 3 does?"), or to summarize what happened or what they accomplished in that group session.

When the leader remains silent, the group is forced to take responsibility for group functioning. Thus, silence can be an effective method of encouraging the group to take responsibility for keeping the group process moving. Here, the leader is able to let go partially of the directing reins. When self-disclosure becomes uncomfortable for her, she again takes firm hold.

The leader takes some or all of the responsibility for the task functions of getting the group going, stating the group purpose, giving information, acknowledging and exploring group members' suggestions, keeping the group moving toward its goal, and ending the group. She demonstrates little direction in terms of restating, summarizing, and teaching the group to solve problems.

The leader fulfills the maintenance functions of accepting, supporting, and promoting attraction for the group by pointing out similarities between group members and by exploring feelings. She does not fill the maintenance functions of voicing group feeling and helping the group to evaluate itself, but she makes some attempt to achieve a balance between task and maintenance functions.

The leader does not use the communication techniques of paraphrasing, behavioral description, or validating. Instead of validating member 6's feeling, she labels the feeling herself. Her statement about noting that no one seems hampered by having diabetes could be viewed as a feedback statement.

One of the leader's questions is of the yes/no variety. When she asks, "Do you resent that?" her wording is ineffective for two reasons. First, the question is one that can be answered with a brief yes or no. Second, the question implies a way member 6 is expected to feel; if he does not already feel that way, the leader may be suggesting how she thinks he should feel. If the group member is quite susceptible to the influence of authority figures, he may answer yes just to receive the leader's approval.

The leader has a tendency to focus on individual problems within the group setting. The result is that she not only promotes dependency on herself (since communications are structured to go between her and another group member) but also carries on a series of one-to-one relationships under the guise of dealing with the group. She may recognize this trait after the fact, because many of her Alternative Action comments suggest ways to involve group members with one another: "Have others had a similar reaction?" "Anyone else feel as 3 does?" and, "What does the group think about what 3 is saying?"

The leader notes three of her reactions to the group. First, she points out that she gave the group a mixed message. She does not identify the feeling that led to the discordant verbal/nonverbal message, but it is likely that she recognizes it as anxiety. Such leader reaction would not be unexpected in the early part of the first group session. Had the leader noted this on her recording, it would have provided even further evidence that she is knowledgeable about group process.

Second, the leader is aware of feelings of protectiveness toward member 3. Awareness of countertransference reactions is helpful; there would be even stronger evidence of the leader's grasp of her reactions if the recording had included a statement concerning need for further supervision in this area and/or intent to pay attention to future interactions of this type with member 3.

Third, the leader recognizes that she may be anxious because the group has a high level of self-disclosure. Perhaps she feels left out or is worried that she will not be able to control how much personal material will be shared. To some extent, the leader does need to balance levels of selfdisclosure so that cohesiveness is increased, yet embarrassment or high anxiety does not result. If only one group member were disclosing secrets, the leader could certainly want either to encourage others to share similar experiences or to defuse the intensity of the disclosure so that other group members will not become frightened. In this case, four of the six group members are openly sharing with one another; it therefore seems that the leader's shift to the more neutral topic of diet is primarily to meet her own inclusion or control needs.

This assessment of leader skills suggests alternative methods of handling similar group situations in the future. One suggested intervention is that the leader should study and ask for ongoing supervision regarding her tendency to overprotect and control the group. In the process of doing so, the leader may be able to encourage more independence among group members by asking them to describe, identify, explore, and suggest alternative ways of dealing with interpersonal reactions to having diabetes. Some statements that illustrate this kind of leader intervention are: "How has each of you reacted when others have . . . ?," "What feeling is it that you all are talking about?," "Let's have all the group members tell a little more about their experiences with . . . ," and "What other ways could you handle that situation in the future?"

The record suggests one comment that might have made the leader more effective in helping the group to summarize the session. Other comments she might have used are: "Today we got acquainted a little bit and began to talk about how people who don't have diabetes react to those who do. We also touched on diet and diabetic reactions. I think all three of these topics are important and that we could expand on them in future sessions." Since this is the first session of the group, it may be too early to expect group members to summarize. It is suggested that the leader act as role model for the group by summarizing the first few sessions. After that, the leader might say, "Who would like to summarize what we did today?" If no one volunteers, the leader can again summarize but add, "Summarizing is an important skill; you learn it through practice, and the group is a good place to begin." This kind of statement does not imply punishment to group members who do not volunteer, but it does point out the leader's expectations and provide a guideline for group behavior in future sessions.

Although many of the alternative action comments are stated well, some could be added or others expanded. For example, the leader could suggest some alternative ways to ask the group to discuss their diabetic reactions. Two examples are: "Who wants to begin talking about his reactions?" and, "Let's go around the group and share experiences in this area."

Assessment of Group Recorder's Skills

The initial information about seating arrangement, date, and so on is adequate. Events and leader actions are clearly recorded. Verbal communication has been placed in quotation marks to differentiate it from nonverbal communication. The analysis of events contains appropriate information, since only the leader's ideas about what occurred are recorded.

The amount of information in columns 2, 4, and 5 provides evidence that the leader and/or group recorder have thought about group, events and leader reactions. They make an effort to separate events—or what is observed in the group—from analysis and evaluation—or what the leader/recorder thinks and feels about what happens in the group. In general, this record shows excellent recording ability.

REFERENCES

Brown, L. D., de Negri B., Hernandez, O., Dominguez, L., Sanchack, J. H., & Roter, D. (2000). An evaluation of the impact of training Honduran health care providers in interpersonal communication. *International Journal of Quality Health Care, 12*, 495–501.

Capafons, J. I., Sosa, C. D., & Vina, C. M. (1999). A reattributional training program as a therapeutic strategy for fear of flying. *Journal of Behavior Therapy and Experimental Psychiatry, 30*, 259–272.

Dai, Y., Zhang, S., Yamamoto, J., Ao, M., Belin, T. R., Cheung, F., & Hifumi, S. S. (1999). Cognitive behavioral therapy of minor depressive symptoms in elderly Chinese Americans: A pilot study. *Community Mental Health Journal, 35*, 537–342.

9
Groups for the Older Adult

THE OLDER ADULT POPULATION GROWS

As the American population ages, the importance of group work grows. Almost 13% of the population in the United States is 65 or older and the 85–and-older group is growing exponentially. With the baby boomers turning senior citizens, the need for gerontological services will be even greater.

A nursing-home resident is an atypical older adult today. Older people are highly diverse in their behavior and interests. Far more typical than ill, nursing-home residents requiring physical care are senior citizens involved in group activities through hospital- or community-sponsored social clubs that combine fitness and recreational activities. Many older adults live at home, and even those who need additional care can choose from a variety of living situations—from sheltered care and assisted living to retirement homes.

Special considerations of communication with groups of older adults who may have cognitive or memory impairment are:

1. Use facial and eye contact to communicate.
2. Directly face the other person and speak slowly, enunciating words so lips can be read.
3. Stay in close proximity or move closer to a hearing-impaired person before speaking. Avoid resorting to shouting or yelling.
4. Experiment with the use of signs, written words, pictures, films, music, or taped recordings as group communication vehicles.
5. Expand the use of gestures, body language, and role playing to enhance the message being communicated.
6. Reinforce a verbal message with a written, auditory or kinesthetic cue.

7. Keep message content relevant and fairly recent in relation to group members' behavior and experience.
8. Have a positive expectation that you and others will be understood.
9. Obtain the professional experience and personal maturity to accommodate loss and death issues since the elderly are frequently preoccupied with them.
10. Be prepared to take an active role in giving information, answering questions, encouraging total group participation, and sharing of self.
11. Ensure that physical complaints are dealt with outside the group and maintain between-session communication with individual members so that they will be less likely to use illness or advancing age as a defense against attending group sessions.
12. Keep yourself well and energetic by eating healthy foods (especially fruits, vegetables, and whole grains), engaging in a daily exercise program, and using stress reduction procedures and affirmations to prepare for each session. For example, write or say the following affirmation up to 20 times daily: "Perfect health is my natural state of being." Consider leading the group in a series of physical warm-up exercises to begin each group. Not only will it reduce anxiety in you and the group members, but it will also stimulate circulation, thereby enhancing thought processes (see Figure 9–1).

Types of group work examined in this chapter include: group work with depressed older adults, promotion of mental health in older adults, writing groups in nursing homes, guided autobiography with older adults, creative communication groups in nursing homes, leadership and personal development groups for the retired, and life review groups for older adults.

THERAPEUTIC GROUP WORK WITH THE DEPRESSED OLDER ADULT

Depression is the most prevalent psychological disorder of the later years (Ivo, Niles, Thiel, Starkowski, & Cowling, 1991). But because depression in the older adult may differ from depression in younger people, specific group techniques are needed.

FIGURE 9-1 Physical warm-up exercises for groups.

Directions: Choose from the list below, adapting them to the group population. Even the most infirm will be able to do most of the following.

- Turn the head slowly to the left and then to the right. Work up to 10 repetitions. After each repetition, relax in your chair and feel the sensations in your neck.
- Shrug the shoulders up toward the ears and then back down again. Add one repetition per week to a total of 10 repetitions. After each shrug, relax in your chair and feel the sensations in your shoulders.
- Rotate the shoulders clockwise and then counterclockwise. Work up to five times in each direction. After each rotation, relax in your chair and feel the sensations in your shoulders, neck and arms.
- Extend the right arm over the head, keeping left arm at the side. If balance allows, extend the arm a little to the left until a slight pull is felt up the right side of the body. Slowly bring down the right arm. Relax into your chair and note the difference between how your right arm and left side feel and how your left arm and right side feel. Then, extend the left arm over the head, (and to the right if possible), keeping the right arm at the side. Then, relax into your chair, feeling the sensations in the upper part of your body. Work up to 10 repetitions.
- Cross the wrists at the abdomen and circle both arms at the same time, first clockwise and then counterclockwise. Work up to 10 repetitions. After each repetition, notice the feelings in your arms and chest.
- Clench the fists tightly and hold for five seconds. Extend the fingers, stretching out the fingers as far as possible from each other. Work up to 10 repetitions. After each repetition, notice the difference in your hands and fingers.
- Make a fist and rotate the thumbs clockwise and then counterclockwise. Work up to 10 repetitions. Notice the difference in the feeling in your thumbs.
- Extend both feet and rotate the ankles, first in a circle to the right, then in a circle to the left. Work up to 5 repetitions, each ankle. Notice the difference in the feelings in your feet and ankles.
- Close the eyes tightly, then open them as wide as possible. Holding the head still, pretend that straight ahead of you is a huge clock. Rotate the eyes around the dial from 12 o'clock to one o'clock and all around the dial. Repeat counterclockwise. Notice the difference in how your eyes feel.
- Open the mouth, stick the tongue out and down toward the chin. Open the eyes as wide as possible. Relax, and feel the sensations in your face. Stick the tongue out and down again, holding for five seconds, with the eyes as wide open as possible. Relax and feel your face come alive.

Ivo et al. (1991) report success with cognitive-behavioral group approaches. Their practice, based on earlier work by Beck, Rush, and Shaw (1979), focused on changing negative- thought% and attitude% *and* on correcting the maladaptive ways information is processed. The six cognitive errors that predominate among older adults are:

1. *Overgeneralizing.* An individual takes one incident and lets it color unrelated present and future situations. For example, "I feel depressed today and I'll always be depressed."
2. *"Awfulizing."* This term implies attaching a great deal of importance to unpleasant, minor events. For example, "I spilled mustard on my blouse and that makes me a bad person."
3. *Exaggerating self-importance.* An example of believing one is the center of everyone's negative attention is "Everyone hates me because I came to the group late."
4. *Unrealistic expectations.* For example, "If my family really cared about me, they'd let me live with them." Unrealistic expectations can also be applied to oneself. For example, "I should have been able to get over losing my husband by now."
5. *Mind reading.* People may assume they know what others think or feel. For example, "You look angry, it must be something I did to upset you."
6. *Self-blame.* For example, "It's all my fault that the group isn't coming on time."

In the cognitive-behavioral approach, the work done in the group is complemented by homework assignments. Tips and procedures for conducting a 24–week experience with depressed older adults reported by Ivo et al. (1991) are summarized below.

Discuss the origins of negative self-talk. Emphasize how values, beliefs, and attitudes are learned in our family of origin. Homework assignments should focus on monitoring thoughts and feelings, with special emphasis on noting or writing down pleasant events and activities. Devote part of the next session to a discussion of homework. Use the words, *sad, blue, down in the dumps* or *stressed out* instead of *depression,* which may be a confusing term for some group members. As with all groups, establish agreed-upon language to be used and then use it. Be aware that it may take up to four months for members to identify and challenge their own and each other's errors in cognition. Point out to the group the benefits of sharing and give examples of what they've accomplished as the group proceeds and especially at termination time.

Make group sessions physically comfortable. Use large print and other forms of magnification for visual materials. A microphone may be needed for the hearing impaired. Lap and shoulder shawls, foot rests, etc. must be provided as needed. Length of group sessions needs to remain flexible; use observation and questioning skills to determine an appropriate length for sessions based on group needs.

Use focused visual imagery to enhance the group experience by discharging suppressed affect. First, use progressive relaxation as a preparation. Tell group members that they can also use this technique to help themselves fall asleep. Ask them to bring in audiocassette tapes to record relaxing messages during the group, and group members can use them between groups for relaxation and sleep purposes. After relaxation is attained, instruct the group members to picture themselves breathing fully, naturally, completely, letting their breathing move toward their navel in an easy, relaxed way. Suggest that they picture a peaceful, relaxing place and themselves in it, smelling all the smells, hearing all the sounds, and feeling all the sensations. Once everyone has a peaceful image in mind, ask them to affirm (either to themselves or aloud), that they can use this image for health promotion purposes. One affirmation that can be suggested is: *I can feel relaxed and at peace anytime I want to. All I have to do is picture my peaceful spot.* Be sure to leave open the possibility that any group member may formulate her own affirmation as long as it is stated in positive terms and is meaningful.

REALITY ORIENTATION

Reality orientation is used in a group or on a one-to-one basis. It provides the best results for reducing disorientation in moderately confused people. The technique is most effective when used consistently throughout the day by everyone who comes in contact with the confused person, using orienting statements such as: "It's Tuesday noon." Daily group sessions of about 30 minutes use simple educational materials such as memory games and sensory-training props (see Sensory Training below). Involvement of staff and family in a total 24–hour experience may partially explain its success.

There has been some criticism of this approach, with some fear that it has been applied in a mechanical fashion that could be insensitive to the needs of individual group members. It has also been suggested that constant relearning of material regarding time, place and person orientation may reduce self-esteem.

Spector, Orrell, Davis, and Woods (2000a) attempted to study whether reality orientation (RT) is an effective treatment. They were only able to find one randomized controlled trial or quasi-randomized trial of RT with extractable data. The results were nonsignificant, so the researchers confirmed the urgent need for more systematic research on the procedure.

REMOTIVATION THERAPY

Remotivation therapy is a highly structured procedure for interactions. It involves the uninvolved and encourages communication skills. Twelve sessions are scheduled over several weeks. The group meets for 30–60 minutes on a prechosen topic or prop. Animals or sports often bring lively discussions. Each meeting includes introductions, reading to the group, discussion, the work world, and expressions of appreciation. Reading to the group and work-world discussion can be deleted.

Done and Thomas (2001) studied whether a short training workshop in communication techniques is more effective than an information booklet for improving communication skills in informal caregivers of people suffering from dementia. At 6-week follow-up, the workshop group demonstrated a significantly greater awareness of communication strategies than the booklet-only group. Both groups reported some reduction in the frequency of communication problems at home and a reduction in the associated level of distress. Satisfaction with the workshop indicated that training was helpful but depended on the stage of illness of the partner. If you're running a remotivation group, you might want to consider providing caregivers with printed communication tips to reinforce what group participants have learned.

Psychoeducative Groups

Although research has not shown the effectiveness of groups for agitated and confused older adults, psychoeducative group intervention for their caregivers has. Haupt, Karger, and Janner (2000) found that a 3–month, expert-based group intervention with caregiving relatives yielded a significant improvement in the anxiety and agitation level in patients. If you work in a setting with agitated and confused older adults and have a chance, provide a psychoeducative group for their caregivers.

HEALTH PROMOTION GROUPS

Health promotion groups can focus on anything from nutrition, fitness, stress management, and positive relation building to specific health topics and self-care. Participants are encouraged to ask questions and share personal experiences. The first part of the session is devoted to a presentation by the leader and the second part to sharing. This kind of session provides a tight structure within which participants can interact and socialize. Healthy snacks such as fresh fruit, sugarless bran muffins, rice crackers, and herb teas can be served.

Sensory Training Groups

Sensory retraining or *sensory stimulation* sessions focus on each of the senses. Such sessions are especially useful for confused, institutionalized older persons who lack stimulation in their daily lives. The leader shares an object, for example, an orange, with the group and invites all to touch and observe using the appropriate senses. Participants are encouraged to describe and discuss their reactions. Interpretations can be provided when needed. Some studies show older adults improve in self-care, cognition, interpersonal skills, and general well-being as a result of these sessions (Paire & Karney, 1984).

Music Therapy

Music therapy provides an interactional method for persons of all levels of function. It may be the method of choice for those unable to speak or interact in other meaningful ways. Music not only soothes, it has been shown to aid healing, stimulate thinking, and assist in neuromuscular control. Singalongs or music listening can develop a sense of tempo, induce reminiscence, and promote relaxation (Glynn, 1986).

Reminiscence Groups

Reminiscence groups usually focus on positive and happy events from the past. Groups can be structured to focus on any of a myriad of topics such as pets, relationships, school, or family, or can be free flowing. Reminiscence groups can assist in image enhancement, problem solving, and self-understanding. Music, pets, poetry, art, and movement can be used in reminiscence groups to enhance the experience. Pet therapy can not only arouse old memories but also provides a friend to a lonely older adult.

Reminiscence therapy (RT) has been defined as a vocal or silent recall of events in a person's life. It typically involves group meetings, at least once a week, in which participants are encouraged to talk about past events. Spector and colleagues (2000b) conducted a systematic review of the available evidence of the effectiveness of RT for dementia and concluded that more research is needed to show a statistical significance for the procedure.

Woodlands Therapy

Woodlands Therapy is a specific type of sensory-motor and play-based training, especially useful with advanced dementia. It is a group method to use when reminiscence or reality orientation are not appropriate. The aim of WT is to enhance well-being among participants, through engaging in sensory-motor experiences and play-based activities, in a social setting (D. Pulsford, 2002 Personal e-mail communication, April 29, 2002).

A WT session uses a number of experiences and activities from the overall menu (depending on what group members decide to use). Specific group experiences to choose from include those listed in Figure 9-2.

Responses to WT are influenced by a number of factors, including individual likes and dislikes, background and culture, and degree of sensory and cognitive impairment. The biggest factor, as validated by Pulsford's (2002) research, is the way that staff facilitate sessions.

When working with people with advanced dementia:

1. Be proactive and directive. It's important that as facilitator you take the lead, and don't expect participants to be self-directive, or to be able to make more than simple choices.

FIGURE 9-2 Woodlands therapy.

SENSORY-MOTOR EXPERIENCES

- Colored patterns projected onto the walls
- Bubble tube
- Fiber optic spray that changes color, and which patients can manipulate
- Different colored and patterned cushions, scarves and textile samples
- Different smells and tastes (though these don't always work well, due to patients' sensory impairment)
- Music

PLAY-BASED EXPERIENCES

- Balls and balloons
- Bubble blowing
- Party blowers
- Dolls
- Soft toys
- Electronic toys (preferably noisy ones)

---

*Experiences suggested by Pulsford (2002).

2. Use person-centered communication strategies. Active listening strategies such as paraphrasing participants' statements and reflecting participants' feelings are very useful with this group of people. Use open questions, but keep them simple. It's often enough to ask questions such as "What colors can you see?" or "Which one of these cushions feels softer to you?"

3. Display emotional and cognitive empathy. Attempt to understand group member experiences as they are filtered through their cognitive disabilities. Pitch your interventions at a level that the group members can understand. It's very easy to overestimate the abilities of people with advanced dementia.

4. Value small achievements. It's unlikely that you will see much (if any) long-term improvement in group members with advanced dementia as a result of group therapies such as WT. Group members may not even remember a session 5 minutes after it has finished. But if there has been even a small improvement in their "well-being" during a session, then that session has been worthwhile.

5. Appreciate the value of "play-based" activities and a "playful" approach. It's rare for group members to feel demeaned by

toys, dolls, and simple games. More likely, they will respond positively to them, if they are presented in a simple, clear, and direct way. Be prepared to shed some of your reserve and inhibitions. Have fun and the group members likely will, too.

6. Use "transferrable skills" derived from working with young children, but avoid treating group members in a patronizing, childlike way.

7. Encourage strongly, but do not coerce. The ethics of group work with people with advanced dementia are complex. Refrain from asking a regular group member, "Do you want to take part in the Woodlands Therapy group today?" The response would most likely be a suspicious look and a refusal, due to inability to remember previous WT sessions or what the letters mean. Pulsford (2002) has found that by persuading group members to participate, they will usually show signs of enjoyment during the session. You may have to coax group members, show them a sensory-motor or play-based item or use other methods of encouragement to get them to the meeting place. Once there, group members often recognize where they are, and are in a better position to make a choice as to whether to stay and take part in the group, or not. At that point, if group members still do not want to participate, allow them that decision.

8. Be aware of, and respond to individual differences. It's a simple but easily forgotten point that dementia does not take away the person's individuality. Get to know each participant as an individual, with an individual personal history, and gear your facilitation to the individuals within the group (Pulsford, 2002).

WRITING GROUPS IN NURSING HOMES

Supiano, Ozminkowski, Campbell, and Lapidos (1989) examined the effect of participation in an 8–week writing group in six nursing homes. The researchers invited residents to a writing get-together—a chance to share ideas, listen to great poetry, and try their hand at writing. Any resident with the physical strength to participate in an hour-long class was welcome. By extending recruitment beyond active residents to disoriented and depressed residents, the researchers hoped to discover who was best served by the writing program.

In all, 62 residents agreed to participate. The program coordinator and nursing home staff selected a control group of 54 other residents from a pool of those considered appropriate for participation. Although the selection was not random, both controls and participants were similar on baseline measures.

The researchers did pretest and posttest assessments of cognitive and affective functions for all participants. They also asked writing group participants about their previous writing experience and perceived ability to convey feelings, ideas, life experiences, and memories.

The group was conducted for eight weeks in each of the six nursing homes by an instructor with a master's degree in counseling and human development and several trained volunteers. Collaborative poetry, individual poetry, and prose comprised the curriculum. The instructor introduced the subject for the week (nature, seasons, music, childhood they experiences, memories of the War and the Depression, love, and aging), then read aloud poetry or prose on that theme. Participants were provided with large-print copies of materials to read. After a discussion, participants wrote down their ideas in class. Because of the frail condition of many participants, volunteers transcribed, repeated, challenged, and shaped what was written. Sessions began the following week with the instructor or author reading aloud what had been written the previous week.

The writing instructor assessed group members on appearance, awareness of self and others, interest, participation, enjoyment, attentiveness, verbal communication, and nonverbal communication every week. Gradually, the instructor shifted from collaborative to individual writing. 'Topics also became less general and more personal and expressive writing was encouraged. The leader also increasingly facilitated dialogue between participants.

Study findings provided evidence that participation in writing groups may reduce depression, particularly among residents with higher cognitive ability and greater depression. A significant number of participants in the writing groups reported an ability to relate feelings and ideas after participating in the group sessions. The cognitively impaired participants and those with high physical function scores showed the most improvement in group process measures. The researchers concluded that there was considerable improvement in residents participating in the writing groups, especially the depressed, the cognitively-impaired, and those without writing experience. A complete curriculum is available on request to Katherine P. Supiano, Dept. of Internal Medicine, University of Michigan

Medical Center, Turner Bldg., 1010 Wall St., Ann Arbor, MI 48109–0714.

GUIDED AUTOBIOGRAPHY WITH OLDER ADULTS

In his work with older adult groups, Wacks (1989) combined reminiscence, life review, Progoff's intensive journal work, guided imagery, and other transpersonal techniques with Hateley's guided autobiography techniques. He suggests that whether autobiographies are taped or written, some form of recording the life history seems necessary if participants are to move beyond simple reminiscence.

Wacks, whose background is counseling psychology, conducted a guided autobiography course that he calls *Psychological Autobiography*. It was conducted at a rural senior citizen's center for one hour of college credit. The course syllabus included the following topics and writing assignments:

- Guidelines/Ground Rules and Life Span Assignments
- Who Am I Now? and Paper Sack Art (collage)
- Who Was I?—Family and Community and Historical Lifeline Poster and Family/Community Commandments
- Roads Not Taken/Songs Yet to Be Sung and Life as a Branching Tree and If Only I Had . . .
- Transitions, Beginning Again and Life as a Book/Movie and Transitions/Turning Points
- Creations/Contributions and Major Accomplishments and Eulogy/Epitaph/Obituary
- Loving Self/Others and Love Letter to Self/Other and Letter to Your Body/Reply
- Forgiveness and Letting Go and Play God for a Day
- What I Have Learned and Letter to a Great-Grandchild
- Finishing Business and One Year to Live and Coming Back Again
- Successful Living/Aging and Images of Successful Aging and Unique Experiences
- The Eternal Now and Peak Experiences/Meditation
- Who Am I?—A Re-Vision and Closure

Wacks (1989) used warm-ups such as *Five adjectives that describe me best are* . . . and *If I were a—(car, animal, house, etc.) I would be a* . Evaluations by participants were very positive. They felt they had gained in self-understanding, and increased closeness to each other. Several in the group evidenced long-term effects: two years later, one participant completed his memoirs and another continued to reflect on the group in her weekly newspaper column.

Wacks (1989) conducted a historical autobiography noncredit course for adults. Participants ranged from age 30 to 80, with most in their late 50s. The class met for ten 90–minute sessions. Early writing assignments included: Genealogy, Circumstances of My Birth, Early Memories, and Lifeline: Birth to Present. Participants were asked to bring in photos and scrapbooks for sharing. They remembered and recorded each year on a historical lifeline. Wacks structured the course topically, focusing on toys, parents, siblings, friends, holidays, illnesses and remedies, lessons learned, first day at school, embarrassments, philosophy of life, pets, vacations, talents, special moments, growing older, and brief encounters. The leader provided time during each class period for participants to share work completed on the lifelines as well as for reading the topical writing assignments for that session.

Wacks (1989) also conducted a reminiscence group for the very old in a local nursing home. Most were in wheelchairs with mild to moderate dementia. The activities coordinator served as coleader. Because of illness, visitation, and treatment, turnover was considerable. On the average, six people attended, with only three regulars. The group leader often went first to model and illustrate possible responses to the topics. Favorite topics of the group were special foods and hymns. When albums of hymns were circulated, two residents who had rarely spoken in the group sang.

Topics introduced by the leader included: childhood memories, farm life, the Depression, hobbies and pastimes, school, changes in lifestyles, transportation, children and grandchildren, church, and special memories.

CREATIVE COMMUNICATION GROUPS

Asmuth and Webb (1990) reported a study of the use of a creative communication group in a nursing home. Residents of three nursing facilities participated. A total of 32 residents volunteered to participate, but only 19 of the total attended four or more of the six sessions. The authors ascribed poor attendance to illness, planned checkout dates, scheduling conflicts, failure of the staff to remind participants of the sessions, and, perhaps, personal choice.

Thirty-five- to fifty-minute sessions were held weekly at each facility. Facility staff and project personnel brought participants to the meeting room. The seating arrangement was a circle of chairs and wheelchairs, except in sessions 4–6, when residents were seated around tables to facilitate the handling of printed materials.

Each of the six sessions was based on a different theme and included: the sea, people, wishes, memories, fantasy, and poetic language. Each session contained a mixture of interpretive reading, creative dramatics, and group discussion activities. For example, during the session on the sea, residents performed the poem "Sea Fever" by John Masefield, practicing for expression of feelings with phrases such as *lonely sea, wild call,* and *quiet sleep.* The choral reading showed potential for stimulating visual imagery. Creative dramatics on the sea theme included pantomimes of beach activities, passing imaginary objects found at the beach, and add-on stories. All the activities were used as bridges to reminiscence and content discussions.

Frequency of participation varied significantly by activity. Residents participated most in interpretive reading and least in creative dramatics. Age was not related to participation. The researchers suggested that a communication course be continued across 10–12 weekly sessions because increased participation only began to appear in the fourth and fifth sessions.

LEADERSHIP TRAINING FOR THE RETIRED

The Third Age, or retirement stage of life, is now commonly accepted as a period when time is available for personal enrichment, fulfillment, and self-actualization. Keeping active after retirement has become a problem for some of the population. One way retired people can continue to be active is by taking on voluntary leadership roles in community groups.

According to Cusack and Thompson (1992), senior leaders have a great deal to offer that younger leaders do not, including: deeper empathy and understanding, dedication and commitment, life experience, freedom of choices, acquired skills, available time, knowledge, patience and wisdom. The authors suggest that leadership training groups for seniors must emphasize:

1. appreciation of individual diversity
2. assessments of individual levels of skill and experience
3. building confidence/self-esteem/the image of self as leader
4. practical application of life experience to leadership situations
5. an appropriate use of audiovisual aids including large print and microphones, and
6. expanded learning time to learn

Of the 24 people who signed up for the group, 18 (4 men and 14 women) completed the course 10 weeks later. The majority of participants were members of one of four seniors' recreation centers in a suburban community in Canada. The average age was 66, with a range of 58–73 years. Educational level ranged from Grade 5 to Ph.D. in psychology.

Two-and-a-half-hour sessions were held to teach and practice the following skills: listening, motivating, encouraging, speaking, decision making, problem solving, assertiveness, and confidence building. Not until the third session on communication did participants show increased comfort with each other. By the fifth and sixth sessions, participants began to express their feelings and face sensitive issues. By the eighth session on group decision making, participants showed a higher level of concentration and leadership behavior.

Some of the comments made by group members may be helpful for future group leaders:

> "Modeling plays a big part. People who have less skill can learn from watching others who have more experience." "One of the roles we need to look at for those experienced leaders is how to help others become leaders. " "I am glad you called it leadership because this draws people with all kinds of experience. It has been good for me to review and to step back." [Cusack & Thompson, 1992, p. 345]

A number of participants experienced personal change as a result of the group. One member took over the newsletter at his center in an emergency and has continued with it on a volunteer basis. Another felt confident enough to speak spontaneously to the group about her personal achievements and contributions to the community. A third realized how important it was that leaders realize volunteers' need for new opportunities. Yet another stated he became much less frightened to stand up and talk in a group.

By the end of the sessions, group members had enlarged their plans for the future, commenting:

"I am going to run for the executive at my center." "I will be more assertive when I recognize a problem brewing." "I plan to take a more active and vocal part at meetings." "I will get more involved with my center." [Cusack & Thompson, 1992, p. 357]

Based on pre- and posttest self-assessments, the two areas showing a significant improvement ($p = 0.05$) were "feeling comfortable expressing my ideas" and "an increased ability to resolve conflicts and problems." Coordinators of the centers from which the participants came also recognized positive changes. Perhaps the best evidence of the program's effectiveness was participants' evaluation of their gains, which included confidence, ability to speak spontaneously, insight into capabilities and limitations, admiration for fellow elders and techniques for use as future group members and leaders.

The group leaders suspected that the group members had not learned so much that was new, but that they had developed a level of confidence and trust that enabled them to work comfortably and successfully together. Cusack and Thompson (1992) stated, "Given the right opportunity, leadership may become a way of life for many adults in the third age" (p. 357).

LIFE REVIEW GROUPS

Life review can be used with either the disturbed or well-functioning older adult (Wilson & Kneisl, 1992; Wysocki, 1983). The therapeutic task with an aged client is to facilitate and support the process of life review. Life review is a means of helping to resolve conflicts of a lifetime in preparation for one's death. Some guidelines (Wilson and Kneisl, 1992, p. 660; Wysocki, 1983) given for lifereview therapy are:

- Describe the characteristics and normality of the life-review process.
- Provide opportunities to recapitulate events in their lives by asking questions such as: What has most influenced the course of your life? Who has most influenced the course of your life? What were your early years like? What was your

first trip away from home like? How many children do you have? What was it like bringing them up?

- Suggest ways to view their life experiences in a broader or different context, for example: How would you have changed your life then? What would you do differently now? What other factors may have contributed to what happened?
- Facilitate connections between past hopes, present events, and future expectations; Would you like to role play with me how to talk to your daughter about that?
- Encourage family members to share the patient's experiences and enrich a recollection or resolve a conflict.

Disturbed older adults are often people who have been disappointed in life, feel they have been manipulated by others, or believe that they have mismanaged crucial life situations. Regrets may become their preoccupation. Those who believe themselves to be victims may blame others and exude pessimism, while others who accept responsibility for their lives may be deeply depressed.

Life review group situations focus on the process of reviewing painful and disappointing life events, ventilating feelings, sharing others' perspectives, and modifying self-perspective by learning to forgive. It is a challenge for group leaders to listen to participants' grief and sorrow. The group leader's acceptance of all verbalizations validates the goodness of those who judge themselves and others harshly. By expressing their grief over lost opportunities, group members win liberate energy to live their remaining days in joy and forgiveness. Those with unresolved anger at life's inequities can regain a balanced perspective by counting their successes and positive life experiences. Relationships that have deteriorated can be rebuilt through role playing and rehearsing new ways of relating with family members and peers.

Guidelines for life review groups include:

1. Begin by explaining the purpose of the group and what life review is. Alert members to the normality of the life review process. The group leader might say, for example, "All of us return in our mind to past experiences and especially to times of trouble or strain. We particularly find ourselves returning to the past as we get older. By talking about our past experiences and unresolved conflicts, we have a chance to survey them, to loosen the hold we may

have allowed negative feelings to take, and to put those experiences in proper perspective among our many achievements and positive life experiences."

2. Use questions to facilitate discussion: *What has most influenced the course of your life? Who has most influenced the course of your life? What situation or relationship in your life do you think you've mishandled? What relationship do you most want to repair? What one incident still makes you feel angry when you think about it? What things are you disappointed about? What would you do differently if you had your life to live over?*

3. Provide positive affirmations and imagery to assist group members to change their perspectives. Some ways to begin the process follow.

   A. Encourage group members to choose an affirmation from a list you supply or to make their own positive affirmation. The following examples have been adapted or suggested by the work of Dackman (1991) but the work of Louise Hay or others could also be used.

Today I pick a phrase to live by, write it down, and hang it up where I can look at it and validate myself every day.

Today I make a list of all the people I admire and put my name at the top of the list.

I borrow the words of others to help me reform my self-image and feelings of self-esteem.

Today I look at the inner and outer me with clarity and love.

Perfection in life comes from living despite it all.

I let the child within me reach out to play, enjoy, love.

I use faith, trust and my inherent creativity to get me over, under, around or through this situation.

I accept what life has given me and pledge to use each precious moment granted me to give hope, love, and joy to myself or someone else.

I trust the Universe, knowing that I am ready to handle whatever comes my way

I let go of old fears, angers and resentments and trust God (the Universe).

What I send out to others, comes back to me fourfold.

I move on with my life knowing I cannot undo what has been done.

   B. Read a guided imagery meditation to the group as a way of helping them heal and recover. Start the group with one meditation and end it with another one. The following guided imagery is suggested by Droege (1992). you can devise your own or build them from group member concerns. Meditations can also be recorded for use between group sessions either by the group leader or members.

Become comfortable in your chair, letting your body sink into your seat . . . letting your breathing drop to your navel . . . letting go of all discomforts, sounds or mind chatter . . . feeling the tension draining away . . . muscles in your forehead, eyes, jaw and face becoming limper and limper . . . muscles in your shoulders and neck limp as a balloon with all the air drained out . . . muscles in your arms and hand free and relaxed . . . drifting . . . relaxing . . . muscles in your chest and abdomen widening, loosening, relaxing . . . thighs, calves and feet, relaxing, loosening . . . letting yourself drift to the center of your being . . . attuning yourself to the world within rather than the world without . . . breathing your natural regular rhythm of your body . . . finding peace and contentment from within the center of yourself . . . [pause for several minutes] . . . Experience that flow of energy that binds us all together as one with God or the Universe, whichever is more meaningful to you . . . let a circle of light surround that image and feel the goodness of you and others in that circle . . . send love and forgiveness around that circle. forgiving all you see whether they deserve it or not . . . feeling the feelings of joy and peace you feel as you forgive. . . take a moment to see the hurt of others who have hurt you and to forgive them and yourself . . . to celebrate the goodness that is within You and others . . . picturing a healing presence within and around you. . . that allows you to forgive, let go, go on, be joyful and well . . . strengthening bonds that have grown loose . . . bringing unity and harmony and love to all . . .

REFERENCES

Abraham, L. L., Niles, & A., Thiel, B. P. Starkowski, K. L, & Cowling, W. R. (1991). Therapeutic group work with the depressed elderly. *Nursing Clinics of North America, 26*(3), 635–650.

Asmuth, M. V., & Webb, L. (1990). Nursing home residents' participation in a creative communication course: The influence of age, activity and attendance. *Journal of Applied Gerontology, 9*(3), 266–282.

Beck, A. T., Rush, A. J., Shaw, P. F., et al. (1979). *Cognitive therapy of depression.* New York: Guilford.

Clark, C. C. (1996). *Wellness practitioner: Concepts, theory, research and practice.* New York: Springer Publishing Co.

Cusack, S. A., & Thompson, W J. A. (1992). Leadership training in the third age: The research and evaluation of a leadership and personal development program for the retired. *Journal of Applied Gerontology, 11,* 343–360.

Dackman, L. (1991). *Affirmations, meditations and encouragements for women living with breast cancer.* New York: HarperCollins.

Done, D. J., & Thomas, J. A. (2001). Training in communication skills for informed carers of people suffering from dementia: A cluster randomized clinical trial comparing a therapist-led workshop and a booklet. *International Journal of Geriatric Psychiatry, 16,* 816–821.

Droege, T. A. (1992). *The Healing Presence: Spiritual exercises for healing, wellness, recovery.* New York: HarperCollins, 84–85.

Glynn, N. J. (1986). The therapy of music. *Journal of Gerontological Nursing, 12*(1), 7–10.

Harrell, A. (May, 1993). Gerontology goes beyond nursing homes. *Center Times,* A 8.

Haupt, M., Karger, A., & Janner, M. (2000). Improvement of agitation and anxiety in demented patients after psychoeducative group intervention with their caregivers. *International Journal of Geriatric Psychiatry, 15,* 1125–1129.

Ivo, A., Niles, S., Thiel, B., Siarkowski, K., & Cowling, W. R. (1991). Therapeutic group work with depressed elderly. *Nursing Clinics of North America, 26*(3), 635–650.

Pulsford, D. (2002). Personal email communication from the Senior Lecturer in Mental Health Nursing, St. Martin's College, Lancaster, UK, April 29th.

Spector, A., Orrell, M., Davis, S., & Woods, B. (2000a). Reality orientation for dementia. *Cochrane Database System Review, 4,* CD00419.

Spector, A., Orrell, M., Davis, S., & Woods, B. (2000b). Reminiscence therapy for Dementia. *Cochrane Database System Review, 4,* CD001120.

Supiano, K. P. Ozminkowski, R. J., Campbell, R., & Lapidos, C. (1989). Effectiveness of writing groups in nursing homes. *Journal of Applied Gerontology, 8,* 382–399.

Wacks, V. Q (1989). Guided autobiography with the elderly. *Journal of Applied Gerontology, 8*(4), 512–523.

Wilson, H. S., & Kneisl, C. R. (1992). *Psychiatric nursing* (pp. 654–664). Menlo Park, CA: Addison-Wesley.

Wysocki, M. R. (1983). Life review for the elderly patient. *Nursing, 83* February: 47–49.

10
Working with Focal and Focus Groups

In the past decade, there has been a tremendous expansion in the area of homogeneous or *focal* groups. Focal groups share characteristics in common including: a high degree of structure, specific target issue, goal-orientation, assigned homework and structured exercises to promote rapid change, inclusion of education components, and discouragement of attention to transference issues. Some of the most popular focal groups discussed in this chapter concern codependency, depression, eating disorders, rape and sexual abuse, domestic violence, parenting, anger and aggression management, anxiety, HIV, cancer, critical incident-stress debriefing, chemical dependence, obsessive-compulsive disorder, pain and fatigue, and hospital transition.

CODEPENDENCY GROUPS

Codependency is characterized by preoccupation and extreme dependence on another person. Dysfunctional parenting passes from generation to generation, teaching children to put their own needs aside, discount their own feelings, and use unclear and confusing communication. The only way to stop codependency is to break the cycle and learn new methods of communication.

There are four primary goals for a codependency group: (1) helping clients understand what codependency is and how it affects them negatively, (2) improving boundaries by helping clients to own their feelings and to identify their own needs and wants, (3) increasing member self-esteem by helping them to learn assertiveness and self-nurturing behaviors and decrease self-critical thoughts, and (4) helping group members begin to express feelings appropriately.

Each session begins with a brief check-in, except the first session, which is used for each group member to make a brief introduction. Next, didactic material scheduled for that week is presented. You can provide written, verbal, or video information concerning the following:

- how codependency operates
- identifying your own co-dependency
- changing the pattern that maintains the turmoil
- you can't really change or control anyone else
- differentiating between problems you can control and those you can't
- learning to be compassionately detached
- identifying feelings
- communicating feelings
- dealing with the difficult feelings of fear, shame, and resentment
- boundaries have to do with what you feel comfortable doing and with whom
- setting limits means defining your limit and stating a consequence for noncompliance
- becoming congruent in feeling, thought, and action
- self-esteem is about honoring your internal reality
- assessing and expressing your wants and needs

Once didactic information has been presented, group discussion and specific exercises are used to identify and practice new behaviors. Following the exercises, the group process is used to engage group members in a discussion of their feelings about what has transpired and what it has been like hearing others share their feelings.

You can develop skill practice exercises for each goal or refer to Amerslav (1992) for ideas including: family sculpting, problem solving, role playing, written exercises, and asking the group members to list problems they want help solving.

An exercise for developing skill in communicating feelings follows:

A good way to start to communicate your feelings is to use this format:

I feel	_____	*(your feeling)*
when you	_____	*(an action)*
because	_____	*(your reason)*

Homework between sessions might include handing out a worksheet and asking that each person fill it out and bring it to group next time for discussion. Some homework suggestions found in Amerslav (1992) include: identifying sources of family turmoil; identifying sources of control within the family system; preparing at least three scripts focused on feelings; making a list of new ways to deal with fear, shame, or resentment; identifying at least one situation in which boundaries with someone close need to be protected; completing a list of wants and needs; and listing ways to expand on a current repertoire of self-care.

FOCAL GROUPS FOR SPECIFIC PROBLEMS OR CONDITIONS

Group Treatment for Depression

A cognitive-behavioral group is effective for a broad range of depressed individuals; however, those with active suicide plans or psychotic symptoms, bipolar disorders, active drug abuse problems, organic brain syndrome, or those who are too hostile, or asocial will not be able to benefit (Miranda, Schreckengost, & Heine, 1992).

The Beck Depression Inventory (Beck, Ward, Mendelson, Mock, & Erbaugh, 1961) is often used to measure depressive symptoms. Permission to use the scale can be obtained by writing the Center for Cognitive Therapy, Room 602, 133 South 36th Street, Philadelphia, PA 19104.

Groups are composed of 6–10 clients and two group leaders, although the initial size may be larger to allow for attrition. Focal groups for depression include weekly 2–hour sessions for 16 consecutive weeks. The primary purpose of the group is to teach clients to control their mood. The four goals of such a group are: (1) diminish feelings of depression, (2) shorten the duration of depression, (3) teach strategies to prevent future depressions, and (4) teach group members to feel more in control of their lives.

According to Miranda, Schreckengost, and Heine (1992) some of the, concepts and skills dealt with in this kind of group are:

1. *What is depression?* (Includes the common symptoms of depression.)

2. *What is cognitive-behavioral therapy?* (Includes learning how thoughts influence feelings in the present only.)
3. *Ways to monitor mood* (How to use The Beck Depression Inventory (Beck et al., 1961), a 21–item questionnaire examining patient perceptions of sadness, discouragement, guilt, disappointments, suicidal thoughts, worrying, decision making, physical appearance, appetite, and sleep patterns.
4. *Examples of thoughts that maintain depression (Ex*amples are given, including members telling themselves they are bad people if someone gets angry at them.)
5. *How depressed thinking differs from nondepressed thinking* (Depressed thinking is inflexible, judgmental, negative, and destructive because it tears down self-esteem and leads to hopelessness. Nondepressed thinking is reasonable, flexible, hopeful, and constructive; it discriminates between who the client is and what she does, builds self-esteem, and focuses on the positive.)
6. *Ways to improve mood* (Includes increasing the number of positive daily thoughts by making a list of good thoughts and reading them over every day, giving mental 'pats on the back,' paying attention to the body's ability to be at peace, and imagining moving forward to a time when things will feel better.)
7. *Decreasing thoughts that lower mood* (Includes "thought stopping" (for example, by picturing the letters STOP when negative thoughts intrude); setting aside worrying time and only worrying during that time; taking fears to the worst possible thing that could happen, and then self-coaching to give instructions for feeling better.)
8. *Using the ABCD Method* (Ellis & Dryden, 1987) to modify errors in thinking:
   A = identify the *activating event* that precedes feeling depressed (e.g., expecting a call from fiancé, but he didn't call).
   B = identify the *belief* about the event that precedes the negative feeling (e.g., he must be with another woman if he doesn't call).
   C = identify the *consequence* of the belief (depression).
   D = *dispute* the belief by offering alternatives (e.g., maybe your fiancé, had to work late, or had an emergency.)
9. *Talking back to negative thoughts. It's nice to be liked, but no one is liked by everyone* (in response to thinking, *I should*

*be loved and approved of by everyone). Not everything will
go the way I want no matter what I do* (in response to
thinking, *If things don't go the way I want, I'll be depressed*).
10. *Learning to increase pleasant daily activities* (e.g., taking a
relaxing bubble bath, sharing examples of activities groups
members enjoy).
11. *Identifying the relationship between expectations and outcome* (by anticipating how much pleasure a certain activity will give beforehand and comparing it afterward with
how much pleasure was experienced).
12. *Setting anti-depression goals* (e.g., I will call one friend
and ask her to lunch, I will structure one day a week so I
am not faced with so much free time).
13. *Using the group to generate ideas for meeting others and
maintaining contact with friends/family.*
14. *Practicing assertiveness skills in the group.*
15. *Practicing listening skills in the group.*

Some homework assignments that may be relevant for depression groups include: complete a daily chart of the member's
moods, read self-help books on depression, practice the *ABCD*
method for a week, keep a list of pleasant activities; make a
personal contract to complete a new pleasurable activity and
write down feelings before and after the event, keep a list enu-
merating positive and negative contacts with people, practice
assertiveness skills in a chosen situation, practice thinking and
behaving differently with someone familiar and report back
results to the group.

A special issue for a depression group is client noncoopera-
tion, which is the visible sign of a psychological mechanism:
resistance. In the first meeting of the group, it may be helpful
to point out, "Thoughts can keep some people from coming to
the group; did anyone have thoughts that almost kept them
from coming here today?" Once group members share negative
thoughts, they can be discussed and worked through as a group
issue.

Group members may also need help in examining and making plans to overcome thoughts that may lead to absences.
Additionally, all homework should be discussed in the group
(as a way to show its relevance) and members who do not
complete their assignments need to be asked questions about
what got in the way of completing homework. Likewise, group

members who complain in the group and insist they can't change need to be challenged by the leader: "This way of thinking may be maintaining your depression. Let's see if we can't turn those negative thoughts into positive expectations."

Groups for adolescent offspring of depressed parents are at a high risk for development of depression. Cognitive restructuring has shown promise for preventing progression to depressive episodes. One randomized, controlled trial of a 15–month follow-up group for at-risk offspring (aged 13–18 years) of adults treated for depression in an HMO showed significant reduction in risk of developing depression (Clarke et al., 2001).

Group treatment can also provide a preventive function for pregnant women. Zlotnick, Johnson, Miller, Pearlstein, and Howard (2001) investigated whether a group intervention based on the principles of interpersonal psychotherapy could reduce the risk of postpartum major depression. Thirty-seven pregnant women receiving public assistance who had at least one risk factor for postpartum depression were randomly assigned to a four-session group intervention or treatment-as-usual condition. Group treatment was successful in preventing the occurrence of major depression during a postpartum period of three months for this population.

Patelis-Siotis and colleagues (2001) used group cognitive-behavioral therapy (CBT) for bipolar depression in an open 14–week trial. Even though all participants had achieved mood stabilization via medication, the CBT group showed significant increase in psycho-social functioning. Providing a CBT group for clients diagnosed with bipolar depression could be an effective treatment for this population.

Group methods can also be useful for individuals diagnosed with a major depressive disorder who have responded to antidepressant drugs during the acute phase treatment. Although drug treatment can be somewhat effective alone, it does not deal with residual symptoms and impaired psycho-social functioning characteristic of depression.

One study (Levkovitz et al., 2000) evaluated the effectiveness of group interpersonal psychotherapy and standard treatment. Group participants showed significant improvement of their depressive symptoms compared to those who received the standard treatment both during the group therapy and in a 6–month follow-up period. Another study (Hellerstein et al., 2001) examined the effect of group treatment following a medication trial with fluoxetine. Results supplied preliminary evidence that group therapy provided additional benefits to medication-responding participants in interpersonal and psychosocial functioning.

Groups for Obesity and Eating Disorders

Food represents emotional and symbolic nurturing (Mishna, Muskat, & Schamess, 2002). When other sources of nurturance are not forthcoming, food can be overconsumed and lead to obesity. When physical activity is minimal and high-fat and high-sugar foods are used to nurture, overweight usually results. With the increase in pediatric obesity, and subsequent diabetes and other potential physical debilitation, the use of group treatment to reduce weight is worth consideration.

Group Treatment for Obesity

A major problem with dieting is that weight that has been lost is nearly always regained. Perri and colleagues (2001) compared the effect of two extended therapy programs for weight management with standard behavioral treatment (BT) without additional therapy contacts. Participants were 80 obese women who completed 20 weekly group sessions of BT and achieved a mean initial weight loss of 8.74 kg. Participants were then randomly assigned to a no-further-contact condition (BT only) or to one of two extended interventions: relapse prevention training (RPT) or problem-solving therapy (PST). Participants who completed the PST intervention had significantly greater long-term weight reductions than BT participants and achieved clinically significant losses of 10% or more in body weight than did BT participants (35% vs. 6%). This study provides evidence that a problem-solving therapy group would be most useful in the long-term management of obesity.

Group methods are more efficient and less costly than individual methods of treatment, even when a client prefers individual treatment. At least one study (Renjilian et al., 2001) showed that group therapy produced significantly greater reductions in weight and body mass than individual therapy, even among those clients who expressed a preference for individual treatment.

Family-based group treatment can also be useful. In one study, twenty-four families with children aged 8–12 years who were at 160% of their ideal body weight participated in a 10–12 session behavioral intervention. Although one-third of the families did not complete treatment, children who did finish lost a significant amount of weight and reported significant improvements in depression, anxiety, and eating attitudes that were maintained over time.

Group Treatment for Food Disorders

Food can also be underconsumed, as in anorexia, or binged and then regurgitated, as in bulimia. Dare, Eister, Russell, Treasure, and Dodge (2001) assessed the effectiveness of various outpatient treatments for anorexia nervosa, including a year of focal psychoanalytic psychotherapy, seven months of cognitive-analytic therapy, family therapy for one year, and low contact or routine treatment for one year (control). At one year, all participants showed some symptom improvement, but it was modest, and several individuals were significantly undernourished at follow-up. Psychoanalytic psychotherapy and family therapy were significantly superior to the control treatment, but the cognitive group experience also showed benefits (Dare et al., 2001).

Cognitive-behavioral therapy, interpersonal therapy, and relational therapy have been shown to be effective approaches for bulimia nervosa. An integrative model using all three shows promise according to Riess (2002).

The intake interview for group members with eating disorders is a major screening tool. Some subjects to cover include: What group experiences have you had; do you identify yourself as bulimic and can you listen to others and to a leader? Because of their physical appearance and the need to identify with those of similar shape, emaciated and restrictive anorectics will probably not be accepted by the group. Be sure to rule out psychosis and those with severely impaired social functioning. Any alcohol or drug abuse problems must also be addressed prior to group membership.

Groups usually run approximately 12 weeks for an hour and a half each session. This is a closed group with the goals of: (1) providing a sense of hope, (2) teaching a series of psychosocial skills that will give group members alternatives to bingeing and purging, (3) establishing an atmosphere of trust, honesty, and acceptance, and (4) reducing group members' isolation, shame, and guilt while increasing self-esteem (Zimmer, 1992).

Some of the main concepts and skills to be covered are:

- People are bulimic because on some level, it works for them—their problem is not likely to disappear overnight, but through working in the group they can develop realistic and manageable short-term goals
- Dieting doesn't work
- The importance of keeping a food journal
- How to distinguish between physical and psychological hunger
- How to set meaningful, manageable goals
- Delineating "good" from "bad" foods
- Learning to identify and override negative feelings, realizing they will gradually pass
- Identifying the inner critic
- Developing alternatives to bingeing and purging
- Learning how to ask for help Learning how to say "no"

Each session includes a discussion of homework and a didactic presentation, followed by group interaction, role playing, and/or group exercises based on the concepts/skills presented that evening. Homework includes practice in each of the concepts or skills discussed.

Denial is the biggest obstacle to overcoming an eating disorder. Signs of denial to watch for in group members include: "I can quit this anytime I want" and "I will change when I'm ready."

Stress is the combination of improper breathing, muscular tension, and a racing mind. The effects from stress include insomnia, hypertension, headaches, fatigue, and poor memory. Teach clients deep-breathing techniques, progressive relaxation, and imagery skills so they can cope with the inevitable panic attacks many people with eating disorders experience.

People with eating disorders tend to be chronic worriers. The three steps to conquering the worry habit are: (1) awareness, (2) learning, and (3) practice. Group members are taught to identify destructive phrases they use, for example, "I should," "I can't "I'll try," and "I dont know." *(Shoulds* are guilt-invoking; *can't* expresses helplessness.) On the other hand, "I will" expresses taking action. *Try* keeps us from commitment, but "I'll conquer this" suggests a positive move in the desired direction. *"I don't know"* frequently means, "I don't want to know," but "I want to know" or "I can find out" expresses striving toward knowledge and maturity.

Teach group members to use affirmations to fight off thoughts urging them to eat. Some affirmations to use are:

1. I may not like it, but I can stand it.
2. I am strong and can control myself in any situation.
3. I have handled myself well in situations like this one before and I can do it again.
4. I am never trapped or helpless because I can leave a situation anytime I want to.
5. I refuse to allow myself to eat something if I don't want to.
6. I refuse to run away from my feelings by eating.
7. I am an adult and I can decide for myself what's right and wrong.
8. I am not responsible for the feelings of other people.
9. I can overcome my guilt by actively fighting against it.
10. If I really hurt another person, I will apologize; otherwise I will not accept responsibility for their reactions.
11. I can be angry without being resentful and full of hatred.
12. Even if I make a mistake, I am still a lovable person.
13. It's okay to feel sad or discouraged without getting depressed.
14. Feelings cannot destroy anyone—especially me.
15. I can develop a plan to deal with anything.
16. I can gain weight and still love myself
17. I can find more effective ways of weight control than bingeing and purging.
18. I do not need the approval of others for my self esteem.
19. I deserve to be happy.
20. Even though I may not like what I do, I like who I am (Sandbeck, 1986).

Any of these affirmations can be written on 3 x 5 index cards, and placed on the refrigerator or any other place where positive messages can counter negative urges to binge or purge. With practice, group members can create their own affirmations.

Maine (1991) examined the relationship between fathers, daughters, and food. She contends father hunger is directly related to the pursuit of thinness. All children strive for an emotional connection with their father. When it is not present, self-doubt, pain, anxiety, depression, and behavioral problems result. "For our purposes, father hunger will refer to this unfulfilled longing for father, which for girls and women, often translates into conflicts about food and weight" (p. 3).

Maine suggests the following questions be posed and answered by those with eating disorders: How do my eating and body image problems keep me from knowing myself.? What feelings about my father have I been trying to avoid? What will happen if I express my feelings directly? What To my father teach me about expressing my feelings? How do my eating problems reflect his messages about emotional expression? What frightens me most about getting better and giving up the masks I wear? How can I find out more about my father's life? How does what I know about my father explain why I have problems being close to him? To other men? What can I change in my relationship with my father now? Who else in the family could support me while I address my father hunger? What keeps me from asking for their help? What is my place in the world?

Michaelson (1993) works with his groups using a "secret attachment" theory. According to him, the addictive personality often feels her life is out of control. He believes that the underlying problem is a secret attachment to feeling controlled. Midnight munching may be a passive-aggressive defense to this attachment. "With this secret attachment, a person feels that when he is not in control of some person or situation, then he is *being controlled* by that person or situation" (p. 96).

In order to learn more about their hidden attachments to control, members of eating disorders groups are assigned to write a letter to the part of themselves attached to control. One woman saw this part as a hairy monster with saliva and scum dripping from its mouth. This approach allows the group member to imagine the nature of the part that has control, speak to that part, say how it makes her feel, and intuitively listen for its reply.

Landgarten and Lubbers (1991) suggest ways to incorporate art productions into eating disorder groups. Some suggestions include:

1. Have the group create a mural together, using media of their choice. By working together to solve a problem, members may break through barriers of isolation.
2. Have the group members work together to create an art object from a cardboard box and then discuss their problem-solving procedure. Boundary maintenance and other

communication problems can be confronted and discussed as they emerge during this activity.

3. Group members can work in pairs to trace around their bodies on large sheets of papers. This exercise can help participants break through body-image maladaptive coping mechanisms and address body-image distortions. Group members must wear form-fitting clothes during the tracings. Large sheets of butcherblock paper are taped on the walls or doorways of the room. Once outlines are completed, group members portray their feelings within the frame of their body tracing using crayons, paint or other available media. Group members then share their self-portraits along with feelings that have been evoked by the task.

Rape and Sexual Abuse Groups

Rape Survivors Group

According to statistics of the National Crime Bureau, one in three women has suffered the traumatic victimization of sexual assault at some point in her life. Social convention continues to stigmatize raped women as being responsible for their own assault (Conyers-Boyd, 1992).

Very recently raped individuals are probably not good group candidates. Their inclusion may lead other members to minimize their own needs and focus on the acute pain of the woman at the beginning stage of her crisis. As with other focal groups, anyone who is actively psychotic or abusing a substance is not an appropriate member. Conyers-Boyd cautions that group members should be as homogeneous as possible in terms of age, ethnic background, individual sexual preference and variables surrounding the assault so that all members can receive an equal measure of support.

Twelve-week groups of one-and-one-half hour sessions are suggested. Each session is divided into four parts: (1) check-in (to briefly establish each member's feelings), (2) theme of the week, (3) sharing of personal stories and reactions, and (4) closure, including a guided imagery exercise and preview of next week's agenda. Goals of the group include providing information about sexual abuse, validating members' feelings, assisting in the development of self-esteem, and providing a safe environment for sharing where the feeling of isolation is decreased. Conyers-Boyd suggests that the leader go around the group initially and ask each member to verbally commit ' to confidentiality, to abstaining from alcohol or drugs in group, and to notifying the group about missed sessions or late arrival.

Some of the concepts and skills covered in a rape survivors group include:

- Sexual assault occurs on a continuum so that it's not always immediately recognizable (from suggestive comments or gestures to rape).
- Symptoms reported by victims are similar to those associated with posttraumatic stress disorder, but other forms of coping behaviors, such as emotional shutdown, dissociative behavior, amnesia, and unreasonable anxiety around certain people or situations are also common; the victim is not responsible for the attacker's behavior.
- It takes courage to survive the rape and the subsequent feelings the trauma sets off.
- The importance of acknowledging and accepting specific coping responses developed after the attack.
- The only common traits that all sex offenders share are treating women as objects, blaming the victim, and refusing to take responsibility for their own behavior.
- Giving yourself permission to experience uncomfortable feelings. There are ways to deal' with uncomfortable feelings (e.g., hitting pillows, screaming in a safe place, performing a demanding physical task, writing an angry letter that isn't mailed, fantasizing retaliation).
- Recovery may take up to 6 months or more—it is equivalent to having open heart surgery.
- Using affirmations to deal with flashbacks and other uncomfortable feelings.

Sexual Abuse Groups

Young children ages 2 to 8 who had been sexually abused and their nonoffending mothers participated in either a supportive or a cognitive-behavioral therapy group. Mothers who participated in cognitive-behavioral groups reported greater reductions at posttest in intrusive thoughts and negative parental emotional reactions about the sexual abuse. The children treated with cognitive-behavioral therapy demonstrated greater improvement in their knowledge of body safety skills at posttest than did the children who received supportive therapy (Deblinger, Stauffer, & Steer, 2001).

Feeling dysregulation is pervasive among women with histories of childhood sexual abuse. It is an important indicant of posttraumatic stress disorder (PTSD), a disorder that frequently characterizes survivors of childhood abuse. Wolfsdorf & Zlotnick (2001) found support for an affect-management group experience that taught mindfulness, crisis planning, and challenging distorted thinking.

Domestic Violence

Offender Groups

According to Mackenzie and Prendergast (1992), domestic violence follows a particular pattern—the abuse becoming more frequent and severe over time. Violence-prone relationships go through cycles: (1) the honeymoon period after an abusive incident when partners try to be nice to each other, wanting to believe it won't happen again; (2) the tension-building phase when buried issues inevitably surface; and (3) the blowup, when violence again occurs.

Not all clients who are violent with their families are appropriate for group membership. Use a screening interview and ensure there are no "drop in" members because safety and trust are fundamental concerns. Although men who are domestically violent may also abuse their children, sexually or otherwise, and participate in street violence, these issues need to be dealt with separately by other treatment providers. Remember to follow legally mandated reporting procedures when working with this type of group (Mackenzie & Prendergast, 1992).

You must have experience with this population to feel confident confronting denial, minimization, manipulation, and inconsistency. You also must be able to set a tone of warmth and caring and be assertive enough to point out group member behavior, role modeling the goals of honesty, support of others, and accountability.

Members displaying any of the following behaviors should be referred for individual treatment prior to group membership: psychotic, sociopathic, or sadistic symptoms; ritualized abuse, the use of weapons, rape, or a history of serious injury to the partner; untreated substance abuse; unclear motivation of entrance into counseling or solely because of an order by a judge or the threat of divorce; and language or cultural barriers. Additionally, those involved in child custody suits who may come for counseling in order to be given approval need to be told prior to group membership that you will not provide a guarantee to the court or anyone else because of group membership.

Unlike some other focal groups, battering behavior is not easily changed. A minimum of 6 months in a weekly 2–hour group is necessary. Additional enrollment in one or more 12–week programs should be an option for men who are not able to stop battering behavior within the 24–week format. Group members need to be told initially that they've spent a lifetime developing these behaviors and should not expect to learn new ones quickly. Encouragement from the leader about the necessity of staying with the format and not expecting easy solutions can be beneficial. If issues of their own abuse in their family of origin, depression, or suicidal ideation surface, these need to be dealt with in individual treatment.

Mackenzie and Prendergast (1992) suggest an ideal group size of 8–10 men and two facilitators. Coleaders afford safety for both clients and facilitators and ensure continuity due to leader illness, vacation or leave of absence. Group members need to be alerted to the fact that attendance alone does not constitute fulfillment of court-mandated group membership.

Members have not successfully completed the format until they are able to own responsibility for their violence, apply behavioral techniques to stop violent behavior, and show an understanding of the skills and concepts presented in the group. Because more poor and minority men are apt to be arrested for this offense, issues of race and class need to be explored in the group, along with the anger accompanying poverty and discrimination, frequent contributors to male violent behavior (Mackenzie & Prendergast, 1992).

Ground rules for such a group include: no weapons in the group, no drug or alcohol use for the 24 hours preceding the group meeting, no verbal disrespect of partners or other group members, no more than three absences in any 24–week format, timely arrival and fee payment, and no violence of any kind during sessions.

According to Mackenzie & Prendergast, the main concepts and skills for a domestic violence offender group are:

1. *Self-reporting.* Group members are coached to narrate violent incidents, reporting only how the incident started, what was said, how the member felt, what he did, his responsibility in the incident, how the violence ended,

and what the consequences were. For example, when a member says, "My hand just flew out and hit her," the leader says, "I'm going to help you start to take responsibility for your behavior. Your hand didn't just fly out and hit her. Who's in control of your hands?" Through painstaking restatement of member self-reports, they learn how to think differently about the violence based on the words they speak.

2. *Time-out.* Offenders practice appropriate ways to take time-outs by saying to their partner, "I'm starting to feel angry, I'm going to go out, but I'll be back in one hour to check in." (No drugs, alcohol or driving allowed during a time-out. At check-in, the group member can discuss what provoked the anger or take another time-out if anger begins again.)

3. *Recognition of Warning Signs.* Group members learn to use imagery to picture exactly what happened inside of them just prior to their violent behavior.

4. *The Cycle of Violence.* A didactic presentation is made of the honeymoon/tension-building and violent outburst cycle. In an early phase of the cycle, the man may feel remorseful and affectionate toward his partner (honeymoon), but as day-to-day tensions arise, violence may once again occur. The presentation also includes how healthy alternatives such as time-out, deep breathing and feeling statements can interrupt it.

5. *The Emotional Funnel.* A didactic presentation shows that learning to identify one's own feelings of powerlessness, fear, tension, shame, and sadness, and expressing a sense of vulnerability and willingness to accept a partner's expressions of vulnerability, will prevent anger from building to violence.

6. *Three-Breath Technique.* On first in-breath, notice any tension or unusual physical sensations; on out-breath, ask, "Am I angry?" On second exhale ask, "Am I feeling afraid?" On third breath, ask, "Am I feeling sad?"

7. *The Feeling Statement.* "I feel _____ when you _____ because I _____. I would like _____.

8. *Setting Goals.* Useful goals that refer to the group member's behavior are specific, and contain a statement of what the group member will do, for example, *I will use feeling statements three or more times a day when I'm tempted to be verbally abusive.*

9. *Taking Responsibility.* Teach group members to take responsibility for their behavior, for example, "I have been violent" (not "she provoked me") and "I control my own actions' (not "my hand just flew out and hit her") and "I choose not to be violent again" (not "I'll try not to be violent").

10. *Gender Roles: How Boys Get to Be He-Men.* Discussion of group members' concepts of "the person I want to be involved with" versus "what it takes to be a man." Discussion of how men are constricted by being "he-men" and how to claim a broader, more flexible gender role.

11. *Empathic Listening.* Presentation of qualities of empathy and then practice in paraphrasing what the speaker has said.

12. *How Abusive, Violent and Controlling Behaviors are Related.* Didactic presentation shows that the same underlying beliefs give a violent offender permission to use the silent treatment, withhold child support, take away car keys or other objects, and battering.

13. *Male Socialization and Adult Battering Behavior.* Didactic presentation of how boys are taught to numb or deny their pain and how this leaves men desensitized to the pain inflicted on others.

14. *How Parents Teach Violence.* Group members speak in their fathers' and mothers' voices about who they are and how they discipline their children.

15. *Relationship of Dependency and Isolation to Violence.* Didactic presentation of how violent men may be isolated from others and dependent on their partner for understanding. When she is unavailable or unwilling, unmet needs for support can yield violence. Discussion of how group members can reduce isolation, reduce their dependency, build closer relationships with other men, and analyze what prevents men from being close to each other.

16. *The Relationship between Homophobia, Racism, and Sexism.* Didactic presentation of how fear leads to all three. Role playing of related situations.

17. *Attitudes about Sex.* Discussion of how the way men and women are brought up affects their ability to enjoy sex.

A study of spouse abusers (Rondeau, Brodeur, Brachu, & Lemire, 2001) examined the variables associated with dropout and completion of treatment among spouse abusers. Data were collected on 286 men in eight community programs. Results showed that men who completed the program were older, better educated, and had better economic conditions than men who dropped out. They also had a more stable family life, had been in a relationship for a longer period of time and had more children with their spouse. Men who completed treatment also showed more commitment, better working capacities, and a higher level of agreement with the group leader, leading to a stronger therapeutic alliance. Social and judicial pressure were not related to completion, but support provided by people in the abuser's environment was.

Kim and Kim (2001) developed a group intervention model for battered women and tested its effectiveness. Women who participated in the group learned to assess trauma, identify major problems, deal with their feelings, understand themselves, identify the batterer's characteristics, improve their stress management strategies, develop action plans, and promote empowerment. Their level of trait anxiety also decreased significantly in the treatment group, but not in the control group.

Parenting Groups

There is no certification or licensure necessary to become a parent, yet it is the hardest task facing adults today and one for which most parents have no training. To grow to maturity, children need structure from nonabusive parents. The goal of parenting groups is to help parents elicit more appropriate behaviors from the children. Through membership in a parenting group, participants begin to recognize the systemic nature of families. They learn that changes in their behavior will facilitate changes in their children. Specific goals include learning about and practicing communication, problem solving and limit-setting skills.

Although it is preferable to have both parents in the group, it is not always possible. Aim for a group between 8 and 16 adults. Run separate groups for parents of teens and those with younger children. Parents who are referred by the courts or who have children involved in the juvenile justice system should be carefully screened for disruptive potential and possibly referred for individual counseling.

Parenting groups meet for an hour and a half weekly for eight weeks. A coleader, preferably of the opposite sex, will help encourage verbalization from the same-sexed clients. A coleader can also model parenting skills.

According to Paleg (1992), the following concepts and skills should be emphasized:

1. *Parenting Styles.* Present the authoritarian, permissive, and mutual respect models of parenting.
2. *How Children Change.* Discuss how when parents act differently (e.g., making Susie's play activities contingent on completing homework versus yelling at Susie for forgetting her homework), children act differently (Susie calls a friend for the assignment versus Susie slams her door and refuses to come out).
3. *Children Want to Belong.* When children don't feel they contribute to the family in a valuable way, they become discouraged and may evoke scolding to get attention, start a power struggle with a parent, take revenge or act inadequate in order to belong.
4. *Diagnosing Your Child's Misbehavior.* When a child's goal is attention, the parent can diagnose it because he or she will feel irritation. An example is the child who pesters the parent, not letting up. When a child's goal is power, parents experience anger. An example is when children curse even more after being told not to use a swear word again. When a child's goal is revenge, parents experience deep feelings of hurt and a desire to hurt back. An example is when a parent yells at a child for pulling his sister's hair and the next time he slaps her in the face. When a child's goal is to avoid expectations by being inadequate, a parent's feelings will be despair and helplessness. In this case, parental attempts to spur a child on to study may result in the child failing a course.
5. *How to Increase Positive Behaviors in Children.* Didactic presentation of how reinforcing a behavior (smile, caress, criticism, or a slap) will increase its chances of being repeated; the importance of being specific about behavior expectations ("I want Timmy to set the table when asked" *not "I* want him to do what I tell him!"). Rewards ought to be appropriate and well-timed. Shape behavior by reinforcing behavior that approximates the desired action. Increase positive behaviors by rewarding a behavior incompatible with the one to eliminate. Discourage a par-

ticularly unacceptable behavior by rewarding every response *but* that behavior.

6. *Separate the Child from Her Behavior.* "I'm disappointed you didn't clean your room, Ruthie" *not* "Ruthie, you're a slob."

7. *Provide Encouragement.* Point out children's strengths and contributions, expect them to be responsible, let them do as much as they can for themselves (that is appropriate for their age), ask for their advice or opinions and let them make decisions, ask them what they think they should do to solve a problem they come to you about, remind children (when they disparage themselves) of their positive traits.

8. *Acknowledge Feelings.* "Everyone gets angry, and it's okay to feel anger, but yelling, screaming and hitting aren't okay; hit a pillow or talk about your feelings instead"; "It hurts and it's okay to cry"; "I hear your disappointment at not being included."

9. *Solving Problems.* Teach a problem-solving model that includes defining the problem, brainstorming alternatives, choosing the best solution, developing a plan, putting it into effect, evaluating the results, and choosing another alternative if necessary.

10. *Punishment Doesn't Work.* Punishment is not a useful parental response because it teaches children that coercion is the way to get what you want, it only stops the undesired behavior temporarily, it may teach behavior that is inconsistent with a desired message (e.g., spanking a child for hitting a sibling), it reinforces the behavior by giving it attention.

11. *Provide Children with Choices.* Even very young children can have a say in when a task is done, how it's done, or with whom the task is done. When they have some say in a task, they are less apt to engage in power struggles or misbehave to get attention.

12. *Set Consequences.* Children need to learn their behavior has consequences. Instead of bringing lunch to children who forget to bring their lunch, let them experience the consequences of forgetting. Missing lunch once will not be detrimental but it will teach children how hunger is the direct result of forgetting to take their lunch. Other examples: If a child breaks a neighbor's window, the child,

not his parent, should find a solution for replacing it; if children are late to school, instead of nagging or threatening, calmly announce the time their ride is leaving and let them scurry to get ready or else miss breakfast, leave without combing their hair, or other routines.

13. *Use Time-Out.* Time away from whatever is happening, usually spending time in his or her room for a specified number of minutes, can be presented as one of two alternatives or as a logical consequence of behaving inappropriately around others.

14. *Deciding Whose Problem Is Whose.* Although parents may want their children to share behavior, tastes and opinions, separateness in dress, hairstyle, and political opinions is necessary if children are to become autonomous and independent. Children need to make their own decisions, provided they're old enough to decide and their health or safety isn't at risk. On the other hand, if a teenager is consistently breaking curfew, the parents' right to a good night's sleep is being violated and a joint problem-solving session is called for. With grown children, it is perfectly appropriate to decide where to draw the line on financial support: "We're happy to let you live at home without paying rent if you go to school, but if you are not in school you'll have to find a job or somewhere else to live."

15. *The Importance of Fun.* To reduce power struggles, increase the frequency of pleasurable activities including a special time alone with each child at bedtime to review the day or tell a story and a family day each week for the family to do something together.

Another family project that can enhance parent–child relationships is turning off the television one day a week and assembling the family in one room to do anything they like. Music, puzzles, crafts, reading, writing, playing games, etc. can enhance skills in the children and increase cohesion. So can starting a dialogue journal: buy a special notebook and write a letter, family story, or note of praise to each child. Tuck the child's notebook under his or her pillow and encourage each to write back to you. This develops a special kind of nonverbal communication process. Collect family stories in a book and read them aloud to each other.

Musculoskeletal Disorders

Gignac (2000) reported the results of an 8–9 week group intervention for persons having difficulty coping with musculoskeletal disorders. The participants were 64 community-dwelling adults who completed questionnaires at the beginning, end, and three months after their final group session. Significant changes from pre- to postintervention were found in mastery, depression, and coping efficacy. Individuals who had concerns or reservations about participating in the groups gained from the intervention in the same ways as others who were more positive at the group's outset.

Pain

Kolip and colleagues (2001) developed a group training for chronic back pain patients in a rehabilitation clinic to enhance coping, activate internal and external resources, and make transfer to everyday life easier. The training consisted of either 12 physiotherapy sessions or 12 psychologically oriented sessions. The treatment group rated transfer possibilities to working life higher than the control group and reported more satisfaction with the psychological aspects of rehabilitation. Revisions, such as strengthening the topic of employment, were suggested by participants and implemented by the researchers.

Obsessive-Compulsive Disorder

Concerns about isolation, partial pharmacotherapy response, compromised development, inadequate cognitive-behavioral therapy (CBT) and therapist scarcity led Thienemann, Martin, Cregger, Thompson, and Dyer-Friedman (2001) to adapt a CBT protocol to a group format for adolescents with obsessive-compulsive disorder (OCD). Adolescents aged 13 to 17 years with OCD participated in a 14-week group CBT. OCD symptoms measured by the Children's Yale-Brown Obsessive Compulsive Scale improved significantly, both statistically and clinically.

Critical Incident Stress Management

A Critical Incident Stress Management (CISM) program can reduce the cost of workers' compensation claims for stress-related conditions and the number of lost work days. Occupational health professionals need to be ready to develop and implement a comprehensive critical incident stress management process in anticipation of a major event. The ability to organize, lead, or administer critical incident stress debriefings for affected employees is a key role for the occupational health professional (Lim, Childs, & Gonsalves, 2000).

A group experience can decrease traumatic symptoms among adolescent survivors of a close relative or friend's homicide. Forty-five inner-city adolescents between the ages of 11 and 19 years participated in a 10–week, community-based therapy group designed for youths who had a loved one die because of violence. On completion of the group, the adolescent participants reported an overall significant decrease in traumatic symptoms on an index of posttraumatic stress, especially in the areas of reexperiencing and avoidance symptoms (Salloum, Avery, & McClain, 2001).

Eid, Johnsen, and Weisaeth (2001) studied the effect of a Group Psychological Debriefing (GPD) on acute stress reactions following a traumatic event. A group of military personnel and voluntary civilian firefighters were exposed to severe stress during rescue work in a tunnel following a fatal traffic accident. Both groups participated in an operational debriefing, going over what they saw, thought, and felt during and after the incident. In addition, both groups received brief stress management counseling and the military personnel also participated in a structured 2 1/2-hour GPD after the accident. Two weeks later, the GPD group reported a lower frequency of symptoms related to emotional arousal and more positive personal outcomes than the nondebriefed group.

Childhood Aggression

Aggressive behavior on the part of children can result in isolation from others and poor school performance. August, Realmuto, Hektner, and Bloomquist (2001) developed The Early Risers prevention program to alter the developmental trajectory of children with early onset aggressive behavior. The program features a six–week summer school program, child social skills groups, a teacher consultation and student mentoring program, and a parent education and skills-training group. Following two years of intervention, program children showed significant improvement relative to controls in academic achievement and school behaviors while parents with high program attendance showed improvement in discipline methods.

Anxiety Reduction

Shortt, Barrett, and Fox (2001) conducted a randomized clinical trial evaluating the efficacy of the FRIENDS program, a family-based group cognitive-behavioral treatment for anxious children. Children aged 6 to 10 who fulfilled the criteria for separation anxiety (SAD) were randomly allocated to a 10–week wait-list control group or FRIENDS. After ten weeks, 69% of the students in the FRIENDS group were diagnosis free, compared to 6% of the control group. After a year, 68% of the treatment groups were symptom free.

Muris, Mayer, Bartelds, Tierney, and Bogie (2001) also studied anxious children. The students who participated in group or individual cognitive-behavioral experience showed a significant decline in symptoms. Group and individual approaches were equally effective. Since group methods are more cost effective, consider using them for anxiety in children.

Social skills training (SST) in a group setting may be the more effective approach to generalized social phobia than cognitive group therapy (CGT). Both are effective in reducing social and general anxiety, but psychiatric patients benefited more from SST (van Dam-Baggen & Kraaimaat, 2000).

Anxiety and Depression Related to HIV

Most HIV-infected patients show symptoms of anxiety and depression. Blanch and colleagues (2002) found that a 16-week group psychotherapy program led to an improvement in both depression and anxiety.

Petry, Martin, and Finocche (2001) described how contingency management was used to help clients complete treatment goals. In the HIV drop-in center, groups were held on Tuesdays and Thursdays for 35 weeks. They used a drawing associated with the possibility of winning a prize as a reinforcer to get clients to attend group sessions. Overall, the procedure increased attendance and the percentage of activities completed also rose from 25% during baseline to 65% during reinforcement phases. The findings show that group-based contingency management is effective.

Facing and Reducing Breast Cancer

Supportive-expressive group therapy can reduce distress about the metastatic breast cancer experience (Classen et al., 2001; Hosaka et al., 2001). Group treatment that enables breast cancer patients to express their feelings can result in enhanced immune function (van der Pompe et al., 2001). Group treatment that encourages support and the expression of feelings can increase survival for patients with metastatic cancer (Cunningham, Phillips, Lockwood, Hedley, & Edmonds, 2000; Goodwin et al., 2001). Group treatment for family members of patients with childhood cancer has also been shown to reduce anxiety when five sessions were offered to siblings aged 7–18 (Houtzager, Grootenhuis, & Last, 2001).

Reducing Stress in Infertile Women

Infertile women express higher levels of distress than fertile women. A 10-session support group or cognitive-behavioral group effectively improved mood in participants as compared to a control group (Domar et al., 2000).

FOCUS GROUPS

Focus groups are unique because they allow for group interaction and greater insight into why certain opinions are held than face-to-face interviews or questionnaires, and can be more efficient. For example, it would take many hours to individually interview all clients at a center about the benefits of specific programs, but by taking a random sampling of clients and forming them into one- to two-hour focus groups, the same information can be obtained in less time (Krueger, 1988).

Uses

Focus groups can be used in many ways. Some ways you might consider using them are to:

1. Improve the planning and design of new programs
2. Provide the means of evaluating existing programs
3. Produce insights for developing marketing strategies
4. Strengthen quantitative research designs by adding a qualitative component

Focus groups often precede quantitative research procedures. When used this way, focus group information can help the researcher learn the vocabulary and discover the thinking pattern of the target audience. Focus groups can also help researchers identify illogical sequence of questions that confuse respondents, or search for the omission of critical questions that need to be asked. By conducting a focus group, you can get in tune with participants and discover how they see reality. Insights you gain can help you to develop more efficient follow-up quantitative procedures like telephone or mail-out surveys.

Focus groups can also "triangulate" with quantitative measures. In this approach to research, you would use focus groups at the same time as you collect quantitative data and use *triangulation,* (two or more different research methods to confirm findings and obtain both breadth and depth of information).

Focus groups can follow quantitative procedures when you want help interpreting the results of your study. They may be especially useful when you've collected needs assessment information and find it's incomplete.

Advantages

Focus group interviews offer many advantages. First, people are social creatures and focus group are socially oriented. Because focus groups occur in natural, real-life situations, inhibitions are relaxed and the dynamic nature of group interaction is emphasized. Second, focus groups allow you to probe. When unanticipated issues or opinions evolve, you can explore them, something that can't be done in a structured interview or mail-out survey. Third, your results are fairly easy to understand and present. Fourth, focus groups are relatively low in cost. Fifth, speedy results can be obtained. You don't have to wait to see if there is a one-year (or longer) effect of your intervention. Your results are available when the focus group ends. Sixth, they provide qualitative data without the limited sample size and time and cost constraints of individual interviewing (Krueger, 1988).

Validity

How valid are focus groups in obtaining results? *Validity* is the degree to which a procedure measures what it is supposed to measure. Any measure can intentionally or unintentionally distort results. Focus groups are valid when they are used carefully for a problem that is suitable for focus group inquiry. The procedure has one type of validity that is called *face validity*. The results look valid on the face of them. This is because people open up and share opinions and insights that may not be available in individual interviews, questionnaires, or other measures. Results are generalizable to similar populations no matter what tool you use. Just as in other research methods, you must be careful to whom you generalize your results. If you used a group of older adults, you can't generalize to teens.

Limitations

All measuring and data collection procedures have limitations. Focus groups do, too:

1. You have less control than during an individual interview. Participants interact and influence one another.
2. Care must be used to keep data in context and not lift comments out of context and sequence so that you come to premature conclusions.
3. The technique requires practice to know when to pause, probe, or move to a new topic.
4. Because groups may vary, it is wise to include enough groups to provide a balance.
5. Finding an environment conducive to comfortable self-disclosure may be difficult.
6. Getting participants to attend focus groups requires perseverance; consider providing a reward for participation (Krueger, 1988).

How Focus Groups Can Be Used

Here are some examples of how focus groups can be used:

1. To generate information for questionnaires
2. To conduct an assessment of client needs
3. To evaluate the benefits of new programs
4. To discover what prevents clients from engaging in specific health-enhancing behaviors
5. To explore how to reach a new clientele
6. To find ways to recruit clients to a new program
7. To understand a program's image

8. To assess a new product
9. To provide feedback for administrators

Finding Group Members

Most focus groups are composed of members from an existing list. Alternative strategies are to contact other groups for names, ask participants in focus groups for names, ask invited participants to bring a friend ("snowball sampling"), randomly select names from a phone book and screen them to make sure their characteristics match your criteria, advertise your needs in chat rooms or in a local newspaper, or intercept a random assortment of people visiting a hospital or organization.

Focus Groups for Research

Although randomization of selection is important in many studies, the intent of focus groups is not to infer, but to understand. You will not be trying to generalize to other populations, but to determine the range. You will also not be trying to make statements about the population under study, but to provide insights about how people perceive a situation. As a result, randomization is not the primary factor in selecting participants.

When compared to quantitative survey methods, the number of focus groups you will need in order to conduct a study is surprisingly small. One rule is to continue conducting interviews until little new information is provided. Usually two focus groups will provide the information you need. Plan for four groups, but evaluate after the third group. If new information does not emerge in the third go-around, eliminate the fourth group.

Making Sure Participants Attend

If you want to ensure that focus group members participate, you must follow a few simple rules. Be sure to personalize your invitations. Try to make all members feel they are needed and wanted at the session. Establish meeting times that don't conflict with other important events. You may have to overrecruit during your initial screen, then, one week before the session, send a personalized invitation that contains your name on an official letterhead and details about the session, location, and topic of discussion. Be sure to phone each member the day before the group meets to elicit each one's agreement to participate.

Specific Focus Group Techniques

With enhanced access to the Internet and satellite video transmissions, you can implement new forms of focus groups. They may be conducted in special groups set up on the Internet. Videoconferencing makes it possible to have half the focus group located in one city with the moderator and the other half in another city with a comoderator or assistant.

There are numerous moderating techniques that can help you obtain the information you need. *Personality associations* use photographs to stimulate participant thought and encourage feeling expression. *Expressive drawing* can elicit feelings and reactions participants might not even be aware of until they give their creative side a chance to express itself. Special probing techniques—*attitudinal scaling and laddering*—can provide additional information. Control techniques include *assuring authenticity* and *controlling dominant participants*.

Variable Personality Associations

You can use a series of photographs of people to stimulate group discussion. Choose them based on the topic of discussion. For example, if you are researching the types of homework assistance parents give their children, you could provide a picture of a woman looking proud and happy with her arm around her child, or a man with an exhausted look on his face who is watching from the doorway as his child reads a book, or an angry mother who is arguing with her son about watching TV. You could use these pictures to ask participants to share their feelings about which of the pictures is closest to portraying their attempts to help their child complete homework. When using this technique, be sure to select photos that will ensure a wide range of possible reactions (Greenbaum, 1998).

Fixed Personality Associations

In the fixed association procedure, one set of photos is established and always used. The photos are selected to depict specific characteristics of the people being represented. Over time, you will become familiar with common participant responses to the pictures and be ready to probe any unusual or unexpected reactions you observe. *The People Board* can be used to obtain feeling reactions to various institutions, products, or services.

If you were examining the reactions of parents to school personnel, you might pass out an input sheet on which they are asked to circle the letters (from A to Z) that correspond to the person(s) depicted who definitely are interested in their son or daughter's education. Give participants five minutes to circle as many or as few people as they feel are appropriate and tally their answers on the sheet provided. Total group responses can then be tallied on an easel and used as a discussion point (Greenbaum, 1998).

Situation Associations

This approach is similar to personality associations except in this case situational associations are emphasized. Continuing with the homework situation, to ascertain what types of homework assistance parents want from schools, pictures of parents in the school setting during PTA open houses, or receiving structured assignments from teachers in the mail, or having a high school staff member come to the home to assist, along with other situations could be presented and used as a focus for discussion (Greenbaum, 1998).

Forced Relationships

In a forced relationship, participants are asked to indicate which of several images most closely represents the subject being discussed. The most commonly used categories are colors, animals, and cars. Choose one and then ask participants which color (animal, car) they most closely associate with the problem under study. For example, "Which color do you associate in your mind with trying to help your child with school work?" Participants can then be asked to share with the group why they selected that color (Greenbaum, 1998).

Sentence Completion

Use sentence completion to generate additional discussion, to explore specific aspects of the problem that haven't come up for discussion, and to direct participants to a specific topic. Some examples for the homework problem are:

- When I try to help my child with homework what I usually do is _____

  _____.

- My child reacts to my attempts to help him/her with homework by _____

  _____.

- After I try to help my child with homework, I feel _____

  _____.

When using this technique, be sure to make the sentences clear, short, easy to understand, and specific to the problem under study. Be sure to give participants sufficient time to complete all sentences prior to beginning a discussion of the results.

Expressive Drawing

Bring blank paper and a small box of crayons for each participant. Ask all participants to provide their reactions to the topic under discussion. Give them about three minutes to complete the task. During the discussion period, ask them to show their pictures and explain what they mean and how they relate to the topic (Greenbaum, 1998).

Attitudinal Scaling

This method can be used when the attributes of a service can be identified. To return to the example of homework, in the initial discussion group members try to identify the most important characteristics of effective homework situations from what they've heard, read about, or experienced, for example:

- Teacher provides a written example of what is to be accomplished that homework session
- Child is ready to study
- I focus my full attention on helping child with homework
- Child responds positively to my help
- I feel proud about helping child

Next, the group is asked to discuss the negatives associated with helping their children with homework, including:

- I have no idea how to help
- Child is watching TV and won't study
- Child is irritable and doesn't want to do homework
- Child responds negatively to my attempt to help
- I feel angry and frustrated

Once positive and negative characteristics have been identified, participants are given a piece of paper and asked to put a large cross in the center and write positive effects on one axis and negative effects on the other. The upper end of the homework helping measure is labeled "very effective" and the lower end "ineffective." The right horizontal axis is labeled "frustrating" and the left horizontal axis is labeled "satisfying." Participants are then asked to place their behaviors in relation to their child on the axes.

You draw the scale on the easel and encourage discussion by asking participants to give their reactions and feelings, which are placed on the grid. This exercise forces parents to examine where they might need assistance to help their children with homework.

Laddering

Laddering is a process that can help you probe participants' innermost feelings. It can enable you to get at the hidden reasons participants feel as they do about issues that don't seem that complex or personal (Greenbaum, 1998).

The first step is to ask all participants why they react as they do when homework is not completed. Answers will probably have something to do with the child, such as, "My kid won't do well in school if she doesn't apply herself." The next step is to ask that participant why it's so important that children do well in school. This will probably evoke logical responses, such as, "They won't be able to get a good job or go to college or make a lot of money." Next, ask participants "Why is it so important that your children get a good job or go to college or make a lot of money?" Participant responses could range from "I want my kid to do better than I did," to "I don't want people to think poorly of me as a parent." Next, participants are asked

"Why is it so important that your children do better than you and that people think you're a good parent?" Common responses are that it makes parents feel they are good parents when they see their children doing their homework, and it makes them feel good about themselves and their children.

Assuring Participant Authenticity

A positive attribute of group discussion is that many viewpoints can be expressed and reacted to. This very attribute can also lead to being pushed and pulled about by others' viewpoints and opinions. The very best way to guarantee participant authenticity is to ask each one to write down his or her opinions prior to sharing them with the group (Greenbaum, 1998).

Controlling Dominant Participants

It is not unusual for one participant to vie with you for leadership. You might decide to use any of the following ways to handle this type of situation: call on others for their opinion, ignore the dominant person and omit calling on this person for opinions, explain to the person it's important for everyone to participate and be heard (Greenbaum, 1998).

Setting the Stage

A focus group is typically composed of seven to ten participants who do not know each other. Group members are selected because they have certain characteristics in common and they can relate to the topic under study. Before you select group members, make sure you determine the purpose of the group. Begin by writing down a precise description of the problem at hand. Ask yourself what types of information are of importance, who wants the information, and why this information is needed.

Early on, develop a list of incentives to encourage group participation. This might include a free meal, a gift, or cash. Cash incentives range anywhere from $10 to more than $100. If you are using the focus groups for research, you can include incentives for participation in your grant application. If you work for an agency, there may be money available for marketing or needs assessments. If not, you may be able to provide a free counseling or educational session for participants (Krueger, 1988).

Next, develop your questions. Five or six questions should be sufficient. Avoid questions that can be answered with a yes or a no. Start with open-ended questions, such as, "What did you think of the treatment?" and "How did you feel about the procedure?" Toward the end of the group, shift to close-ended questions that limit the types of responses possible, such as, "What did you like best about the treatment?" and "How did you feel about Dr. Smith's presentation at the conference?" or "Where do you get new information on parenting?" Avoid asking "why" questions that are often pointed and sharp and can sound like interrogation. Instead, break "why" questions down into "influence" questions ("What influenced you to go to the doctor?") and "attribute" questions ("What features of the self-care book do you like the best?").

Brainstorm and write down all the questions you can think of. Then, read them over and have experts review the questions. At a minimum, they should be familiar with the purpose of your study, but it would be better if they were experts in leading focus groups. Ask them if the questions have a logical and sequential flow and whether the probes will elicit the information desired. Here is an example of questions structured to obtain information about helping children with their homework:

1. Tell us about your favorite way to help your child with homework.
2. Describe the last time you helped your child with homework.
3. Some of you mentioned activities that were coordinated by the school. What comes to mind when you think about the school?
4. If you could change one thing about your relationship with your child's teacher and his or her homework assignments, what would it be?
5. Thinking back to the last time you volunteered to help your child with homework, what were you thinking at the time that led you to choose to help your child?

The next portion of the pilot test is to try the questions out with a small number of people out of the intended audience. If necessary, use an assistant moderator to note nonverbal behavior, respond to unexpected interruptions, provide refreshments, take notes, operate the tape recorder, and handle environmental conditions (lighting, seating, heat/air conditioning). Prepare yourself to talk casually with participants as they arrive. You may have a short registration form for them to answer or maybe just focus on being a good host. If a meal is served prior to the group, you can begin to pick up clues and to mentally formulate who should sit next to whom while you're talking to participants prior to eating. If possible, use place cards and casually seat participants next to each other in a way conducive to their talking.

Work out any problematic forces prior to the group. Alcohol, smoking, and group discussions don't mix. Small children can also be distracting. If children must be present, ask the assistant moderator to provide puzzles, crayons, and coloring books, or take the children to a separate room. Be sure to either tape record or jot down notes. It is better to use both methods in case one or the other might fail. Prepare yourself mentally to be alert and free from distraction. As you listen to participant responses to your questions, ask yourself:

- What do I need to ask now to understand what this participant means?
- Is there a question on the guide I developed that I should omit?
- How much time do I have to cover the rest of the questions?
- What am I learning and what else needs to be asked?
- How do I help participants get past intellectualizations and reveal their real feelings?

Be sure to use the pause to the best advantage, waiting an extra thirty seconds prior to asking the next question. Silence will often propel a participant to say something important. Use the probe to elicit additional information, such as, "Please explain further," "Please give us an example of what you mean," "Anything else?" or, "I don't understand. Please explain it to me."

Anticipate the unexpected. Always bring a list of participants and their phone numbers with you to the focus group. If no one shows up, call them and see if they are coming. It would be better to confirm their participation the day before the group meets. If only a few people show up, hold the group anyway. Afterwards, call the others to see if they received the invitation. Arrive at the meeting place in advance and make sure it is adequate. If the group isn't very talkative, bring some extra questions that add interest and use them to warm up the group. Consider using warm-up exercises (Clark, 1997). End by saying, "Is there anything I forgot to ask?" The information garnered may give you good ideas for revising your question list for a future focus group.

After the group ends, reflect once again on the wording and sequencing of the questions. Also evaluate the room arrangement, composition of participants, and the steps you took to encourage participants to speak. If you are conducting a research study and no major changes are made in the questions or procedure, you can use the pilot group as part of the analysis.

Next, decide who will provide the information. Will you need to engage advisory groups, the organizational decision makers? Do you need employees to answer your questions? Will clients or family members provide the answers to your questions? (Krueger, 1988).

Focus groups work because they tap into human attitudes and perceptions. Some group members may need to listen to the opinions of others before they can form their own ideas.

The questions asked in focus groups are often deceptively simple. The intent of the focus group is to promote self-disclosure. At the beginning of a focus group, be sure to tell participants: *There aren't any right or wrong answers, just different points of view. Please share your opinion even if it differs from what others say. I am just as interested in negative comments as positive ones. Sometimes the negative one are the most helpful.*

If you're planning to lead a focus group, keep in mind that it's important to create a permissive environment that nurtures different perceptions and points of view, without pressuring participants to vote, plan or reach consensus. Encourage group members to respond to each other's ideas and comments during the discussion. conduct the group discussion several times with similar types of participants to identify trends and patterns in perception. Once the discussions are completed, systematically analyze them to find clues and insights about a product, service, opportunity, or process.

FOCUS GROUP RESEARCH

Focus groups are being used more and more in health care situations to increase understanding of client concerns. Weinger, O'Donnell, and Ritholtz (2001) used a focus group format to uncover adolescent perceptions regarding the management of their type 1 diabetes. Parental worry, lack of understanding, and resulting intrusive and blaming behaviors were identified as the major areas of conflict between children and their parents.

Nair and colleagues (2002) used a focus group study to determine what patients wanted to know about their medications. Both client and clinician perspectives were identified. While clients wanted more general and specific information about their medications, physicians and pharmacists questioned the amount of side-effect and safety information patients wanted and thought that too much information might deter patients from taking their medications.

Wilson and colleagues (2002) used focus groups to identify lay beliefs about high blood pressure in a low- to middle-income urban African-American community. Participants identified the following problematic aspects of physician communication about cardiac testing: it was confusing, lacked substance, and was vague. The researchers concluded that the feelings of mistrust toward physicians that resulted may be a source of some of the documented racial variation in health care utilization.

Leask, Hawe, and Chapman (2001) compared naturally-occurring vs. constructed focus groups. They found that natural groups were generally flatter and less enthusiastic and displayed a higher level of conformity to conventional wisdom. The researchers suggested avoiding natural groups when a range of opinions about a potentially controversial topic is needed.

Young, Gittelsohn, Charleston, Felix-Aaron, and Appel (2001) conducted focus groups with four distinct groups of African-American women including currently physically active, currently sedentary, successful weight loss and unsuccessful weight loss. They found that motivators for the exercisers to start exercising were health concerns, weight control, stress reduction, and the influence of others. Motivators to continue exercising included feeling good and having energy. In contrast, sedentary women reported that social support and enjoyment would motivate them.

Mothers are in an important position to prevent obesity in their children, but only if they are worried about their children's weight gain. One study explored mothers' perceptions about how they determine when a child is overweight, why children become overweight, and what barriers exist to preventing or managing childhood obesity (Jain et al., 2001). Mothers did not define obesity in terms of weight, but considered being teased about weight or developing limitations in physical activity as indicators of their child's being overweight. Mothers found it difficult to deny their children food, even if they had just eaten when the child's diet was challenged by other family members. The researchers concluded that health professionals may be more effective in preventing childhood obesity by focusing on goals they share with mothers, rather than on labeling children overweight.

Even children as young as age 6 can successfully participate in focus groups. Advantages of such a measure is that it captures perspectives, original ideas, and insights, which are often neglected in more traditional pediatric research; can serve as an innovative approach to understanding children's experiences from a developmental perspective; and frees research from the data-gathering limitations placed by literacy/reading levels that plague quantitative methods using self-report.

Focus groups have been used to identify factors influencing participation of African-American elders in exercise behavior (Walcott-McQuigg & Prohaska, 2001), collect perceptions of women living with coronary heart disease (Lisk & Grau, 1999), examine adolescent mothers' beliefs about parenting and injury prevention (Bennett, 2001), develop a questionnaire to improve medical communication (Steine, Finset & Laerum, 2001), examine consumer attitudes about key messages and the format of the 1995 *US Dietary Guidelines for Americans* (Geiger, 2001), identify older cardiac patients' preferences for treatment and perceptions of risk (Kennelly & Bowling, 2001), uncover the gulf between teenage opinions of health care services and the opinions held by primary care providers (Jacobson, Richardson, Parry-Langdon, & Donovan, 2001), measure the impact of solution-focused communication training on nurses' communication skills, obtain data on the differences between the behaviors and perceptions of inner-city women and the general population about obesity and cardiovascular risks (Covington & Grisso, 2001), prevent obesity in African Americans (Dietz, 2001), explore how education may enhance pain management in children (Simons, 2002), and determine rural women's perceptions about cardiovascular disease prevention and behavior change (Krummel, Humphries, & Tessaro, 2002),

REFERENCES

Amerslav, A. (1992). Co-dependency groups, In M. McKay & K. Paleg (Eds.), *Focal group psychotherapy* (pp. 1–27). Oakland, CA: New Harbinger.

August, G. J., Realmuto, G. M., Hektner, J. M., & Bloomquist, M. L. (2001). An integrated components preventive intervention for aggressive elementary school children: The early risers program. *Journal of Consulting and Clinical Psychology, 69,* 614–626.

Beck, A. T., Ward, C. H., Mendelson, M., Mock, J., & Erbaugh, J. (1961). An inventory for measuring depression. *Archives of General Psychiatry, 4,* 561–571.

Bennett, M. L. M. (2001). Adolescent mothers' beliefs about parenting and injury prevention: Results of a focus group. *Journal of Pediatric Health Care, 15,* 194–199.

Blanch, J., Rousaud, A., Hautzinger, M., Martinez, E., Peri J. M., Andres, S., Cierra E., Gattell, J. M., & Gasto, C. (2002). Assessment of the efficacy of a cognitive-behavioral group psychotherapy program for HIV-infected patients referred to a consultation-liaison psychiatry program. *Psychotherapy and Psychosomatics, 71*(2), 77–84.

Bowles, N., Mackintosh, C., & Torn, A. (2001). Nurses' communication skills: An evaluation of the impact of solution-focused communication training. *Journal of Advanced Nursing, 36,* 347–354.

Clark, C.C. (1997). *Creating a climate for power learning.* Duluth, MN: Whole Person Associates.

Clarke, G. N., Nornbrook, M., Lynch, F., Polen, M., Gale, J., Beardslee, W., O'Connor, E., & Seeley, J. (2001). A randomized trial of a group cognitive intervention for preventing depression in adolescent offspring of depressed parents. *Archives of General Psychology, 58,* 1127–1134.

Classen, C., Butler, L. D., Koopman, C., Miller, E., DiMiceli S., Giese-Davis J., Fobair, P., Carlson, R. W., Kraemer, H. C., & Spiegel, D. (2001). Supportive-expressive group therapy and distress in patients with metastatic breast cancer: A randomized clinical intervention trial. *Archives of General Psychiatry, 58,* 484–501.

Collins, T. C., Clark, J. A., Petersen, L. A., & Kressin, N. R. (2001). Racial differences in how patients perceive physician communication regarding cardiac testing. *Medical Care, 40*(Suppl. 1), 27–34.

Conyers-Boyd, J. (1992). Rape survivors group. In M. McKay & K. Paleg (Eds.), *Focal group psychotherapy* (pp. 269–291). Oakland, CA: New Harbinger.

Covington, J. P., & Grisso, J. A. (2001). Assessing cardiovascular disease risk in women: a cultural approach. *Journal of the National Medical Association, 93,* 430–435.

Cunningham, A. J., Phillips, C., Lockwood, G. A., Hedley, D. W., & Edmonds, C. V. (2000). Association of involvement in psychological self-regulation with longer survival in patients with metastatic cancer: An exploratory study. *Advances in Mind Body Medicine, 16,* 276–287.

Dare, C., Eisler, I., Russell, G., Treasure, J., & Dodge, L. (2001). Psychological therapies for adults with anorexia nervosa: Randomised controlled trial of out-patient treatments. *British Journal of Psychiatry, 178,* 216–221.

Deblinger, E., Stauffer, L. B., & Steer R. A. (2001). Comparative efficacies of supportive and cognitive behavioral group therapy for young children who have been sexually abused and their nonoffending mothers. *Child Maltreatment, 6*(4), 332–343.

Dietz, W. (2001). Focus group data pertinent to the prevention of obesity in African Americans. *American Journal of Medical Science, 322*, 286–289.

Domar, A. D., Clapp, D., Slawsby, E., Kessel, B., Orav, J., & Freizing, M. (2000). The impact of group psychological interventions on distress in infertile women. *Health Psychology, 19*, 568–575.

Eid, J., Johnsen, B. H., & Weisaeth, L. (2001). The effects of group psychological debriefing on acute stress reactions following a traffic accident: A quasi-experimental approach. *International Journal of Emergency Mental Health, 3*, 145–154.

Ellis, A., & Dryden, W.A. (1987). *The practice of rational emotive therapy.* New York: Springer Publishing Co.

Fernandez-Aranda, F., Bel, M., Jimenez, S., Vinuales, M., Turon, J., & Vallejo, J. (1998). Outpatient group therapy for anorexia nervosa: A preliminary study. *Eating and Weight Disorders, 3*(1), 1–6.

Geiger, C. J. (2001). Communicating dietary guidelines for Americans: room for improvement. *Journal of the American Dietetic Association, 101*, 793–797.

Gignac, M. A. (2000). An evaluation of a psychotherapeutic group intervention for persons having difficulty coping with musculoskeletal disorders. *Social Work in Health Care, 32*(1), 57–75.

Goodwin, P. J., Leszcz, M., Ennis, M., Koopmans, J., Vincent, L., Guther, H., Drysdale, E., Hundleby, M., Chochinov, H. M., Navarro, M., Speca, M., & Hunter, J. (2001). The effect of group psychosocial support on survival in metastatic breast cancer. *New England Journal of Medicine, 345*, 1719–1726.

Greenbaum, T. L. (1998). *The handbook for focus group research.* Thousand Oaks, CA: Sage.

Hellerstein, D. J., Little, S. A., Samstag, L. W., Batchelder, S., Muran, J. C., Fedak, M., Kreditor, D., Rosenthal, R. N., & Winston, A. (2001). Adding group psychotherapy to medication treatment in dysthymia: A randomized prospective pilot study. *Journal of Psychotherapy Practice and Research, 10*(2), 93–103.

Hosaka, T., Sugiyama, Y., Hirai, K., Okuyama, T., Sugawara, Y., & Nakamura, Y. (2001). Effects of a modified group intervention with early-stage breast cancer patients. *General Hospital Psychiatry, 23*, 145–151.

Houtzager, B. A., Grootenhuis, M. A., & Last, B. F. (2001). Supportive groups for siblings of pediatric oncology patients: Impact on anxiety. *Psychooncology, 10*, 315–324.

Jacobson, L., Richardson, G., Parry-Langdon, N., & Donovan, C. (2001). How do teenagers and primary healthcare providers view each others? An overview of key themes. *British Journal of General Practice, 51*, 811–816.

Jain, A., Sherman, S. N., Chamberlin, D. L., Carter, Y., Powers, S. W., & Whitaker, R. C. (2001). Why don't low-income mothers worry about their preschoolers being overweight? *Pediatrics, 107,* 1138–1146.

Kennelly, C., & Bowling, A. (2001). Suffering in deference: A focus group study of older cardiac patients' preferences for treatment and perceptions of risk. *Quality Health Care, 10* (Suppl. 1), 123–128.

Kim, S., & Kim, J. (2001). The effects of group intervention for battered women in Korea. *Archives of Psychiatric Nursing, 15,* 257–264.

Kolip, P., Czujek, J., Greitemann, B., Rosowski, E., Schmidt, B., & Slangen, K. (2001). "Zest for Life instead of strain of illness"—implementation and evaluation of a program activating chronic back pain patients in a rehabilitation clinic. *Rehabilitation, 40,* 267–274.

Krueger, R. A. (1988). *Focus groups: A practical guide for applied research.* Beverly Hills, CA: Sage.

Krummel, D. A., Humphries, D., & Tessaro, I. (2002). Focus groups on cardiovascular health in rural women: Implications for practice. *Journal of Nutrition Education and Behavior, 34*(1), 38–46.

Landgarten, H. B., & Lubbers, D. (1991). *Treatment of women with eating disorders. Adult art psychotherapy: Issues and application.* New York: Brunner/Mazel.

Leask, J., Hawe, P., & Chapman, S. (2001). Focus group composition: A comparison between natural and constructed groups. *Australian New Zealand Journal of Public Health, 25,* 152–154.

Levine, M. D., Ringham, R. M., Kalarchian, M. A., Wisniewski, L., & Marcus, M. D. (2001). Is family-based behavioral weight control appropriate for severe pediatric obesity? *International Journal of Eating Disorders, 30,* 318–328.

Levkovitz, Y., Shahar, G., Native, G., Hirsfeld, E., Treves, I., Krieger, I., & Fennig, S. (2000). Group interpersonal psychotherapy for patients with major depression disorder—Pilot study. *Journal of Affective Disorder, 60,* 191–195.

Lim, J. J., Childs, J., & Gonsalves, K. (2000). Critical incident stress management. *American Association of Occupational Health Nursing, 48,* 487–497.

Lisk, C. J., & Grau, L. (1999). Perceptions of women living with coronary heart disease: An overview of study findings. *American Journal of Geriatric Cardiology, 8,* 157–161.

Lothstein, L. M. (2001). Treatment of non-incarcerated sexually compulsive/addictive offenders in an integrated, multimodel, and psychodynamic group therapy model. *International Journal of Group Psychotherapy, 51,* 553–570.

Mackenzie, A., & Prendergast, J. (1992). Domestic violence offender groups. In M. McKay & K. Paleg (Eds.), *Focal group psychotherapy* (pp. 419–459). Oakland, CA: New Harbinger.

Maine, M. (1991). *Father hunger: Fathers, daughters and food.* Carlsbad, CA; Gurze Books.

Michaelson, P. (1993). *Secret attachments: Exposing the roots of addictions & compulsions.* Naples, FL: Prospect Books.

Miranda, J., Schreckengost, J., & Heine, L. (1992). Cognitive-behavioral group treatment for depression. In M. McKay & K. Paleg (Eds.), *Focal group psychotherapy* (pp. 135–162). Oakland, CA: New Harbinger.

Mishna, F., Muskat, B., & Schamess, G. (2002). Food for thought: the use of food in group therapy with children and adolescents. *International Journal of Group Psychotherapy, 52*(1), 27–37.

Muris, P., Mayer, B., Bartelds, E., Tierney, S., & Bogie, N. (2001). The revised version of the Screen for Child Anxiety Related Emotional Disorders (SCARED-R): Treatment sensitivity in an early intervention trial for childhood anxiety disorders. *British Journal of Clinical Psychology, 40*(Pt. 3), 323–336.

Nair, K., Dolovich, L., Cassels, A., McCormack, J., Levine, M., Gray J., Mann, K., & Burns, S. (2002). What patients want to know about their medications. Focus group study of patient and clinical perspectives. *Canadian Family Physician, 48,* 104–110.

Ogata, A., & Amano, K. (2000). A psychosocial approach to epileptic patients. *Epilepsia, 41* (Suppl. 9), 36–38.

Paleg, K. (1992). Parenting groups. In M. McKay & K. Paleg (Eds.), *Focal group psychotherapy* (pp. 499–526). Oakland, CA: New Harbinger.

Patelis-Siotis, I., Young, L. T., Robb, J. C., Marriott, M, Bieling, P.J., Cox, L. C., & Joffe, R. T. (2001). Group cognitive behavioral therapy for bipolar disorder: A feasibility and effectiveness study. *Journal of Affective Disorders, 65,* 145–153.

Perri, M. G., Nezu, A. M., McKelvey, W. F., Shermer, R. L., Renjilian, D. A., & Viegener, B. J. (2001). Relapse prevention training and problem-solving therapy in the long-term management of obesity. *Journal of Consulting and Clinical Psychology, 69,* 722–726.

Petry, N. M., Martin, B., & Finocche, C. (2001). Contingency management in group treatment: A demonstration project in an HIV drop-in center. *Journal of Substance Abuse Treatment, 21*(2), 89–96.

Renjilian, D. A., Perri, M. G., Nezu, A. M., McKelvey, W. F., Shermer, R. L., & Anton, S. D. (2001). Individual versus group therapy for obesity: Effects of matching participants to their treatment preferences. *Journal of Consulting and Clinical Psychology 69,* 717–721.

Riess, H. (2002). Integrative time-limited group therapy for bulimia nervosa. *International Journal of Group Psychotherapy, 52*(1), 1–26.

Rondeau, G., Brodeur, N., Brochu, S., & Lemire, G. (2001). Dropout and completion of treatment among spouse abusers. *Violence and Victims, 16*, 127–143.

Salloum, A., Avery, L., & McClain, R. P. (2001). Group psychotherapy for adolescent survivors of homicide victims: A pilot study. *Journal of the American Academy of Child and Adolescent Psychiatry, 40*), 1261–1267.

Sandbeck, T. J. (1986). *The deadly diet: Recovering from anorexia & bulimia.* Oakland, CA: New Harbinger.

Schnurr, P. P., Friedman, M. J., Lavori, P. W., & Hsieh, F. Y. (2001). Design of Department of Veterans Affairs Cooperative Study No. 420: Group treatment of posttraumatic stress disorder. *Controlled Clinical Trials, 22*(1), 74–88.

Shortt, A. L., Barrett, P. M., & Fox, T. L. (2001). Evaluating the FRIENDS program: A cognitive-behavioral group treatment for anxious children and their parents. *Journal of Clinical and Child Psychology, 30*, 525–535.

Simons, J. M. (2002). An action research study exploring how education may enhance pain management in children. *Nurse Education Today, 22*, 108–117.

Steine, S., Finset, A., & Laerum, E. (2001). A new, brief questionnaire (PEQ) developed in primary health care for measuring patients' experience of interaction, emotion and consultation outcome. *Family Practice, 18*, 410–418.

Thienemann, M., Martin, J., Cregger, B., Thompson, H. B., & Dyer-Friedman, J. (2001). Manual-driven group cognitive-behavioral therapy for adolescents with obsessive-compulsive disorder: A pilot study. *Journal of the American Academy of Child and Adolescent Psychiatry, 40*, 1254–1260.

Toseland, R. W., & Siporin, M. (1986). When to recommend group treatment: A review of the clinical and the research literature. *International Journal of Group Psychotherapy, 36*, 171–302.

van Dam-Baggen, R., & Kraaimaat, F. (2000). Group social skills training or cognitive group therapy as the clinical treatment of choice for generalized social phobia? *Journal of Anxiety Disorders, 14*, 437–451.

van der Pompe G., Antoni M. H., Duivenvoorden, H. J., de Graeff, A., Simonis R. F., van der Vergt, S. G., & Heijnen, C. J. (2001). An exploratory study into the effect of group psychotherapy on cardiovascular and immunoreactivity to acute stress in breast cancer patients. *Psychotherapy and Psychosomatics, 70*, 307–318.

Walcott-McQuigg, J. A., & Prohaska, T. R. (2001). Factors influencing participation of African American elders in exercise behavior. *Public Health Nursing, 18*, 194–203.

Washington, O. G. (2000). Effects of group therapy on chemically dependent women's self- efficacy. *Journal of Nursing Scholarship, 32*, 347–352.

Weinger, K., O'Donnell, K. A., & Ritholz, M. D. (2001). Adolescent views of diabetes-related parent conflict and support: A focus group analysis. *Journal of Adolescent Health, 29*, 330–336.

Wilson, R. P., Freeman, A., Kazda, M. J., Andrews, T. C., Berry, L., Vaeth, P. A., & Victor, R. G. (2002). Lay beliefs about high blood pressure in a low- to middle-income urban African-American community: An opportunity for improving hypertension control. *American Journal of Medicine, 112*(1), 26–30.

Wolfsdorf, B. A., & Zlotnick, C. (2001). Affect management in group therapy for women with posttraumatic stress disorder and histories of childhood sexual abuse. *Journal of Clinical Psychology, 57*, 169–181.

Young, D. R., Gittelsohn, J., Charleston, J., Felix-Aaron K., & Appel, L. J. (2001). Motivations for exercise and weight loss among African-American women: Focus group results and their contribution toward program development. *Ethnicity and Health, 6*(3–4), 227–245.

Zimmer, S. S. (1992). Groups for eating disorders. In M. McKay & K. Paleg (Eds.), *Focal group psychotherapy* (pp. 237–267). Oakland, CA: New Harbinger.

Zlotnick, C., Johnson, S. L., Miller, I. W., Pearlstein, T., & Howard, M. (2001). Postpartum depression in women receiving public assistance: Pilot study of an interpersonal-therapy- oriented group intervention. *American Journal of Psychiatry 158*, 638–640.

11

When the Organization Is the Group

THE HIGHLY CREATIVE ORGANIZATION

A key question for leaders in organizations is "How do I go about working with people in such a way that it releases their creative energies?" All organizations can benefit from actions that will develop more creative solutions to problems. Although many administrators may say they value creativity, forces often push the organization toward the status quo and short-term solutions. The creative individual may have difficulty adapting to a noncreative work environment. Creative individuals tend to produce a large number of original ideas quickly, are motivated by their interest in a problem, are able to suspend their judgment long enough to make adequate analysis and exploration, are relativistic rather than authoritarian, are playful and undisciplined when working, are independent rather than conforming in judgment, view themselves as different, and have a rich fantasy life and superior reality orientation. Creative organizations have many of the same characteristics; they have open channels of communication, allow eccentricity, evaluate ideas based on their merit not on the status of the originator, use long-range planning, experiment with new ideas without prejudging them, are decentralized and diversified, encourage risk taking and are tolerant of error, allow freedom to choose and pursue problems and discuss ideas, value original and different objectives, and provide a stable, secure environment that allows creators to roam.

Leaders are often rewarded for having a smooth-working, functioning system. How can you encourage creativity, which may at times appear jagged and uneven or even crazy to the uninvolved observer? Unfortunately, many creative individuals are pressured to conform and their creative gifts may not be used. Many organizations of which you are a part may have a

270

reasonable level of trust and do a fine job; their problem may be primarily that they are using old, nonuseful solutions to new problems. Use the following elements to develop a program that stimulates creativity: analyze the current level of innovation and employees' desire or need for more creative work; plan actions for stimulating innovation, including seminars on creative thinking; provide incentives for new, productive ideas; encourage brainstorming in staff meetings; create think tanks; include creativity in performance reviews; develop policies that reduce fear of making a mistake; keep staff openly informed about organizational problems that need solving; have a reward system for the creative person; have an outside observer assess creative output and suggest ways of innovating; rotate people to different parts of the organization so there are new mixtures of people working on old problems; have job enrichment sessions so staff can devise ways of enriching their own jobs (Hawkins & Fillion, 1996; Hogan, Curphy, & Hogan, 1994).

DIAGNOSING ORGANIZATIONAL SYSTEMS

A first step in moving toward a creative, innovative organization is diagnosis. There are three parts of an *organizational system* that need to be assessed: the social system, the operation system and the administrative system.

The *social system* has basic components including: climate or prevailing emotional state (formal, relaxed, defensive, cautious, accepting, trusting), communication network (formal and informal patterns about who talks with whom, when, how often, and about what), status-role structure (division of labor, who holds power, has influence, and how this is achieved), pattern of management (style of handling superordinate and subordinate action), decisionmaking method (consensus, authoritarian, democratic), values and goals (what are the priorities in the system, how are these established, how well do members accept them and work toward them).

The *operation system* includes all the methods of getting the work done. Each organization has a unique way of arranging equipment, people, material, and processes to accomplish the work. Often, it is difficult to separate the social system processes from operation system processes—they interact. However, there are unique elements of the operation system such as how furniture is arranged, how work space is used, where supplies are stored, and so forth. Although all units may be furnished with the same furniture, on one unit the staff may form a circle to meet and on another, most may stand or do their paper work while the leader sits and gives a report. The circular arrangement of furniture (operation system) can affect the level of interaction (social system), but even in a circular arrangement, it is possible for a leader who wants to lecture or carry on a monologue to do so.

The *administrative system* interlaces the social and operation systems and is a network of procedures, policies, reports, and audits. Important elements in the administrative system are hiring, firing and promotional methods, fringe benefits (vacations, sick leave, retirement, insurance, leave time), salaries, bonuses and special benefits, and report-auditing.

ORGANIZATIONAL INTERVENTIONS

Many leaders try to bring about change in organizations by administrative changes. Memos are sent or wages and rewards are manipulated. Sending a memo to the effect that a certain behavior will begin or end at a specified time can backfire.

> Jane Warden, Assistant Director, noticed staff were wasting toilet paper in their rest rooms. She sent a memo that as of that day staff were to be more conservative of supplies. Following the memo, toilet paper waste increased. The staff viewed the memo as a challenge and another sign of being treated as irresponsible children. A whole series of strategy-counterstrategies were played out until Jane decided the use of toilet paper was taking up too much time for its level of priority. She stopped mentioning the item and toilet paper useage dropped to its level prior to the first memo.

The following interventions can affect system output variables:

1. *Social System*
   - Involve workers in setting goals and making decisions.
   - Keep people informed about what is happening in the system.
   - Open communications between all workers.
   - Develop a high level of trust and acceptance.
   - Keep both person-centered and task-centered orientations.
   - Set high performance goals.

- Convey the idea that workers are needed, useful, and doing something worthwhile in their work.
- Develop team spirit.
- Teach supervisors to provide support and recognition.
- Help workers and supervisors identify areas where additional help is needed.
- Refrain from exerting undue pressure on workers.

2. *Operation System*
- Provide an opportunity for workers to use a variety of skills.
- Match the requirements of the work to the personal resources of workers.
- Allow time for workers to interact with one another and build support groups.
- Ensure that physical conditions are comfortable, safe, and excess work is not required.
- Make workers responsible for the quality of output. Ensure that there are not too many conflicting interfaces with other systems.

3. *Administrative System*
- Base promotions on open review between supervisor and supervisee.
- Delegate authority and responsibility
- appropriately.
- Distribute benefits equitably.
- Ensure policies and procedures; do not restrict development of the social system.
- Establish rules and regulations jointly with workers whenever feasible.
- Encourage workers to collaborate with management to set goals and plan work.
- Avoid using restrictive reporting and auditing as control measures.
- Allow for modification in procedures and rules.
- Formally reward appropriate behavior in managers and workers.

To maximize quality output from workers, all three systems must be mutually reinforcing. It will help to work on one or another system, but the best results will be obtained by building a mutually reinforcing organization.

It is not unusual to hear ask, "What can I do to motivate my staff?" Goren and Ottaway (1985) suggest that many teams do not change and appear motivated because of organizational chronicity and collusion. Seemingly unchangeable problem behavior is maintained by the unacknowledged support of the system and because solutions often add to the problem.

Team members rarely admit to supporting the problem solution and tend to scapegoat one individual ("he isn't doing his job") or a subsystem ("physicians are little gods around here"). The physician cannot be authoritarian unless the nurse is passive and acquiescent. The individual who slacks off does so because his coworkers take up the slack.

Team members may want a problem solved, but prefer not to change. Instead, they prefer to make their usual behavior more effective. Often, this is impossible. For example, team members may need to learn to take the responsibility for speaking up and being assertive and to take the risk related to how that change may affect the system.

Organizations may not change for a variety of reasons, including:

1. Leaders and workers collude (or unconsciously agree) not to change. Any of the following can be unconsciously agreed upon decisions that can hamper productivity and goal achievement: vague and unmeasurable goals, unachievable goals, incongruent goals (the director of nursing wants to prevent unionization and the staff wants the director of nursing to change her leadership style), or goals that are incongruent with the available options. "Collusion is the result of trying to achieve success without enduring the pain and difficulty of change" (Goren & Ottaway, 1985, p. 11). Leaders may collude with their staff by publicly valuing a behavior, but secretly valuing another. These hidden agendas will prevent change because lip service will not be sufficient to induce change. It may delude leaders into believing they are making the effort, but no one else is.

2. Staff development and/or other administrators act on the idea that change occurs by sending "troublemakers" for training. This is problematic because those sent for training are not motivated to change and probably will not. It is also problematic because even if a few staff members do change, once they return to their work system, new behaviors will be treated as deviant and pressure will be exerted to return to old behavior patterns. An organizational change program must be one that is mutually agreed upon and entered into by all organizational members.

3. Solutions are focused on understanding the problem rather than changing it. This is evident when the following types of comments are made: "How did we get this way?" "How did this happen?" "Let's see if we can understand the problem." (These kinds of comments focus on insight and history; questions more effective in guiding change are: "How does having this problem maintain the system?" and "What can be done about it?")

4. Competition rather than collaboration is fostered. Leaders who want change must make that expectation clear to staff and must provide the tools and skills needed to effect change. Rewards must be given for collaboration, if collaboration is to occur. For example, publicly acknowledging an ability to teach supportive behaviors to other staff members would enhance collaboration, while publicly praising a unique ability of one staff member would enhance competition (Bragg, 2001; Tjosvold, 1995).

CONDUCTING INTERACTIONS AND "DOINGS"

As formal or informal leader in your organization, you can act to produce a more viable system. It is your responsibility to establish a vision, get assistance with tasks when needed, and work to make your vision a reality. The way you conduct yourself in interactions with other employees, including meetings, can be a first step toward your mission becoming reality.

Establishing a Mission

Effective organizations are client-focused and mission-driven. It is your responsibility as a leader to focus your organization on key goals and values, then get out of the way and let your team devise their own systems and processes. Without a mission, busy work can result. Take a moment now to write down the mission for your organization if it doesn't already have one. Consider a discussion of fairness, integrity, and fiscal responsibility when you're thinking about values. Remember: values drive behavior (Emmerich, 1994).

Without a clear vision of your mission, rules and compliance take over. You may have to teach your supervisees how to set up measures and evaluation procedures to ensure that the mission is carried out and begin to question outdated rules and regulations that are still operative in your organization.

Be sure to ask your supervisees what they need to implement the organization's mission (Emmerich, 1994). Do they need you to delegate authority so they can do their job? Do they need interunit communication to improve? Do they want to make sure the workload is shared fairly? Do they want you to stay out of their work and stop micromanaging what they do? Do they need more evaluation checkpoints built in so you can relax and stop micromanaging? Do they need fewer managers who may be slowing down decision-making processes? Do they need more competent managers?

Value the contributions of individuals in your organization. Provide appropriate training and enhance clear communication and you won't have to do all the work. You will have a prepared and enthusiastic group of employees ready to tackle their jobs.

Successful Delegation

If you are the leader of a team, there are times when you will need to delegate tasks. There are a number of reasons for doing this: (a) you can't do all the work yourself because it's too stressful and will make it impossible to have enough energy left to be a good leader, and (b) as leader, part of your job is to teach others management skills. By demonstrating how to delegate, you will be teaching your supervisees an important lesson and preparing them to move up to the next position. Figure 11-1 provides information on successful delegation.

Facilitating Meetings or "Doings"

Many meetings are unproductive, boring, and despised. Meetings do matter, though, because that's where an organization's culture perpetuates itself. Here are some tips for making your meetings productive, interesting, and well attended.

1. Adopt a mind-set, and work to convince team members that meetings are real work. Consider posting reminders on the walls. Keep your comments focused on the purpose of the meeting. Refer to your agenda and take notes to remind yourself of comments you want to make. If you're conducting a formal meeting, follow the rules for parliamentary procedure (Figure 11-2) and make your comments clear and easy to understand.

2. Make sure your agenda lists the meeting's key topics, who will lead which parts of the discussion, how long each segment will take, and what the expected outcomes are.

FIGURE 11-1. Successful delegation.

A SUCCESSFUL DELEGATION INCLUDES:

1. A clear determination of the task by you

2. A clear statement, preferably in writing, of:
   A. Just what the job entails
   B. End results expected
   C. Suggestions you have for completing the task
   D. What authority or responsibility goes along with the task
   E. When you want a progress report
   F. A specific time you expect the task to be completed
   G. Some idea of how the outcome will be evaluated
3. Clarification with the supervisee of what is expected

4. Establishment of controls and checkpoints

5. Reiterating your expectations as needed

6. Rewarding/praising supervisees' positive movement toward appropriate behavior

7. Ongoing dialogue with supervisees about
   • How they feel about the tasks delegated
   • How they evaluate their work

Points to Keep in Mind When Delegating
   • Use a tone of voice that says, "This is important and I expect you to follow through."
   • Check with the person you've made an assignment to, validating that there has been an agreement/understanding of the assignment.
   • Verbalize the time/date you will be checking back with the person to evaluate his/her performance.
   • Make sure you do check back with the person at the time agreed upon.

Remember:
Consistency of word and action is the hallmark of building trust.

   • When checking with supervisees, find out exactly what has and has not been accomplished to date.
   • Work out a plan for supervisees to complete the assignment. If you take over and complete the task you are teaching the delegatee to be dependent.

Remember:
Leadership includes teaching others management skills
so they can learn to be effective.

   • Provide praise and direction as needed.

FIGURE 11-2 Tips on Parliamentary procedure.

You're facilitating a group where minutes are taken, officers are elected and motions are made and seconded. Here are some tips based on Jones' *Parliamentary Procedure at a Glance.*

MOTIONS:

*Motions occur in order of precedence from 1 (privileged) to 18 (main). After addressing the chairperson, the group member waits for recognition prior to speaking. When a vote is taken, the chairperson pauses after calling for the Ayes prior to asking for the Noes.

1. **Fix the time of the next meeting**. This motion is in order after a vote to adjourn has been taken but has not yet been announced by the Chair, may be amended by time and place, is not debatable when another motion is before the group, is not subject to any other motion except amendment, and has no privilege if the time and place has been set for the next meeting. The motion requires a second; the mover may interrupt a member who has the floor, but must first be recognized.

   MEMBER: "Mr./Madam Chairperson, I move that when we adjourn, we meet Tuesday, 10 a.m. in the conference room."

   CHAIR: "It is moved and seconded that when this group adjourns, it will meet again (repeats above). Is there any discussion?"

   MEMBER: "The vote is on the motion that when this group adjourns, it meets Tuesday at 10 a.m. in the conference room. Those in favor say 'Aye.'" Pause. "Those opposed say 'No.'"

   CHAIR: either, "The 'Ayes' have it and the next meeting will be held. . . . Mr./Ms. Secretary, is there any other business?" or "The 'Noes' have it and the motion does not carry." Consult Secretary for other business.

2. **Adjourn or recess**.

   MEMBER: "Mr./Madam Chairperson, I move that we adjourn (recess)."

*It's possible to have many motions before a group at one time if they are made in the following sequence: a main motion was moved, then an amendment was put forth, then a motion to refer was made, then a motion to postpone consideration was voiced, then a motion to close debate was heard, then a motion to table the motion, then a point of order was raised, and a movement to adjourn occurred (Jones, 1991).

CHAIR: "It is moved and seconded that we adjourn. Those in favor of adjournment say 'Aye.'" Pause. "Those opposed say 'No.'"

"Aye" vote: "The 'Ayes' have it and you stand adjourned." (sound gavel.)

"No" vote: "The 'Noes' have it. Ms./Mr. Secretary, what is the next business?" or, "Is there further discussion on the motion before us when it was moved to adjourn?"

3. **Questions of privilege** include bad heating or ventilating, disorder, illness, threats, desire to be excused, tampering with papers, and so on.

MEMBER: "Madam./Mr. Chairperson, question of privilege."

CHAIR: "Please state your question."

MEMBER: "I request that the air conditioning be turned on because the room is too warm."

CHAIR: "Privilege granted. Will the person closest to the thermostat please check to make sure it is turned on."

4. **Call for orders of the day**. An "order" is something the majority of the group has requested. It could be to have the topic of refreshments be considered. That "order" takes precedence over a new motion sponsored by only one or two members of the group.The command to "postpone" is a general "order" while the command that the topic of refreshments be considered immediately after the reading of the minutes is a "special order." A group member calling for orders of the day may interrupt a member who has the floor. A general order may be postponed by a majority vote, but a special order may be postponed by a two-thirds vote. No second is required and it is not debatable or amendable. As group leader, ensure that the secretary has a copy of all orders of the day available for that meeting. If you neglect some item of business, a group member may call for orders of the day.

MEMBER: "Mr. Chairperson, I call for the order of the day."

CHAIR: "If there is no objection, the Secretary will read the order of the day."

A group member may call for a special order without being recognized and does not require a second. A special order can be postponed until the business before the group has been concluded. A special order is not debatable or amendable and if it isn't taken up at the time specified, the order is nullified. A call for orders cannot be used until any pending question has been resolved.

(continued)

FIGURE 11-2 *(continued)*

---

5. **Point of order.** A group member may interrupt a speaker without being recognized or seconded to call for a point of order when a motion is processed out of order or clear violation of the by-laws is noted.

MEMBER: "Madam Chairperson, I raise a point of order."

CHAIR: "State your point."

MEMBER: "The motion just proposed is a clear violation of our by-laws."

CHAIR: Either, "Your point is well taken," or "Your point is not well taken."

Requests for information must go through the chairperson, e.g.,

MEMBER: "I would like to ask _____ (group member who is speaking) a question."

CHAIR: "State your question."

If a second inquiry is made, the chairperson asks the group member who has the floor, "Are you willing to be interrupted?"

6. **Appeal.** For an appeal to the decision of the Chair, a member may interrupt a member who has the floor, but a second is required. All appeals must yield to questions of privilege, adjournment, and orders of the day. A motion to table can kill the appeal without debate if it is sustained. A tie vote sustains the Chair's decision. An appeal can only be made immediately after the Chair's decision and is not in order when another appeal is pending.

MEMBER: "Madam Chairperson, I appeal the decision of the Chair."

CHAIR: "There is an appeal from the decision of the Chair." (If a motion to table or to close debate has not been made.) "Is there any discussion?" If there is no discussion or the question has been called, "Those in favor of sustaining the decision of the Chair say 'Aye.'" (Continue resolution as #2 above.)

7. **To suspend the rules.** This motion cannot be debated or have a subsidiary motion applied to it. The member cannot interrupt a member who has the floor and must first be recognized and seconded. The motion cannot be reconsidered for the same purpose except at a later meeting and only by unanimous consent. Motion to suspend requires a 2/3 vote unless otherwise specified in the by-laws.

MEMBER: "Madam Chairperson, I move to suspend the rule that interferes with present rule ____ (by-law or constitution).

CHAIR: "It is moved and seconded that we suspend the rules interfering with rule ____. Those in favor of suspension signify by saying 'Aye.'" Those opposed to the suspension of these rules signify by saying 'No.'" (Follow #2 above, adding "by a two/thirds vote.")

8. **To create special orders.** Once established, orders of the day are established rules and can only be changed by a 2/3 vote. The member moving to create special orders may not interrupt a member who has the floor, and must first be recognized and seconded.

MEMBER: "Mr. Chairperson, I move we postpone consideration of this matter until our next meeting and make it a special order at that time."

CHAIRPERSON: Asks for a second, reports it has been moved and seconded and repeats the move, asks for discussion, puts it to a vote and reports the findings. Requires a 2/3 vote to create a general order, it cannot interfere with established rules.

9. **To withdraw a motion.** A member may not interrupt the person who has the floor and must first be recognized to withdraw a motion or ask that a motion be withdrawn.

MEMBER: "I withdraw my motion."

CHAIR: "Is there any objection to the motion being withdrawn?" If not, "Is there any other business.

If there is an objection, another member can say, "I move that Mr. Y be allowed to withdraw his motion." The Chair calls for vote and reports the findings.

10. **Vote by ballot.** If voice vote or hand raising leaves questions in the mind of the chair or any group member, a *division* can be called and the Ayes asked to stand and be counted, then the Noes. If a vote by ballot is called for in the by-laws, the Chair should appoint two or more tellers to distribute, collect, and count the ballots, and report in writing to the secretary. The chair will then read the vote.

11. **Objection to consideration.** A group member can rise without being recognized or seconded to "object to the consideration of this motion." The chair will then call for a vote and report the outcome; 2/3 vote against the motion is needed to carry.

12. **Motion to table.** Tabling a motion requires recognition and seconding. It cannot be debated or amended or have a subsidiary motion applied to it, cannot be moved when another motion is before the group, and requires a majority for it to carry.

(continued)

FIGURE 11-2 *(continued)*

MEMBER: Mr. Chairperson. I move we table the main motion," or "I move we take from the table the motion that was tabled to _____.'

Chair asks for a second, calls for a vote, reports the vote and asks for further business.

13. **Close debate.** "I move the Previous Question," is a call for an end to debate. The mover must first be recognized and then seconded. A member can also limit the debate: "Madam Chairperson, I move we limit the debate to 10 minutes" (or whatever). The chair will then call for a second and then a vote. A 2/3 vote is needed to carry and more than 1/3 Noes can defeat a motion to limit debate or close debate. Informally, one or more members may call, "Question!" when the chair asks if the group is ready to vote on the question.

14. **Postpone to a certain day.** Main motions can be amended by altering the time and require a 2/3 vote. After the vote, the chair can call for any discussion as to the advisability of postponement and a definite time for the motion to be reconsidered is stated. After a discussion, it is put to a vote.

15. **To refer or recommit.** A question can be referred to a committee or person if more information is needed. The member must first be recognized and seconded prior to referring the motion or amending a motion to refer.

16. **To amend.** The chair decides the propriety of amendments and may demand that they are submitted in writing. Amendments to an amendment are not permitted but the chair's decision is subject to appeal. Amendments take the form of adding, striking out, inserting, substituting, and so on. Once accepted by the chair, it is put to a vote and the chair calls for a discussion on accepted amendments. If not accepted, the amendment is lost and the chair calls for further discussion on the original motion.

17. **To postpone indefinitely.** When an important matter is unexpectedly brought to the group, the opposition can move to postpone indefinitely. This opens the main question to debate and provides the opposition with information about how many members are in favor of the main motion before it actually comes to a vote. Once the motion is made, the chair asks for a second and then asks for discussion on the motion. It is put to a vote and requires a majority to pass.

18. **Main question or motion.** This motion should be in writing if it's complicated. It provides for a substitute to the original motion. The member who makes the motion cannot interrupt a member who has the floor, must first be recognized, and requires a second to proceed. Once the motion has been stated, the chair can call for a discussion, a vote, and then for further business.

3. Change your meetings to "doings" by using technology to record comments, outline ideas, generate written proposals, project them for the entire group to see, and print them out before participants leave so they have real-time minutes. Don't think or talk "meeting;" think and talk "creating a document" and "productive interaction." Make sure your meeting room has access to Internet resources and articles, prices, consultation, or whatever else you need to make good decisions during meetings. Build project clusters and colocate desks around them. Post information, goals and works-in-process around the clusters. Instead of having debates, ask participants to respond to questions you ask by typing in their responses. Spend some time asking participants to brainstorm an idea (maybe why meetings don't work) and then post them on a big screen and everyone's monitors, if possible. Let them vote electronically, too, if possible. If you have the right software, you can sort any of the many responses, find the mean and standard deviation, and display how each person's rating of ideas, decisions, and soon varies from the group consensus. Also make sure there is a space in your meeting room for teams to store materials (flip charts, models, etc.).

4. Stick to the agenda. Refuse to allow participants to wander. If necessary, appoint a task person to call "time" and "let's get back on track" when members stray.

5. Embrace anonymity so participants will be more honest. Ask participants to enter comments onto laptops and then project each comment onto a screen without attribution.

6. Monitor what works and what doesn't and hold people accountable. Appoint an observer to record what went right and what went wrong and make sure it gets included in the minutes. Over time, you'll create an agenda for change.

7. Time is money. Make sure no meeting lasts longer than 90 minutes; productivity slumps after an hour and a half. Track the cost of your meetings. Consider using a computer-enabled simultaneity to enhance productivity (Matson, 2002a, 2002b).

LEAD FROM WITHIN

Frustrated with your work relationships? You can learn to lead from within. When your boss storms into your office and berates you or does it in front of your colleagues, you have several choices: walk into her office, tell her where to go, and then resign, bite your lip, silently curse and stuff the anger until you can binge eat later; yell at one of your supervisees; get back at your boss by using the grapevine to spread a rumor; or lead from within.

Leading from within provides a long-term solution to work relationships. Here are the steps to being a better leader in your organization:

1. Treat all people with respect even if they berate you or lie to you. Find a way to build rapport with each member of your team. Put forward your opinions and viewpoint without contradicting others, for example, "Here's another way of looking at things. What do you think?"
2. Remember your vision and do something to share it with colleagues, then stick to it, act on it and envision others joining your bandwagon. If possible, spend time visualizing and meditating together with colleagues to make the vision reality.
3. Be passionate about your vision. It refuels people. Don't try to outdo or outlast everyone; find out what moves you, what matters to you, what you care about, and then translate that into action.
4. Be bold, try something new, be vulnerable even when your colleagues razz you. Stay on course. Take deep breaths to energize yourself, picture yourself being successful, then go for it!
5. Communicate your vision with passion when discussions turn to office politics or how nothing ever changes. Say, "I feel frustrated. Let's talk about how to get this organization on track. I have a few ideas I'd like to share with you."
6. Ensure that team members have a sense of ownership and family.
7. Appreciate each team member often, even for small things, and do it publicly whenever you can.
8. Work to recruit team members who share your vision.
9. Notice when your boss is angry and having a rough time. Think about how to turn it around. Take a risk, show you care and say, "You must feel terrible. You've been through a lot, haven't you? How can I help?" (Bender, 1998; Bhatnagar, 2001).

POWER AND POLITICS IN ORGANIZATIONS

Organizations are composed of people who are constantly vying with one another for power, status, and prestige. Information, resources, and support are the commodities necessary for accumulating power. Successful managers often have to overstep the limits of their formal positions; power helps them do this. Power is rarely, if ever, given; it must be taken. Others must be convinced to go along with the manager's ideas. *Coalitions* must be formed during which there is a temporary joining of individuals with a common purpose or goal formed to exert pressure on others. Space, personnel, support, or ideas can be traded to develop power. Posturing or bluffing is used to provide power; more is asked than is ever expected, creating fall-back positions. Posturing is an attempt to keep others off balance or keep them guessing about what is expected. Participation in committees, task forces, social gatherings, or special projects of powerful individuals increases visibility and increases the possibility of being seen in the right place at the right time.

Those who are politically vulnerable or expendable are those who get set up and blamed, becoming organizational scapegoats. Politically astute leaders may wish to consider using some or all of the following skills and tactics to increase power, although you will have to decide if they are ethically and morally sound for you.

- Build a team, being careful there are not disgruntled, disappointed, or jealous subordinates on it.
- Choose your second in command carefully; aggressive, ambitious, or upwardly mobile workers may seize power.
- Establish alliances with both superiors and peers.
- Establish both upward and downward channels of communication; without them, an executive may become isolated and subject to being ousted or preempted.
- Be aware of powerful people's biases. This is crucial to predicting how a decision will be made; decisions rarely stand on their merit alone.
- Identify priorities for the, organization and follow them; three kinds of routines found in organizations are: survival tasks done to protect self and position, camouflage routines done to disguise the use of survival routines, and task routines.
- Identify when to be fair; being fair to aggressive, manipulative individuals may lead to a takeover of one's power or job.
- Be courteous; when others feel good or powerful, they will not have a need to retaliate.

- Compromise on small issues and only have a few issues that are ethically or morally essential; this will provide a flexible position and maneuverability.
- Use passive resistance when under pressure to perform on demands that cannot be openly challenged, yet are not in one's best interests.
- Project an image of power, status, and material success; others may mistake modesty and democracy for lack of power and influence.
- Divert an organized attack by initiating internal dissension or introduce an issue or rumor that sets your adversaries fighting among themselves (Del Bueno, 1986).

HEALING BETRAYAL OF TRUST

Trust is betrayed often in organizations and the effects can be long-lasting. Betrayal experiences range from not showing up at an agreed time to deliberate sabotage.

Rebuilding trust after betrayal has occurred takes effort and time. If trust is not rebuilt, distrust, cynicism, and disillusionment are sure to follow. Individuals who feel their trust has been violated watch for examples of continuing betrayal, put their guard up, and thus resistance to mending the hurt increases. Bragg (2001) suggests seven steps that must be taken to repair the damage betrayal has caused:

1. Acknowledge that betrayal has occurred. It is being whispered about in private. Raise the issue to open discussion level by saying it aloud.
2. Allow the venting of betrayal and hurt. Listen. Empathize. Understand. Give up judging who is right or wrong. These steps are crucial for individuals and organizations if morale is to be high.
3. Bring in a consultant to facilitate the healing process. Employees may need supportive counselors to guide them through a change process and/or rebuild trust.
4. Acknowledge that you can't change what has already transpired, but talk with everyone about what has been learned from this experience, what can be done differently next time, and how this can be prevented in the future.
5. Take responsibility for your part in any betrayal, including acknowledging your motives and expectations.

6. Vent, then forgive and release yourself and the other person(s) from the event. Anger and resentment are counterproductive and unhealthy. If necessary, seek counseling yourself so you can move on.
7. Remember the situation and what you learned, but move on and focus on the future. Don't expect miracles, because rebuilding trust takes time and effort.

REFERENCES

Bender, P. U. (1998). Frustrated with work relationships? Lead from within. *Canadian Manager, 26*(3), 23–25.

Bhatnagar, A. (2001). Great teams. *Executive Excellence, 18*(10), 12.

Bragg, T. (2001). Healing betrayed work relationships. *Industrial Management, 43*(3), 29–31.

Del Bueno, D. (1986). Power and politics in organizations. *Nursing Outlook, 34*, 124–128.

Emmerich, R. (1994). What will it to take to save your organization? *Savvy: A Resource For Personal & Professional Development, 1*(4), 1–4.

Goren, S., & Ottaway, R. (1985). Why health-care teams don't change: Chronicity and collusion. *Journal of Nursing Administration, 15*(7/8), 9–16.

Hawkins, K., & Fillion, B. (1996). *Perceived communication skill needs for small work groups.* East Lansing, MI: National Center for Research on Teaching Learning. (ERIC Document Reproduction Service No. ED399592.)

Hogan, R., Curphy, G. J., & Hogan, J. (1994). What we know about leadership: effectiveness and personality. *American Psychologist, 49*, 493–504.

Jones, O. B. (1991). *Parliamentary procedure at a glance.* New York: Dutton.

Matson, E. (2000a). The seven sins of deadly meetings. *Magazine.* Accessed 3/12/02 at http://www.fastcompany.http://www.fastcompany.com/online/02/html

Matson, E. (2000b). Have I died and gone to meeting heaven? *Magazine.* Accessed 3/12/02 at http://www.fastcompany.com/online/02/meetings2.html.

Tjosvold, D. (1995). Effects of power to reward and punish in cooperative and competitive contexts. *Journal of Social Psychology, 135*, 723–736.

12
When the Community Is the Group

COMMUNITY ORGANIZATION

Community organization is the process of building a broad-based constituency, involving citizens in a program, or creating a new, community-based program. Support for a program will logically emerge if community needs and concerns are understood and focused upon. Sometimes, issues for community organization surface naturally. You must be ready to mobilize the community around the issue of concern, set a meeting to discuss the situation, and involve the community's leaders to build momentum for programs. Community members often have different goals than you; it is often necessary to work on community issues as defined by the community in order to develop a meaningful organizational structure. Discussing drug or alcohol abuse or prevention of hazardous situations may be irrelevant to community members until they recognize the need for intervention.

At times, you may need to identify issues by drawing attention to existing community problems and providing statistics that may generate enough concern to bring community members to a meeting to discuss ways of addressing the problem.

Strong grassroots community organizations rarely spring up spontaneously. You may talk to community members informally for months before sufficient concern is generated to warrant a meeting. A crisis situation like a death or major injury is often the focus for immediate mobilization. Seize the moment when a crisis occurs and use it to mobilize community members.

Another useful way of involving the community is by developing a neighborhood festival or health fair. Many health issues involve (or should involve) children. Gain access to public schools. Schools in some communities, often in low-income ones, have developed adversarial relationships with community groups and may resist school-community partnerships. One way to develop a working relationship with a school is to meet with the principal. If the principal is known to be antagonistic to community groups, the school's parent group can be approached first and asked to support a meeting with the principal. Sympathetic teachers are another group that can be approached for initial contact.

It may be difficult to involve members of low-income communities. They may be too concerned with survival needs to respond to long-term planning. It is wise to seek out a few parents with potential for becoming strong community leaders and concentrate efforts on making sufficient home visits to cajole them to attend or sponsor community meetings. Become familiar with information networks and natural helpers in a community, including: well-known house wives and service providers such as post office workers, barbers, hairdressers, grocers, pharmacists, religious leaders, and elderly citizens.

A WELLNESS VIEW OF COMMUNITY

Communities are believed to evolve toward wellness by learning to (Clark, 2002):

- manage life experiences
- seek out challenges
- self-assess level of wellness
- identify wellness self-care goals
- relate to others in a flexible, differentiated, assertive manner
- use self-care strategies
- examine and readjust beliefs and practices into an integrated whole
- develop successful coping procedures

During the evolutionary process of moving toward wellness, communities interact with stressors more rationally and more efficiently by perceiving and managing situations differently. Although biological, historical, social, and cultural factors seem to be givens, they can be readjusted. For example, perceptions of traumatic situations can be readjusted and the immune system (a genetic given) can be strengthened by using self-care strategies.

Some assumptions underlying this model are that communities:

- are capable of self-assessing their own wellness needs
- are capable of setting their own wellness goals
- are capable of taking action to meet their wellness goals
- are capable of evaluating their progress toward wellness
- are in the process of moving toward wellness
- are capable of displaying characteristics of wellness even when stressed
- have innate self-healing processes that can be activated to enhance wellness
- can learn to move to a higher level of wellness
- can learn from modeling, clearly structured goals, means to meet those goals, and peer support

In this model for practice, *motivation* is intrinsic because the community chooses a goal that has meaning. Compliance becomes irrelevant because the community takes control over decision making. The process of moving toward wellness assumes top priority over the outcome: wellness.

Your role in assisting communities toward wellness includes:

- being an effective role model for wellness
- facilitating consistent community involvement in assessing, implementing and evaluating wellness and wellness goals
- teaching communities to perceive life experiences as manageable and meaningful
- increasing community self-responsibility and commitment to self-care
- teaching self-care strategies to enhance fitness, nutritional status, and environment: manage stress, build positive relationships, and develop coherent belief systems (including spiritual beliefs)
- teaching creative problem solving
- facilitating self-assertion
- teaching communication skills
- facilitating richness of community social supports
- teaching effective learner, family, and work role behaviors to communities

In a health promotion and wellness approach, you are a *facilitator.* Your task is to aid in the removal of obstacles to energy flow in the community, resulting in enhanced well-being and self-actualization.

In this model, you are also a *master teacher* who provides self-assessments and shows communities how to self-assess their wellness, decide on wellness goals, plan self-healing/self care actions to meet their goals, and self-evaluate success. You focus on the whole community, helping to determine what is interrupting the smooth flow of energy and action.

You may also play the role of *creator of sacred space* (McKivergin, 1997). In this role, you devise a sacred space in which healing work can occur. You may shape the physical environment or provide a relationship-focused environment to evoke healing. Natural light, plants, fresh air, pleasant sounds or music, comforting smells, and comfortable surroundings are some of the elements of creating sacred space.

Another health and wellness promotion role is *collaborator*. Together, you agree on ways to remove obstacles, and you support the community toward rechanneling energy flow. As balance is approached, enhanced well-being and self-actualization of potential result.

Another part of your wellness role is *role model*. Giving information about suggested change is often insufficient. From a very early age, human beings watch others' behavior and often mimic it. For this reason, being a positive role model is an extremely important role for community health practitioners.

Prior to becoming a role model for communities, you will be setting goals for your own wellness behavior and taking action to meet these goals. Self-assessing your own wellness may involve finding a supportive peer to assist you in this role.

Another role you may become involved in is *researcher*. See Figure 12–1. It describes a wellness study undertaken with members of one community.

Changing Community Priorities

Community disillusionment with medical care has led to the use of complementary practices that are wellness oriented, holistic, less intrusive, and have fewer side effects (Clark, 1998; Eisenberg et al., 1998). The U.S. government followed consumer interest and established the Office of Alternative Medicine (OAM), now called the Center for Alternative and Complementary Medicine, within the National Institutes of Health.

FIGURE 12.1 Community wellness study.

Clark (1998) reported using Orem's self-care theory to develop a questionnaire to examine older adults' self-care. A key-informant sample of 30 active older adults, ages 57–83, was sought. Fourteen participants were members of a line-dancing group known to the author. The remaining were members of a local community whom the author knew to be active, relatively healthy, and busily engaged in daily activities. Twenty-five respondents reported eating fresh fruits and vegetables, little meat, and low-fat foods to stay healthy and 19 participants reported taking vitamins and minerals, including vitamins B,C,E, calcium, or a multivitamin. Twenty-four informants reported that eating a low-fat, fresh fruit, and vegetable diet resulted in "feeling healthy and alert." Twenty-six elders reported sleeping 6 to 8 hours a night and 14 older adults said they rested one-half to 2 hours a day. The most frequently reported stressor was family problems (n=9), specifically problems of children or grandchildren. All respondents believed they were handling stress well and used a wide range of techniques to manage it, including refusing to think about things not under their control, reading, keeping busy, forgiving others, praying, sharing feelings with a friend or spouse, thinking positively, exercising, playing the piano or organ, singing or dancing, going to the movies, and setting priorities. Respondents kept safe from environmental harm by using common sense and then not worrying. Every informant claimed that keeping in touch with friends and family resulted in positive feelings, including joy, lightness, reawakened interests, prospects for future actions, and confidence. The majority believed that keeping active was the key to feeling energetic and independent. Except for one informant, all respondents attributed their enhanced quality of life and zest for living to remaining active, eating healthily, exercising, pacing themselves, doing what they liked to do, getting weekly phone calls from family, reading the Bible, and "feeding the life of the mind."

Clark C.C. (1998). Wellness self-care by healthy older adults. *Image: Journal of Nursing Scholarship, 30*, 351–355. Copyright material of Sigma Theta Tau International. Used with Permission.

Cultural Factors Affect Health Promotion

Health beliefs and wellness are affected by the forces of culture. Efforts to promote health and wellness must identify cultural factors and consider them when working with communities. Three important actions are: (1) attempt to enter the community's world to enhance your understanding, (2) suspend your personal biases and judgments about community beliefs, and (3) observe and talk to members of the cultural group until you have sufficient data to verify your Impressions (Huff, 1999).

The Aging of America Affects Health Promotion

According to the U.S. Department of Health and Human Services, by the year 2030, about 22% of the population will be 65 or older. Up to 80% of these older adults will be healthy, engaging in everyday activities. Only about 5% of older adults will live in nursing homes. Those who live in the community may be quite active, engaging in self-care activities (Clark, 1998).

Disease Factors Affect Health Promotion

The major causes of death are chronic illnesses, including cardiovascular disease and cancer. Both can be modified and, in some cases, eliminated by changes in life style. As a community health promoter, your biggest task is to find ways to convince your targeted community to take action to modify its lifestyle, environment, and government to reduce the incidence and symptoms of chronic illness. A first step in that direction is to assess progress toward wellness.

Wellness Self-Assessment

Take a look at Table 12-1: Wellness Self-Assessment. Later on, you can use this self-assessment with targeted communities. Before you do, it is important that you assess your own level of wellness, choose some wellness goals, and take action to meet them. Not only will these actions allow you to better understand what community members are going through, they will also enhance your level of wellness and assist you to become a more effective role model. If you were part of this community action, what other solutions would you offer to the group?

Facilitating movement toward community-chosen goals may require a change in your beliefs. The model also suggests that you, as a whole person and group leader, examine your beliefs for their consistency, choose wellness goals, facilitate movement toward those goals and evaluate your success.

When mind, body and spirit are in harmonious balance, a high level of wellness evolves. The *collaborative process* enables you to assist communities to assume ownership of the dynamic health–illness interchange.

TABLE 12.1 Wellness Self-Assessment

DIRECTIONS: Read the statements for each dimension of wellness. Circle the number that most appropriately resembles the importance of each statement to you and your well-being, as well as your current interest in changing your lifestyle as follows:
1. I am already doing this. (Congratulate yourself!)
2. This is very important to me and I want to change this behavior now.
3. This is important to me, but I'm not ready to change my behavior right now.
4. This is not important in my life right now.

NUTRITIONAL WELLNESS

I maximize local fresh fruits and uncooked vegetables in my eating plan.	1 2 3 4
I minimize the use of candy, sweets, and sugars.	1 2 3 4
I eat whole foods rather than processed ones.	1 2 3 4
I read labels and avoid foods that have color, artificial flavor, or preservatives added.	1 2 3 4
I avoid coffee, tea, cola drinks, or other substances that are high in caffeine or other stimulants or depressants.	1 2 3 4
I eat high fiber foods daily.	1 2 3 4
I have a good appetite, but I eat sensible amounts of food.	1 2 3 4
I avoid crash diets.	1 2 3 4
I eat only when I am hungry and relaxed.	1 2 3 4
I drink 8–10 (or more) glasses of water daily.	1 2 3 4
I avoid foods high in saturated fat, such as beef, pork, lamb, soft cheeses, gravies, bakery items, and fried foods.	1 2 3 4
I obtain sufficient minerals from my food or supplement my nutrition so that my muscles do not spasm or ache.	1 2 3 4
I drink distilled water or use a reverse osmosis filtration system to ensure my drinking water is safe.	1 2 3 4
I use muscle testing, food rotation methods, or the pulse test to make sure I don't eat foods I am sensitive to.	1 2 3 4

FITNESS AND WELLNESS

I weigh within 10% of my desired weight.	1 2 3 4
I walk, swim, garden, dance, or engage in some form of exercise I enjoy daily.	1 2 3 4

I digest my food well (no gas, bloating, diarrhea,
   constipation, irregular bowel movements, etc.).   1 2 3 4
I urinate or have a bowel movement when my
   body tells me it is time to and never hold back
   from using the toilet.   1 2 3 4
I take steps to keep my organs (liver, intestines,
   heart, etc.) well.   1 2 3 4
I wear clothes that do not leave marks on my skin
   or inhibit my breathing (no push-up or tight
   bras, tight jeans or pants, girdles, etc.)   1 2 3 4
I breathe easily from my abdomen most of the time.   1 2 3 4
I take regular breaks (at least every hour) from
   strenuous or repetitive movements.   1 2 3 4
I do flexibility or stretching exercises daily and
   always prior to and following vigorous exercise.   1 2 3 4
I am satisfied with my sexual activities.   1 2 3 4
I obtain sufficient daily touch (massage, hugs, sex,
   hand holding, etc.).   1 2 3 4
When I am ill, I am resilient and recover easily.   1 2 3 4
I have a good memory.   1 2 3 4
When I look at myself nude, I feel good about
   what I see.   1 2 3 4
I use imagery to picture myself well and healthy
   daily.   1 2 3 4
I use affirmations and other self-healing measures
   when ill, injured, or to enhance my fitness.   1 2 3 4
I avoid smoking and smoke-filled places.   1 2 3 4
My balance is good.   1 2 3 4
I rarely experience pain and when I do I know   1 2 3 4
how to reduce it without taking drugs or alcohol.   1 2 3 4

STRESS AND WELLNESS
I sleep well.   1 2 3 4
I live relatively free from disabling stress or
   painful, repetitive thoughts.   1 2 3 4
I laugh at myself occasionally and I have a good
   sense of humor.   1 2 3 4
I use constructive ways of releasing my frustration
   and anger.   1 2 3 4
I feel good about myself and my accomplishments.   1 2 3 4
I assert myself to get what I want instead of
   feeling resentful toward others for taking
   advantage of or intimidating me.   1 2 3 4

(continued)

TABLE 12.1 *(continued)*

I can relax my body and mind at will.	1 2 3 4
I feel accepting and calm about people or things I have lost through separation.	1 2 3 4
I live with a sense of joy and a zest for life.	1 2 3 4
I have a peaceful expectation about my death.	1 2 3 4

WELLNESS RELATIONSHIPS

I have at least one other person with whom I can discuss my innermost thoughts and feelings.	1 2 3 4
I can ask people for help when I need it.	1 2 3 4
I keep myself open to new experiences.	1 2 3 4
I listen to others' words and the feelings	1 2 3 4
behind the words. I can give and accept love.	1 2 3 4
What I believe, feel, and do are consistent.	1 2 3 4
I allow others to be themselves and to take responsibility for their thoughts, feelings, and actions.	1 2 3 4
I allow myself to be me.	1 2 3 4
I live with a sense of purpose.	1 2 3 4
I believe in something or someone.	1 2 3 4
I can forgive myself and others.	1 2 3 4
My life has meaning.	1 2 3 4

WELLNESS AND THE ENVIRONMENT

I have designed a wellness support network of friends, family and/or peers.	1 2 3 4
I have designed my personal living, playing, and working environments to suit me.	1 2 3 4
I work in a place that provides adequate personal space, comfort, safety, direct sunlight, and fresh air; and limited air, water, or material pollutants; or, I use nutritional, exercise, and stress reduction measures to minimize negative results.	1 2 3 4
I avoid cosmetics and hair dyes that contain harmful chemicals.	1 2 3 4
I avoid pesticides and the use of harmful household chemicals.	1 2 3 4
I use muscle or pulse testing to make sure I use safe household and lawn products.	1 2 3 4
I avoid x-rays unless serious disease or injury is at stake, and I have dental x-rays for diagnostic purposes only every 3 to 5 years	1 2 3 4

I keep up with the latest research and follow a
safe course related to sunscreen use and other
environmental protections.   1 2 3 4

I use the earth's resources wisely.   1 2 3 4

I meet the challenges of my environment.   1 2 3 4

COMMITMENT TO WELLNESS

I examine my values and actions to see that I am
moving toward wellness.   1 2 3 4

I take responsibility for my thoughts, feelings, and
actions.   1 2 3 4

I keep informed of the latest health/wellness
knowledge rather than relying on experts to
decide what is best for me.   1 2 3 4

I wear seatbelts when driving and insist that
others who ride with me also do so.   1 2 3 4

I ask pertinent questions and seek second opinions
whenever someone suggests surgery, medication,
or other treatment.   1 2 3 4

I know which chronic illnesses are prominent in
my family and I take steps to avoid incurring
them.   1 2 3 4

I work toward achieving a balance in all wellness
dimensions (nutrition, fitness, stress, relationships, environment, and commitment).   1 2 3 4

I look beyond my needs to the needs of society.   1 2 3 4

The scope of health promotion encompasses you and the community no matter what the targeted settings. This model encourages you to serve as a wellness role model for communities, taking care to cherish your own well-being while celebrating your ability to help others. The quality of the relationship is enhanced by the processes of communication, education, participation, research, and self-responsibility. Figure 12-2 provides information about a community project that used all these processes.

FIGURE 12-2 Girls against violence.

Saddened after the murder of a teenage mother and her child by an ex-boyfriend, the mothers of a small Midwest town gathered together to find a solution to the violence that was plaguing their city. They invited prominent business people and teenage girls to discuss the problem and come up with solutions. Before the meeting date, they sent out educational fliers, summarizing the effects of violence on communities and some possible solutions. One of the mothers was a mental health professional with experience in group facilitation. She was chosen to help the group come to consensus. She had developed a violence solution questionnaire, which she asked the participants to fill out. While the group discussed solutions, the group facilitator tallied their responses. When the group members exhausted their ideas, the facilitator read aloud the findings of her questionnaire. The group chose several solutions to implement that were not stated during the discussion. They established leadership teams, pairing young teenage girls with adult mentors from the business community, and decided to have a booth at a local health fair and hand out information on ways to prevent dating violence; verbal, psychological and sexual abuse; neglect; and murder. They also wrote a grant and obtained funding from their county juvenile welfare association to teach a course in violence prevention at the local schools and develop a peer protection program for young teenage girls.

This section is adapted from chapter 1, *Health Promotion in Communities,* by Carolyn Chambers Clark, Springer Publishing Co., 2002.

COMMUNITY ASSESSMENT

A community assessment provides you with information about a community's needs, unique character and flavor, leadership and communication networks, culture, and history. The process of needs assessment can also bring you and the community closer together, thus developing mutual respect and trust.

Traditionally, a *needs assessment* is a systematic survey of a community's social, political, economic and demographic composition. Problems and variables related to the issues a program will address are also assessed. A community assessment has two components: process (the various methods used to collect information about the community) and product (a report that summarizes community needs).

On the surface, a needs assessment appears scientifically objective. However, biases can creep in. The kind of information sought implies a set of assumptions about both the problems the community wishes to deal with and ways of solving them. One way to protect against bias is to openly recognize that biases and assumptions exist and try to balance them by examining a wide variety of community variables.

In middle-class communities, you may be able to rely heavily on data collected by community surveys, the juvenile justice system, the census bureau, the schools, and similar human service agencies. In low-income communities, residents are often involved in adversarial relationships with agencies so that their data may be highly biased.

In low-income communities, residents may be highly suspicious of anyone who plays an investigating or questioning role. One way of overcoming this obstacle is for teams of staff members to select streets or blocks in the community and go door to door, introducing themselves and asking for an opportunity to describe the kinds of services they offer. This method enables the staff to gather information as well as to provide it. Community forums focused on discussing and prioritizing community needs may be useful.

In a low-income community, a wide range of formal and informal community information networks must be accessed. These include the official leaders (church leaders, school officials, civic leaders, law enforcement and court officials, representatives of the media, and elected officials), as well as leaders who emerge in school yards, parks, church gatherings, social gatherings, nightclubs, bars, pool halls, and street corners.

Dyson (1986) suggests helping communities develop neighborhood health watches similar in structure to neighborhood crime watches. He contends that public tabulations on arrests, abortions, teen pregnancies, divorces, school dropouts, and truancy citations become public several months after actual events. "Measuring neighborhood illness rates shows up *quackery*, which I define as spending private and public resources for health without asking what good is obtained" (Dyson, 1986, p. 3).

One of the issues of such a program is confidentiality and privacy. Dyson agrees that privacy must be preserved, but insists there are nonpublic, hidden tragedies that call for immediate remedial action because they create dangerous family and community imbalances. Some of the hidden tragedies to assess are:

- Inappropriate admission to a nursing home
- Students failing in school
- Job loss

- Arrest
- Injury from assault
- Premature birth
- Infant death
- Chronic illness complications

Dyson suggests that weekly counting visits to identify disability days in a sample of families in each block would give timely local information for addressing local needs Privacy would have to be protected by keeping names anonymous. Figure 12-3 provides a community assessment.

EXAMPLES OF COMMUNITY ORGANIZATION EFFORTS AND RESEARCH

There are numerous examples of community organization efforts. This chapter presents a few, including a lay health promotion program in a Hispanic community, diabetes programs in Hawaii, conducting a survey in a youth service organization, a model violence-prevention center, and the Colorado Health Promotion Initiative.

Lay Health Promoter Program in a Hispanic Community

Hopper (2002) wrote about a lay health promoter program in a Hispanic community that improved communication between community members and health care providers, bridged cultural gaps, improved the delivery of health services to vulnerable populations (low-income, ethnic, and rural and neighborhood groups), and assisted communities in problem solving and increasing individual and community empowerment.

The first step was to assess whether a lay health promoter program was viable and valuable. If this information is not available, Hopper (2002) suggests looking to existing agencies that provide services to vulnerable populations for statistics to determine problematic areas (morbidity and mortality) and access to services. Key informant interviews and focus groups can be set up to discuss with health care providers and members of targeted populations their perception of needs.

Once the need is established, the second step is to find a place for the program to be housed. Consider the location, open-

FIGURE 12–3 Community assessment.

Who and What Is the Community?

1. How is space distributed and used? (buildings, crowded areas, natural and physical barriers to social interaction, parks, playgrounds)
2. How safe and healthful are work and school environments? (Are smokers and nonsmokers segregated? Are junk food and cigarette vending machines highly accessible? Are alternatives offered? Is the use of stairways promoted? Are they accessible? Well lit? Is car pooling encouraged? Is flex-time used to allow employees time to engage in wellness activities before work or during lunch? Are high-quality child care services available for residents? Are buildings well-ventilated and do they have adequate natural light and sufficient work/learning space?)
3. What are the cultural mix and stability of the population? (Are there one or more cultural groups living in harmony or in conflict, and how much acculturation and stress occur due to people moving in or out of the area?)
4. What are the community's age, sex, and family groupings like? (elderly population, single-occupancy commuter group, young-marrieds with children, singles, a mix)
5. What income levels are represented and to what extent? (wealthy, middle-class, poor who receive governmental or charitable assistance for health care, or a mix)
6. What are the occupational levels? (Are they hard-driving executives who leave the family's health concerns to their wives, action-oriented population who learns by doing, a mix?) What does the occupational level tell you about the population's education, health problems, problem-solving patterns, and methods of learning?
7. What community resources are available and where are they? (Where are the schools, hospitals, shopping areas, and clinics located in relation to available transportation? What self-help or supportive groups and services exist in the community? What facilities are there for wellness programs? What space could be developed to provide further wellness services? What skills or resources do the residents have that could be shared through a wellness program exchange? Is there any way to trade unused sick leave for a well day? Could unused sick leave be converted to cash? Do faculty, bosses, or town legislators support personal health promotion objectives? Can additional rewards or incentives be built into the current health illness insurance programs without taking away existing benefits? If there are company- or school-subsidized cafeterias, could wellness-promoting foods be more subsidized than junk foods?)

(continued)

FIGURE 12–3 *(continued)*

How Are Needs Met?

1. Are needs met or prevented from being met by space, culture, age, sex, family, income, occupation level, or community resource factors?
2. What do the community's clergy, health care practitioners, welfare agencies, and clients know about what needs are not being met?
3. What do records of health services, worker's compensation claims, and accident and safety records tell you about how needs are met and what wellness needs are not being met?
4. What do questionnaire or survey methods tell you about what community residents say the type of wellness activities they would participate in if offered?
5. What specific risk factors exist in this population and how are they being addressed or not?
6. How can family members of community residents be considered in planning wellness programs and be used to provide needed support systems?

How Are Deviance and Disturbance Handled?

1. Are those with psychiatriclmental health difficulties rejected by the community? If so, in what way?
2. How are homosexuals, delinquents, the homeless, or those who abuse alcohol, drugs, or food treated by community members? If so, in what way?
3. What political, educational, or social views lead to rejection of those who deviate from the norm?
4. Are there humane or highly institutionalized agencies available in the community to help deal with deviant members? What are they?
5. Does the community reject the idea of placing treatment facilities for its deviants within the community? How?
6. Is there a prevailing view that people who deviate from accepted behavioral patterns should be punished? How is this belief put into practice?

How Are Identities Developed?

1. How do families, faculty, administrators, etc. teach their members to act?
2. What kinds of religious/spiritual organizations or groups exist in the community and what is their prevailing view of human motivation?
3. What youth agenciesihelpers are there and how do young people relate to them?
4. What kind of formal and special education programs are available and how are they used by the community?

5. How could already existing agencies or groups be used more effectively?

How Are Community Functions Accomplished?

1. Are community decisions made before adequate information has been obtained? What possible effect(s) might this have?
2. Are decisions made by default, based on the personal concerns of a few, or made by consensus? What are the consequences of this type of decision making?
3. Is communication fragmented and inefficient? How does such communication seem to affect the community?
4. Are communication messages based on a sense of community (we're all in this together) or on stereotypes and the establishment of distance between groups (It's us against them)? What is the effect of both types of communication messages?
5. How accurately does the local media portray information to the community?
6. Are there informal (rumor) communication channels?
7. Are problems solved informally with board and committee meetings used only to record earlier decisions? How might this affect the community or the decisionmaking process?
8. How are ad hoc, neighborhood, or block associations used in decision making?
9. How readily are newcomers accepted by the community?
10. Is leadership concentrated among a few groups or is it widely distributed in the community?
11. Are there wide vacillations in power or frequent changes in the power base that could affect health planning or treatment?
12. Where is power located, how is it perceived, and how is it used?
13. What overlapping areas and missing links are there in wellness services?
14. What segments in the community are receptive and hostile to outside influence?
15. Is there a sense of trust between community members and leaders?
16. Is there community disintegration? (Has a recent disaster, widespread ill health, extensive poverty, confusion of cultural values, weakening of religious affiliations, extensive migration of new groups, or rapid social change radically affected the community?)

What Are the Resistances to Change in this Community?

1. What factors in the system will be affected as a result of a change toward wellness?
2. What forces are operating to inhibit change toward wellness?
3. What information or experiences must precede the change toward wellness?

(continued)

4. What new procedures or experiences will need to be developed as a result of a movement toward wellness?
5. Who is likely to suffer from the change?
6. How aware are community residents of the need for change?
7. Are community residents sufficiently involved in planning for the change?
8. What is the relationship between the change agent and community residents?
9. What past relationship between the change agent and the community might be influencing resistance to change now?
10. How open have community residents been to the introduction of change in the past?
11. How can free and open communication, administrative support of and reward for problem-solving efforts, shared decision making, sufficient time to problem solve, written statements of what the change goals will be, professionalism, concern for long-term planning, cohesiveness among change agents, and feelings of security among residents, timing, and resident confidence in ability to change be enhanced to lower resistance to change?

ness to program partnership through in-kind and rent-free contributions, adequate physical space, and trust and respect of the targeted community.

Step 3 is to obtain community support. If you've completed a community assessment, you already know who the trusted key players in the health and human services area are and the informal and formal community leaders, too. The more the community buys into the program, the more likely you are to be successful. Include local businesses that can provide in-kind donations and will soon learn the benefits of your program.

Step 4 is to design the program. Hopper suggests a 40-hour program with two-hour classes once a week. Provide child care and lunch if the class is held over mealtime. Bring items such as blood pressure equipment and a thermometer for demonstration and playback practice. Have a graduation, certificates of achievement, refreshments, and a commencement speaker for *promotoras* who have attended at least 80% of the classes. After graduation, encourage *promotoras* to share what they've learned with their communities.

Step 5 includes designing the program evaluation. It is best to think of this step at the time you plan the program, especially the *process evaluation,* so you can collect ongoing data about what was done, when it was done, who did it and to whom, how often it was useful, and how well it was done. *Outcome evaluation* examines the program's effects on program goals, including changes in health status.

Step 6 includes preparing a budget and obtaining funding. A minimal budget is required for this kind of program, but a nurse or health educator with experience working in the community is mandatory. This person should probably be bilingual. Many pamphlets and handout materials are available from the Red Cross and the American Heart Association. Check state and federal agencies, too. Be sure to allow funds for meals, graduation ceremonies, curriculum materials, salaries (director, health educator, and childcare coordinator), and equipment. Travel, awards, and follow-up may require additional monies.

Step 7 includes the actual development of the program and marketing it to find students. Volunteer to make presentations to community meetings, churches, libraries, and anywhere community members congregate to tell them about your program. Write an article and work with the editor of a local newspaper to have it published.

Step 8 includes developing and implementing strategies to keep the program graduates involved and connected. Consider a newsletter, monthly support groups, or continuing education workshops.

Diabetes Programs in Hawaii

Wang (2002) reported the developed of community diabetes programs in Hawaii. Noting the lack of hospital partnerships with the community for chronic illnesses such as diabetes, this professor at the University of Hawaii hoped to bridge this gap.

Wang offered her services to a Chinese community called the Golden Ager Association of Hawaii. She met with volunteers and established rapport by asking about their needs and offering her services, then developed and used a demographic questionnaire based on her knowledge of the community. Other measures she used included a diabetic self-care practice instrument, and the Denyes health status instrument.

Wang negotiated with the leader of the Golden Ager Association to teach community members about blood pressure and glucose monitoring in exchange for collecting research data. She also facilitated community leaders to develop their own capacity for action by using focus group interviews and group workshops.

Conducting a Survey of a Youth Service Organization

Strack (2002) reported a community project that assessed the health risks of youth residing in group homes and shelters throughout the state of Maryland. The need for the Monitoring Adolescents in Risky Situations (MARS) Project had already been established by state statistics on behavioral risk data on adolescents.

His first step was to set up a *steering committee* or group of individuals from external organizations or areas who can provide guidance. This process was important because it is often a prerequisite for funders, but it is also a great mechanism for obtaining insight, support, and direction. To establish a steering committee, make a list of organizations that could benefit from the results of your survey and those that have insight into the population you're going to survey.

Before you begin your project, make sure that you will give something to the community, possibly in the form of useful information it can use to enhance health and wellness. If you are the *principal investigator* or lead researcher, manager, or person responsible for the study, you will be establishing the grand plan for conducting the survey, including how to monitor activities and progress while adhering to quality standards. One of your tasks will be to establish a timeline for the project, including goals; finding an *institutional review board* (IRB) to okay your project; time to prepare and plan the survey, collect data, and analyze it. Be sure to allow sufficient time to pilot your project through an IRB, which will probably require a study protocol (check with the review board of your institution in case it requires a specific format), participant consent forms (possibly a parental consent for underage participants), and any instruments you will be using. For more information access the Office for Protection from Research Risks at http://www.nih.gov/grants.oprr/oprr.htm.

It is wise to do a pilot study, field testing your instruments with a sample that is comparable to the population you will use in your larger study. You will also need to hire and train data collectors, contact organizations you will be surveying, collect data using the survey, and track the data collection process.

Strack found the youth in his sample were more than willing to share information and wanted to know how the data being collected were going to be used. Many participants stated that they agreed to be surveyed because they thought it might help someone else.

A Model Violence-Prevention Center

DiNapoli (2002) reported on the development of a model violence-prevention program in a school. Recent violent incidents in Arkansas and Colorado spurred the development of a violence-prevention center in one school.

One component of a successful violence-prevention center is education (identify students who may be potentially at risk for violence as perpetrators or victims, advise faculty and staff of students at risk ([socially isolated, experienced recent situational stressors, product of a disrupted upbringing, been a witness or victim of a previous violent action including suicide]).

Training included a series of initial in-service training sessions for the school related to the risk, identification, prevention, and postintervention of adolescent violence. Core concepts included risk identification, resource identification, and crisis intervention.

A critical component of the program was to bring students to the decision-making table (DiNapoli, 2002). A *gatekeeper* (community practitioner with a broad multidisciplinary education and holistic view of health) met with the advisory board and students, faculty, staff, and parents on an ongoing basis to discuss the school climate, study risk, and help design prevention strategies. The gatekeeper also encouraged students to join support groups and addressed media issues after violent incidents.

DiNapoli learned some lessons from the program she established.

1. Be sure to involve the entire community and keep in mind that the essential element is training, training, and more training.
2. Plan for an ongoing evaluation of programs to help identify effective approaches to violence prevention.
3. Choose a viable method for disseminating information. DiNapoli's Center used parent-teacher groups that may be too small an audience.

Evaluating the Colorado Health Promotion Initiatives

Judge and colleagues (2002) evaluated the Community Action for Health Promotion Initiative (CAHPI), a five-year $5.2 million initiative designed to increase local health promotion and disease prevention activities in Colorado. The specific health issues were those listed by Healthy People 2000, including physical activity and fitness, diet and nutrition, tobacco use prevention, substance abuse prevention, violence prevention, child injury prevention, heart disease prevention, diabetes prevention, healthy habits for children and adolescents, and adult wellness.

Because there was little research available about such an ambitious project, Judge and her colleagues had to begin learning what happened in the smaller projects, continually refine their approaches to data collection, and efficiently analyze data, making sure they were capturing what was important.

Their first step was *scouting*. During this phase, they conducted interviews with project directors and other key staff, community leaders, project officers from the management agency, and program participants. They visited the project sites to observe program activities and talk with people.

After two years of scouting, they modified their qualitative instruments to capture the life cycle of projects. As their funding cycle changed, they had to make corresponding changes in their evaluation tools. They added more information about the history of health promotion in the project communities, leadership development, technical assistance provided by the management agency, and the dynamics of working with others to implement the programs.

They took turns *cleaning the data,* making sure that it was consistently and accurately entered. Now that qualitative measures were not the only ones being employed, they took steps to find ways to compare earlier measures with more quantitative tools.

Lessons they learned included:

1. Be open to what else is going on in the community.
2. Strike a balance so you stay in touch with project staff, but don't get in the way.
3. Think and talk about what types of methods are most appropriate for each stage in the evaluation process.
4. Develop meaningful relationships among and between key stakeholders if you want a successful outcome.

REFERENCES

Clark, C. C. (1998). Wellness self-care by healthy older adults. *Image: Journal of Nursing Scholarship, 30*, 351-355.

Clark, C. C. (2002). A model for health and wellness promotion in communities. In C. C. Clark (Ed.), *Health promotion in communities, holistic and wellness approaches,* (pp. 3–14). New York: Springer Publishing Co.

DiNapoli, P. P. (2002). Violence prevention in schools: A model violence- prevention center. In C. C. Clark (Ed.), *Health promotion in communities: Holistic and wellness approaches* (pp. 433–438). New York: Springer Publishing Co.

Dyson, B. (1986). Measuring neighborhood health. *Network 12,* 2-3.

Eisenberg, D. M., Davis, R. B., Ettner, S. L., Appel, S., Wilkey, S., Von Rompay, & Kessler, R. C. (1998). Trends in alternative medicine use in the United States, 1990–1997. *Journal of American Medical Association 280,* 1569–1575.

Hopper, S. K. (2002). Establishing a lay health promotion program in a Hispanic community. In C. C. Clark (Ed.), *Health promotion in communities: Holistic and wellness approaches* (pp. 383–399). New York: Springer Publishing Co.

Huff, R. M. (1999). Cross-cultural concepts of health and disease. In R. M. Huff & M. V. Kline (Eds.), *Promoting health in multicultural populations* (pp. 23–39). Thousand Oaks, CA: Sage.

Judge, K. A., Main, D. S., Tressler, C., Fernald, D., Parker, J., Corbett, K., & Horton, J. (2002). Evaluating small community-based health promotion programs: Lessons learned from Colorado Health Promotion Initiatives. In C. C. Clark (Ed.), *Health promotion in communities: Holistic and wellness approaches* (pp. 439–460). New York: Springer Publishing Co.

McKivergin, M. (1997). The nurse as an instrument of healing. In B. M. Dossey (Ed.), *The American Holistic Nurses' Association (AHNA) core curriculum for holistic nursing* (pp. 17–25). Gaithersburg, MD: Aspen.

Strack, R. W. (2002). Conducting a survey: The example of a youth service Organization. In C. C. Clark (Ed.), *Health promotion in communities: Holistic and wellness approaches* (pp. 421–432). New York: Springer Publishing Co.

Wang, C. (2002). Diabetes programs in Hawaii. In C. C. Clark (Ed.), *Health promotion in communities: Holistic and wellness approaches* (pp. 401–408). New York: Springer Publishing Co.

Glossary

GLOSSARY OF SELECTED GROUP TERMS

aggressiveness behavior that has an element of control or manipulation of the other person.

anxiety unexplained feeling of discomfort that occurs when expectations are not met.

apathy a withdrawal response that can be used to cover tension and discomfort.

assertiveness setting goals, acting on those goals in a clear and consistent way, and taking responsibility for the consequences of those actions.

behavior description a statement of what was observed, without including a comment on the meaning or motive for the behavior.

behavioral modification an approach to change that focuses on principles of learning, such as reinforcement, that can decrease unsatisfying or disruptive behavior and on increasing satisfying, goal-directed behavior.

closed group a group to which new members are not added when others leave.

coalition a temporary joining of individuals with a common purpose or goal formed to exert pressure on others.

cognitive-behavioral focuses more on thoughts than feelings, precursors to behavior.

cohesiveness the measure of attraction of the group for its members.

community organization the process of building a broader-based constituency, involving citizens in a program, or creating a new, community-based program.

countertransference leader response in an over- or under-active way to group members because they evoke remembrances of earlier personal relationships of the leader.

covert content the deeper, symbolic meaning of words.

feedback letting group members know how they affect each other.

focal groups are highly structured, target one issue, discourage attention to transference, and use homework and structured exercises designed to promote rapid change.

focus group face-to-face interaction of selected clients to obtain their opinions of pre-chosen questions, products or programs.

group conflict reaction to being given an impossible task, having contradictory loyalties, jockeying for power or status, disliking others, or involving oneself in the task.

group contract a written or verbal operating agreement between leader and group members.

group event behavior of all group members except the designated leader,

group process constant movement as group members seek to reduce the tension that arises when people attempt to have their individual needs met yet work to help meet group goals.

hidden agenda individual member or leader goals that are at cross-purposes to group goals.

"I" messages verbal communication that conveys the way the individual thinks or feels.

incompatible response one that cannot be performed at the same time as the desired behavior.

maintenance responses those that are directly related to improving interpersonal relationships within the group.

manipulation attempt by group member to have his own needs met.

modeling demonstrating desired behaviors.

monopolizing a group problem wherein one group member agrees in some way with other group members to talk and thereby to protect them.

needs assessment a systematic survey.

norm rule for behavior in the group.

open group a group to which new members can be added as others drop out.

organizational system composed of the social system, operation system, and administrative system of an organization.

orientation phase early group phase when anxiety is high, levels of self-disclosure are low, bids for the leader's attention or care are made, group goals are refined, and the leader models effective group behavior.

overt content superficial, agreed-upon meaning of words.

pairing behavior whereby group members pair off in twos to provide mutual support for one another through having subconversations; characteristic of the orientation phase.

prompting telling a person how to behave next.

reinforcers rewarding events that immediately follow a behavior and thus maintain its occurrence.

resistance phenomenon that occurs when people fear change or lack knowledge of or participation in the change.

scapegoating a group process wherein one or two members of the group are singled out and agree consciously or unconsciously to be targets for group hostility or advice.

shaping the reinforcement of successive approximations toward the desired behavior.

silence a communication that has various meanings.

supportive group a group whose main purpose is to share thoughts, feelings, and reactions to crises, health conditions, or interpersonal relationships.

task functions those that are directly related to the accomplishment of group goals.

task group a group with a main purpose of completing a task.

teaching group a group whose main purpose is to impart information.

termination phase the last phase, wherein the group focuses on evaluating and summarizing the group experience.

themes linkages and underlying consistent meaning in group interaction.

time out removing the person from a pleasurable activity immediately, once undesirable behavior occurs.

Index

token system symbolic reward for desirable behavior that can be turned in at a later date for more concrete rewards.

transference member response whereby aspects of former relationships are projected onto current figures in the group setting.

validating checking with the other in a tentative way to see whether one's perceptions are correct.

warming-up exercises exercises used to decrease group anxiety.

Woodlands therapy a specific type of sensory-motor and play-based training especially useful with advanced dementia.

working phase the middle phase in a group, when members know how to work together cooperatively, thoughts and feelings are shared more openly, and the leader needs to intervene less frequently to move the group along.

"You" message aggressive verbal communication in which blame is placed on the other person.

ＳＰ *Springer Publishing Company*

Nursing Leadership Forum

Harriet R. Feldman, PhD, RN, FAAN, Editor
Joyce J. Fitzpatrick, PhD, RN, FAAN, MBA,
Consulting Editor

This quarterly is designed for professional nurses who perform leadership functions with clients, colleagues, health care institutions, and communities. It addresses the many facets of leadership through debate, interviews and thought-provoking current articles. This unique forum discusses the vital importance of nursing leadership in the public debates of health care reform.

"A substantive journal for practicing nurse leaders. Solid content, timely, and a welcome source of relevant information." **—Dr. Maryann F. Fralic**
The Johns Hopkins University, School of Nursing

"No concept is talked about in these turbulent times more than 'leadership,' but often in very surface ways. Nursing Leadership Forum provides a regular opportunity, by contrast, to have focused and extended discussion in this area."
—Angela Barron McBride, PhD, RN, FAAN
Indiana University School of Nursing

"...NLF consistently engages the reader in sharing an appealing vision of nursing leadership." **—Olga Maranjian Church,** PhD, FAAN
University of Connecticut, School of Nursing

Sample Contents:

POINT/COUNTERPOINT

- Point: Telehealth: Can Nursing Values be Preserved?
  Counterpoint: Telehealth: A Challenge to Preserve Nursing Values
- Point: Primary and Secondary Prevention Point: Are Nurses Making a Substantial Contribution?
  Counterpoint: Isn't Primary Health Care Synonymous With Nursing Practice?

ARTICLES

- Where Will I Go? Displaced Nurses Relate Their Experiences
- Evaluating On-Line Continuing Education for Nurses

INDEXED / ABSTRACTED in: CINAHL, International Nursing Index, Social Services Abstracts, and Sociological Abstracts.

Volume 7 (2002-2003) • 4 issues • ISSN 1076-1632
Fall, Winter, Spring, Summer

536 Broadway, New York, NY 10012 • Telephone: 212-431-4370
Fax: 212-941-7842 • Order Toll-Free: 877-687-7476 • Order On-line: www.springerpub.com

Springer Publishing Company

Encyclopedia of Complementary Health Practice

Carolyn Chambers Clark, EdD, RN, ARNP, FAAN, Editor in Chief;
Rena J. Gordon, PhD, Contributing Editor
Barbara Harris, RN, LMT and **Carl O. Helvie**, RN, DrPH
Advisory Contributing Editors

This comprehensive resource of key terms and concepts in complementary health care addresses practices, conditions, and research-based treatments. With over 300 entries by distinguished contributors, coverage includes such alternative therapies as naturopathy, homeopathy, chiropractic, nutrition, and massage.

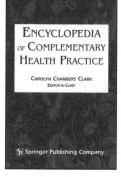

ENCYCLOPEDIA
OF COMPLEMENTARY
HEALTH PRACTICE

CAROLYN CHAMBERS CLARK
EDITOR-IN-CHIEF

One section is devoted to pertinent issues in complementary health practice including economics, legal ramifications, education, and historical perspectives. Other valuable features are the extensive cross references and a directory of practitioners and institues relevant to complementary health practice.

Partial Contents:

- A Theory for Complementary Health Practitioners
- The Role of Science in Complementary Health Care
- Complementary Health Practice: A New Paradigm
- The Economics of Complementary Health Practices
- Complementary Health Centers and Networks
- Complementary Health Practitioner Locations
- Effects of Complementary Health Practices on Medical Education
- The Education of Homeopaths
- Education and Research Conducted at CAMPS
- Legal Rules Affecting Complementary Health Practice: Malpractice and Vicarious Liability
- National Center for Complementary and Alternative Medicine
- Wellness Promotion: Historical Aspects
- Self-Care in American History

1999   664pp   0-8261-1239-0   soft • *1999   664pp   0-8261-1237-4   hard*

536 Broadway, New York, NY 10012 • **Telephone: 212-431-4370**
Fax: 212-941-7842 • **Order Toll-Free: 877-687-7476** • **Order On-line: www.springerpub.com**